SOLDIERING ON

SOLDIERING ON

BRITISH TOMMIES AFTER THE FIRST WORLD WAR

ADAM POWELL

The
History
Press

I dedicate this book to my late father
Corporal Roy Powell, who served
in the Second World War, and to
Carmen and Francesca Powell for
their love, support and patience.

First published 2019

The History Press
97 St George's Place, Cheltenham,
Gloucestershire, GL50 3QB
www.thehistorypress.co.uk

British Library Cataloguing in Publication Data.
A catalogue record for this book is available from the British Library.

ISBN 978 0 7509 9147 6

Typesetting and origination by The History Press
Printed and bound in Great Britain by TJ International Ltd

CONTENTS

PROLOGUE

The Grand Theatre, Wolverhampton, 23 November 1918. David Lloyd George, the prime minister, announced an election would be held only a month after the Armistice. He hoped for a thumping majority as the 'man who won the war'. Lloyd George told the audience:

> What is our task? To make Britain a fit country for heroes to live in. I am not using the word 'heroes' in any spirit of boastfulness, but in the spirit of humble recognition of fact. I cannot think what these men have gone through. I have been there at the door of the furnace and witnessed it, but that is not being in it, and I saw them march into the furnace. There are millions of men who will come back. Let us make this a land fit for such men to live in. There is no time to lose. I want us to take advantage of this new spirit. Don't let us waste this victory merely in ringing joybells. Let us make victory the motive power to link the old land up in such measure that it will be nearer the sunshine than ever before, and that at any rate it will lift those who have been living in the dark places to a plateau where they will get the rays of the sun. We cannot undertake that without a new parliament … We have seen places we have never noticed before, and we mean to put these things right.[1]

'A fit country for heroes to live in' soon became 'a land fit for heroes' in popular parlance. It has since descended into a cliché but was widely believed at the time. Soldiers expected decent treatment and recognition for what they had done – for they *had* marched into the furnace. Yet the fine words of 1918 were not matched by actions. The interwar years saw some improvements in the treatment of veterans but these were tepid reforms, hampered by inadequate funding and a lack of political will. The sight of soldiers begging in the street became commonplace in many British cities. Veterans were disproportionately unemployed; the disabled and shell-shocked often badly neglected.

Soldiering On examines how and why this happened. Books about soldiers in the aftermath of the First World War have tended to focus on one particular aspect of the ex-servicemen's struggles, shell shock being a recent and fertile field; or they have looked at the politics of the period as a whole, with the veteran being relegated to little more than a footnote. There's a need to look at the range of experiences returning soldiers went through in a single volume.

Soldiering On deals primarily with British Army veterans from 1918 to the eve of the Second World War, but also compares how other belligerent nations treated their ex-servicemen. The precarious state of Britain's economy meant reconstruction plans were never properly implemented but other countries faced similar difficulties and managed rather better. The failure to support veterans adequately was a political choice as well as a financial challenge. True, ex-servicemen were treated better than in the Edwardian era, but that is not saying much. Unlike other European nations, the British Government had always relied on volunteers. A conscripted army meant young men across the social spectrum experienced some form of military service, but Britain recruited from a narrow base: the officers were upper-middle and upper-class products of the public school system; the men were from the lowest rungs of society. The Duke of Wellington said during the Napoleonic Wars, the 'French system of conscription brings together a fair sample of all classes; ours is composed of the scum of the earth'.[2] Little changed in the next 100 years. Ex-officers were sufficiently wealthy to look after themselves. Rankers were not expected to do anything except re-enlist until their health packed in, and then charity or the workhouse were the most likely destinations. They had no statutory right to a pension, regardless of how many years they'd served.

It was not until 1916 that the British Government introduced conscription. Britain now had an army comparable to other European nations but without the experience or institutions to reintegrate large numbers back into civilian life. There was another problem: the pre-war attitudes that had tolerated ex-servicemen begging on the street never fully disappeared. Rudyard Kipling summed up the public's view of the ordinary soldier in his poem 'Tommy' (1890):

> O it's Tommy this, an' Tommy that, an' 'Tommy, go away';
> But it's 'Thank you, Mister Atkins', when the band begins to play.

Soldiers were necessary for fighting in remote parts of the Empire but in peacetime a pest, especially after a few drinks on a Saturday night. General Robertson, Chief of the Imperial General Staff, had joined the army as a private in 1877. His mother told him, 'I would rather bury you than see you in a red coat.'[3] But in the First World War, ordinary soldiers had come from all walks of life. Kitchener's original volunteers were disproportionately middle class, improving the reputation of the average soldier among the public but not by enough for meaningful political reforms. The large amounts of money military charities raised after the war showed a degree of sympathy for the veteran, yet soldiers often found it difficult to obtain work, particularly in the old industrial heartlands. The disabled and shell-shocked often had to eke out an existence on inadequate pensions. British political attitudes during these years limited any changes that might have benefited ex-servicemen. All the main parties rhetorically committed to helping veterans but none were prepared to do much in practice. Nor was the main ex-servicemen's organisation, the British Legion, able, and sometimes even willing, to force concessions from governments more concerned with balancing budgets.

But the interwar years were not always negative for veterans. Most managed to find employment, did not suffer from shell shock or beg on street corners. This isn't minimising the traumatic effects of the war on many ex-servicemen but acknowledging that others went on to lead fulfilling lives. It is wrong to generalise about the 5 million British servicemen who survived the war; instead, one should look for discernible trends, while being aware that there were always exceptions. Just as experiences differed so did attitudes. Some hated their time in the army, while others regarded it as a worthwhile experience. Some grew disillusioned with the peace, particularly as Europe slid towards another war in the 1930s. But from letters, testimonies and interviews, most veterans remained proud of having fought in a war they regarded as just.

Finally, it is worth noting that the British Army was a truly multinational force taking in troops from across her huge empire. The men from the dominions of Canada, New Zealand, South Africa and Australia have received considerable attention – and their contribution was enormous. However, other men fighting in British uniforms – African, Caribbean, Asian and Irish – have often been ignored. This book helps redress this by showing how they were also profoundly affected by the First World War.

Introduction

'GENTLEMEN' AND 'PLAYERS': BRITAIN ON THE EVE OF WAR

'The lost golden age ... all the more radiant because it is on the other side of the huge black pit of war.'

J. B. Priestley[1]

The farthings and sovereigns,
And dark-clothed children at play
Called after kings and queens,
The tin advertisements
For cocoa and twist, and the pubs
Wide open all day

'MCMXIV', *Philip Larkin* [2]

When Queen Victoria died in 1901, Britain had the largest empire the world had ever seen. It had pioneered the Industrial Revolution. London was the centre of finance, sterling the world currency. Yet there was a sense that a golden age was ending. *The Economist* wrote of 'a perceptible note of apprehension in the public mind.'[3] There was an ambiguity about whether to embrace change or stick with what had served Britain so well.

International exhibitions are the face a nation wants to present to the world. The Paris Exposition Universelle in 1900, which finished two months before Queen Victoria's death, was a consciously modern affair, introducing the escalator, the diesel engine and talking films to the public. But the British delegation constructed a mock-Jacobean manor house.[4] Its designer, Edwin Lutyens, was a brilliant purveyor of nostalgia who would later play a major role in shaping First World War memorials. The stained glass was by William Morris, the tapestries by Edward Burnes-Jones, both members of a group that raged against the machine.

At the start of a new century, the world's first industrial nation chose to celebrate the age before steam.

Contrast this to the Great Exhibition of 1851 where the Crystal Palace in Hyde Park astounded foreign visitors with its daring. But if the mid-nineteenth century was an era of confident progress, Edwardian Britain was dogged by uncertainty. Britain was losing the economic race to Germany and the United States. The British economy was slow in diversifying during the Second Industrial Revolution (1870–1914) when technological developments boosted the chemical, electricity, petroleum and steel industries. Its manufacturing base was still reliant on old staples like textiles, coal and shipbuilding but even these were suffering from a lack of investment. A dangerous dependence on Germany for many imports was exposed during the war. *The Times* argued that, 'Others have learned our lessons and bettered our instructions while we have been too easily content to rely upon the methods which were effective a generation or two ago'.[5]

The Boer War (1899–1902) revealed Britain's military deficiencies and her unpopularity. 'As a nation we are not greatly loved by the world at large,' *The Economist* admitted.[6] Lord Salisbury* used the phrase 'splendid isolation' to describe Britain's policy of staying out of European affairs, but being isolated was no longer an option. Nations were making alliances and rearming at an alarming pace and Britain wasn't strong enough to stand alone. After some hesitation it allied with France, her traditional enemy, and Russia, the nation she had most feared only a few years before. This marriage of convenience was brought about by a mutual dislike of Germany. Unified in 1871, the German Reich had industrialised rapidly while building the best army in Europe. Now she looked for opportunities overseas. In an era where colonies defined a nation's power, Germany wanted its 'place in the sun' but Britain and France had taken the lion's share. Germany resented any lectures about aggression from the two nations that had conquered so much of the world; however, her decision to build a large navy was bound to alienate Britain. After all, Germany's army was supreme, so why did it need a large navy? It was obviously aimed at Britain, the leading maritime power whose empire depended on her naval dominance. Relations with Germany grew frosty, exacerbated by the new Emperor, Kaiser Wilhelm II, an

---

* British prime minister from 1885–86, 1886–92, 1895–1902.

unstable man who, despite being part British,** developed a loathing for his mother's country. It was heartily reciprocated.

Britain was a deeply stratified society before the war, but many were starting to question their place in it. Militant trade unions were flexing their muscles – over 40 million days of work were lost through industrial action in 1912.[7] Some wanted to improve pay and conditions, others hoped to bring down capitalism through strikes. Suffragettes turned to violence when peaceful tactics failed to secure women the vote. Shop windows were smashed, acid was poured into letterboxes and the Chancellor of the Exchequer's country house was blown up. In Ireland, a civil war between Catholics and Protestants was looming, only delayed by the onset of the First World War. This was an era of Joseph Conrad's *The Secret Agent* as well as *The Wind in the Willows*.

It was a country edging towards democracy. The last Reform Act (1884) gave the vote to ratepayers and homeowners: about 60 per cent of the adult male population. The idea that all men should have a right to vote was not yet fully accepted by the authorities. The link between the franchise and property ownership meant businessmen could vote multiple times if they owned premises in different constituencies. Female suffrage was given even shorter shrift. However, changes were happening, albeit glacially. In 1907 some women gained the right to be elected to local councils. In 1911 a large majority of MPs supported a private members' bill to enfranchise 1 million affluent women, but parliamentary wrangling stopped the bill from becoming law. A franchise bill to extend male suffrage met a similar fate.

The election of a left-leaning Liberal government in 1906 exposed another constitutional problem. The Conservative-dominated House of Lords started blocking legislation, notably the People's Budget (1909–10), which introduced progressive taxes to pay for an extension of welfare. It raised the question: could Britain be truly democratic if the hereditary aristocracy, the bulk of the Lords, held a legislative veto? The issue was rancorously settled a year later in favour of the House of Commons. The Lords became a revising chamber; it was a retreat for the ruling class, for it was still possible to talk of a ruling class or 'The Thing', as the radical William Cobbett called it. Britain was a country run by some 600 families who dominated politics, the economy, the professions, culture and fashion. It had never completely calcified. Successful industrialists had been entering its portals for decades, marrying their offspring to grander, if sometimes poorer,

---

** His mother was Queen Victoria's eldest daughter.

families, or buying landed estates and sending their children to the right schools. There were mavericks like the politician Joe Chamberlain or William Robertson, who went from footman to the army's Chief of Imperial General Staff. But they were exceptional men, in both senses of the word. And 'The Thing' had an ability to co-opt them; to blunt any desire to change the system once they rose high enough to be able to do so.

For most, the class system ensured you remained where you were born. People could be instantly classified by their clothes, accents and even height, due to differences in diet. The huge wealth divide meant a solicitor or doctor could earn £1,000 a year, a maid perhaps £20. A middle-class lifestyle cost at least £160.[8] For Britain's working class, destitution, or the threat of it, was always present. In Seebohm Rowntree's *Poverty, A Study of a Town* he found that 28 per cent of York's population were living on less than was 'necessary to enable families to secure the necessities of a healthy life'[9] – half of them through low wages and a quarter through unemployment, disability or the wage-earner's death. For millions just above the poverty line, an injury, a period of sickness or an economic downturn could bring disaster. There were many Leonard Basts, E.M. Forster's struggling clerk in *Howards End*, who 'stood at the extreme verge of gentility. He was not in the abyss but he could see it, and at times people whom he knew had dropped in, and counted no more.'[10] Rowntree's study shocked many readers and helped Winston Churchill leave the Tory Party and join the Liberals. 'For my own part,' he commented, 'I see little glory in an Empire which can rule the waves and is unable to flush its sewers.'[11]

The disparities in wealth were starkly illustrated by the infant mortality figures. In 1910, 60 children per 1,000[12] infants died in affluent Hampstead but it was 148 on the other side of London in Shoreditch.[13] For Bournemouth, the figure was 77 per 1,000; for industrial Burnley, 172.[14] This was higher than Afghanistan in 2017 (estimated at 116 per 1,000),[145] the world's worst country for infant mortality. After the Taliban's disastrous rule and almost thirty years of war, Afghanistan's rate was still better than areas of Edwardian Britain. The Boer War saw many potential recruits rejected on health grounds. In cities like Manchester, up to half the men[16] who volunteered could not pass the low-level medical examination. As the working class made up 80 per cent of the population, the military implications were not lost on the government.

Class snobbery was pervasive. Even a sensitive liberal like John Maynard Keynes could note in his diary that he had to 'go to tea now to meet some bloody working men who will be I expect as ugly as men can be'.[17] E.M. Forster summed up this attitude: 'We are not concerned with the very poor. They are unthinkable and only to be approached by the statistician or the poet.'[18] Members of the propertied classes rarely spoke to their social inferiors other than as servants, shopkeepers or tradesmen. There was little social mixing even on the same sports teams. In cricket matches the 'gentlemen' (men from the middle and upper classes) had separate dressing rooms to the 'players' (men from the working class). On cricket scorecards, gentlemen were marked as 'Mr', a distinction not reserved for the plebeians. It wasn't until 1952 that a 'player', Len Hutton, finally captained England.

There was a growth of working-class consciousness, mostly in the form of trade union activity. This culminated in 1914 with the Triple Alliance. Formed from unions representing miners, dockers, seamen, railway and transport workers it contemplated using a general strike as a political weapon. Many members were syndicalists who argued for the workers' ownership of production. The formation of the Labour Party marked another political change. The first avowedly national party for the working class, it announced that some workers no longer believed their interests lay with Liberals or Conservatives. It made steady, if unspectacular progress, gaining twenty-nine seats in 1906 and forty-two by 1910. It supported the Liberal government in return for measures that would benefit the poor, like free school meals.

The liberation of women from their Victorian straightjackets did not start in the First World War. Attitudes were already changing. The 'New Woman' first made her appearance in the 1890s. Well educated, independent and sexually autonomous, she probably supported women's suffrage and other radical causes. She may well have owned the new transport sensation: a bicycle. She was usually from a privileged background, unconventionality being a luxury the poor could rarely afford. With changing lifestyles, practicality now informed the fashion of the middle class. The traditional bustles were no longer in vogue, looser dresses were preferred.[19] Hair was cut shorter for the same reason[20] and straighter silhouettes replaced the 'S' shape of the Victorian age.[21]

The role of government had also changed by the eve of the war. Both main parties had differed little in the nineteenth century in their belief that the state was not there to help the vulnerable. Any straightened circumstances were largely their own fault. What they needed was correction not coddling. The mainstay of Victorian social policy was the Poor Law Amendment Act (1834), which forced the desperate into workhouses that were little better than prisons. The 1905–15 Liberal government passed legislation that marked the first major step towards a welfare state: pensions, labour exchanges, boards to enforce minimum wages, compulsory health insurance for workers earning less than £160 a year, limited unemployment pay, school clinics and health inspections, wage boards for the sweated industries. There was opposition: hereditarian doctors argued that this was money wasted on the 'residuum' of humanity; free marketers saw this as an assault on hallowed principles; the aristocracy resented the tax increase. The reforms themselves were limited in the scale and number of people who could qualify but a Rubicon had been crossed. More would follow after the war.

The years before the First World War were not the 'long sunlit afternoons' that are often portrayed. Shooting parties with the Prince of Wales, the Ascot opening day, debutante balls, they all happened, but there was political and social ferment too, which the First World War sometimes delayed, often amplified, though did not create. Some people feared and some people embraced these changes, but most recognised their world was changing nonetheless.

PART I

COMING HOME

I

'THE DEAFENING SILENCE': THE ARMISTICE AT THE FRONT

'Only those men who actually marched back from the battle line on 11th November, 1918, can ever know or realise the mixed feelings then in the hearts of combatants.'

Frank Crozier[1]

November 11, 1918. It was a grey, miserable day when Bugler Corporal Sellier sounded the end of the First World War. At least 16 million people had died and another 20 million wounded; the British losses alone totalled 722,785 servicemen.[2] Yet the reaction to the Armistice was often more subdued at the Front than in Britain. Lieutenant Colonel Roberts noted this contrast: 'One cannot but remark on the absolute apathy with which the end was received over here. England seems to have had a jollification, but here one saw nothing but a disinterested interest in passing events.'[3] It seems surprising that soldiers were less enthusiastic than those out of danger. Brigade Major Oliver Lyttelton thought the feeling of anti-climax was widespread: 'We rode round the troops; everywhere the reaction was the same, flat dullness and depression ... This readjustment to peace-time anxieties is depressing, and we all felt flat and dispirited.'[4] At Le Cateau, W.F. Browning 'joined the queue and went up to the board, in silence like the rest and read the stupendous words "An armistice will be signed and fighting on the Western Front will cease today, November 11 1918 at 11 a.m." Not a word was spoken'[5] Deneys Reitz of the Royal Scots Fusiliers later commented, 'A few cheers were raised, and there was a solemn handshaking and slapping of backs, but otherwise they received the great event with calm.'[6] Colonel W.N. Nicholson wrote: 'on our side there were only a few shouts. I had heard more for a rum ration.'[7] Partly this was because men of that generation were not encouraged to show their emotions. They thought self-control a stoical response to life's vicissitudes. It helped many cope with conditions in the trenches.

Soldiers also had to contend with a different range of emotions to civilians. Troops had been killed on the last day, and the sadness and anger were still palpable. There was confusion about what an armistice exactly was – a surrender or a temporary truce? The agreement stated that the Armistice was initially to last only thirty-six days and either side could renew hostilities if the terms were not carried out. This helps explain the decision by some senior officers to gain as much ground as was possible on the last day, as many didn't trust the German High Command. These suspicions continued for weeks. When Brigadier General Hubert Rees returned from a prisoner of war (POW) camp in December he met people at the British Embassy in The Hague who firmly believed General Hindenburg, Germany's Chief of the General Staff, 'was collecting a great army near Hanover to renew the war'.[8] But the price paid for fighting until the end was a heavy one. There were almost 11,000 casualties on the last day of the war, a higher rate than D-Day.[9] Officially, the last British soldier killed was Private George Ellison. He'd been a pre-war regular and served since 1914, only to die at 9.30 a.m. on the day of the Armistice. Some British soldiers were killed even after the Armistice. In the Middle East and Africa, news of the war's end sometimes took several days to reach the troops, enough time for a few more telegrams home.

Another reason for the ambiguous mood was that this wasn't the decisive victory soldiers had hoped for. The Allies were pushing back the Germans, but the task remained unfinished. There was no equivalent of Waterloo. The Germans were still on foreign soil so the sudden ending frustrated some. One soldier complained, 'Why the bloody hell couldn't we have chased him right through Berlin while we had a chance …?'[10] Others thought the Germans would not accept they had lost – and would be more willing to fight again. Hubert Essame, a battalion adjutant, 'had an uncomfortable feeling that it would all have to be done over again'.[11] Joe Cottrill, Siegfried Sassoon's friend and a battalion quartermaster, presciently realised the dangers of an early peace even before the war had finished: 'it must go on – in the interests of our own preservation – till we are in a position to make a peace which will give us a certainty of the war not being resumed as soon as Germany thinks she is strong enough.'[12]

'Armistice? Armistake,' was a joke doing the rounds.

Some soldiers remembered comrades who hadn't made it, their sadness tinged with survivor's guilt. Lieutenant Patrick Campbell recalled all the dead he had served with who he would soon be leaving: 'we should become aware of their loss, we had hardly done so until now, we had still been with them, in the same country, close to them, close to death ourselves … they would stay behind, their home was in the lonely desolation of the battlefield.'[13] These feelings explain why many veterans would return to the Front after the war. Sergeant Cude's thoughts were with 'the good chaps who were with us but have now departed for all time'. He added, 'I have a keen sense of loneliness come over me, for in my four years out here almost, I have missed hundreds of the very best chaps that have ever breathed.'[14]

Others were so tired they couldn't register much at all. Stuart Dolden wrote, 'Frankly I had had enough, and felt thoroughly weary and in that respect I was not alone.'[15] Gunner Pankhurst recalled: 'We were so war weary that we were just ready to accept whatever came. When I read of the dancing in the fountains in Trafalgar Square ... my mind always goes back to us few men and the quiet way we took the news.'[16] Soldiers, often in the middle of their regular duties, like transportation or trench repair, had little time for contemplation. The enormity of what had happened would sink in later.

The sudden peace was strange. Soldiers had to adjust to walking upright along the front line, many still continued to lower their heads to avoid bullets hours after the fighting had ceased. When the guns stopped, the silence seemed overwhelming to those used to the sound of shot and shell; soldiers described it as 'deafening', 'uncanny' even 'oppressive'. This was in contrast to the final barrage before 11 a.m. as the artillery let off unused ammunition. 'It was the appalling new silence of things that soothed and unsettled them in turn,' wrote Kipling in his history of the Irish Guards. 'They did not realise till all sounds of their trade ceased, and the stillness stung in their ears as soda-water stings on the palate, how entirely these had been part of their strained bodies and souls.'[17]

Some were genuinely sorry the war was over. They would miss the intense bonds of friendship that cut across class barriers, which they would probably never experience again. Captain Herbert Read later wrote that it was only the 'public-school snob' or the 'worse snob ... from the fringes of the working-classes' who could not 'develop a relationship of trust and even ... intimacy with his men'.[18] Read described the unity in his company as 'compact, unanimous' forged in the 'heat of combat'.[19] The belief that it was a war worth fighting gave them a shared purpose. Sapper Arthur Halestrap spoke for many when he said, 'Straightaway we felt we had nothing to live for. There was nothing in front of us, no objective. Everything you had been working for, for years, had suddenly disappeared. What am I going to do next? What is my future?'[20] Fighter Pilot Cecil Lewis confessed 'to a feeling of anti-climax, even to a momentary sense of regret ... when you have been living a certain kind of life for four years, living as part of a single-minded effort, its sudden cessation leaves your roots in the air, baffled and, for a moment, disgruntled'.[21] 'What are we going to do now?' was a common reaction. 'It was like being made redundant,' recalled one ex-serviceman, another felt like 'we'd been kicked out of a job'.[22]

However, it would be wrong to run away with the idea that the end was greeted with universal disappointment. There were over 3 million men still in the British Army when the fighting stopped, so any generalisation is dangerous. Many soldiers later testified to the joy they felt at the end of the war. 'This is probably the best letter you have received in a long while! No more war! For the present at any rate.'[23] C.P. Blacker, near Mauberge, wrote of 'Faces radiating with joy emerged from blankets and everyone struggled to their feet. Pandemonium!'[24] Lieutenant A.S. Gregory wrote to his mother on the last day stating, 'Never again, I hope, shall I wear tin hat and box respirator.'[25]

Many were relieved to have survived the conflict; the British Army had been experiencing huge losses in the last 100 days. Frederick Hodges' first thought was, 'I'm going to live. I was stunned, total disbelief, and at the same time a secret and selfish joy that I was going to have a life.'[26] Soldiers could start to contemplate what many had not thought possible – a life outside the trenches. 'Each man had but one thought in those miraculous first hours: "I – even I myself, here – have come through the war!" … So mad with joy we don't feel yet what it all means.'[27] Very lights were set off and alcohol was issued. Drink played a part in how great the celebrations were. Some regiments offered a double rum ration, though enough alcohol for a booze-up could be hard to obtain. If a British soldier had more than his share he might have to contribute it to the general fund. Captain G.B. Jameson remembered how the veterinary officer's case of whiskey was broken into, he got drunk and went to sleep on a stretcher.[28] But others could find nothing. Cecil Lewis was cut off in a remote village and had to settle for a bonfire of some old German Very lights,[29] though some locals had saved a bottle or two for this occasion, often hidden for years from the Germans. There was music, flowers and dancing; sedate, respectable old women would hug and kiss British soldiers. George Littlefair remembered locals 'coming out shoving drinks on to us, you know, happy that the war was over'.[30] Private Doug Roberts was going to fetch a deserter from Dieppe with a sergeant, but knew the war was over when a Frenchman smashed the train window and threw in two bottles of wine. They never bothered about Dieppe or the deserter. When he went back to camp 'everyone was getting drunk.'[31] The luckiest were those on leave in Paris. The celebrations became legendary. As one journalist for *The Times* wrote, Paris 'went charmingly off her head'.[32] Tommies were welcomed by Parisiennes for their contribution to victory and British troops never went short of a free drink or a kiss. '*Vive les Anglais!*' was yelled throughout the night, not a cry often heard in that city today.

But for some, alcohol couldn't help lift their spirits. J.B. Priestley wrote thoughtfully, 'I can remember trying to work myself up into the right Bacchanalian mood, trying to ignore the creeping shadows, the mysterious rising tide of regret and sadness, which I think all but the simplest men suffer on these occasions.'[33]

2

'A BIT OF SHOUTING': THE ARMISTICE IN BRITAIN

'We have won a great victory and we are entitled to a bit of shouting.'
Prime Minister David Lloyd George, five minutes before the Armistice began[1]

The *Daily Mirror* reported that there had been quite a lot of shouting: 'London went wild with delight when the great news came through yesterday. Bells burst forth into joyful chimes, maroons were exploded, bands paraded the streets followed by cheering crowds of soldiers and civilians and London generally gave itself up wholeheartedly to rejoicing.'[2] It was understandable. Civilians were no less nationalistic than in August 1914 when crowds gathered in front of Downing Street to urge their leaders to declare war. And now the Allies had won, when for so long it seemed the Germans had the upper hand.

The British abandoned their customary restraint. Respectable businessmen banged on the side of buses with their shoes. Students burnt the Kaiser in effigy. American newspaperman, Edgar Bramwell Piper, saw revellers commandeer taxis and 'pile in and on anywhere, preferably on top. One car, with a prescribed capacity for four, had exactly twenty-seven persons sardined in its not-too-ample proportions.'[3] Crowds sang old favourites like 'It's a Long Way to Tipperary' or new ones like 'Good-bye-ee'. War worker Alice Kedge ran into the street after hearing the maroons* and saw:

> people everywhere, stopping the traffic, clambering over the trams, hanging out of windows, waving flags. I remember seeing the French tricolour and the American 'Stars and Stripes' as well as Union Jacks. We 'choir' girls linked arms

---

* The maroons were a signal for an air raid. Some people thought the German air force were about to bomb them again.

and started singing at the tops of our voices. I can't remember what we sang but we were soon leading a procession all the way down the Gray's Inn Road towards Holborn.[4]

The epicentre was around Piccadilly and Trafalgar Square. There was a food fight involving Canadian troops. Someone lit a fire that scarred the base of Nelson's Column. Young women were liable to be grabbed, kissed and even tossed in the air. Strangers embraced and, according to legend, openly had sex in the streets. It took four days for the Armistice celebrations to end. The police eventually had to clear out the hard-core revellers.

There was plenty of drink of course. Pubs ignored wartime restrictions and stayed open all night. Bramwell Piper thought that there were few displays of drunkenness on the street, though there was a lot in the city hotels and restaurants. Others remember plenty of windows broken and public vomiting. A parrot called Polly in Ye Olde Cheshire Cheese pub became a celebrity for her ability to imitate the sound of popping champagne corks. She reportedly did this 400 times before passing out with exhaustion. When she died in 1926, 200 newspapers gave Polly an obituary.[5]

Despite London's wartime restrictions on lights, many shops and restaurants 'did not trouble to draw blinds and curtains'[6] reported the *Daily Mirror* but the coal shortage meant only half the lights could be turned on. The odd firework was let off but they were mostly confined to officially sanctioned displays, another of the many wartime regulations.

For the religious-minded, churches were packed for thanksgiving services. St Paul's, despite its size, had to hold two. Lloyd George was mobbed and carried shoulder high as 'the man who won the war'. The King and Queen received an even greater reaction. Crowds descended on Buckingham Palace chanting, 'We want the king' and singing the national anthem. George V had to make numerous appearances from the balcony, though no one in the noisy crowd could hear what he said. The royal couple was driven around London in an open carriage, cheered wherever they went. The King was genuinely moved. He had been an exemplary head of state and deserved the accolades. French Premier Clemenceau later said to Lloyd George that he envied him George V compared to President Raymond Poincare.*

Not everyone was in a celebratory mood. Mourners could be seen in the crowd. Arthur Conan Doyle had just lost his son Kingsley and was disgusted when he saw a 'civilian hack at the neck of a whiskey bottle and drink it raw. I wish the crowd had lynched him. It was the moment for prayer, and this beast

---

* The French president was the head of state, the premier was the head of the government.

was a blot on the landscape.'[7] Sir Henry Wilson, Chief of the Imperial General Staff, tried to comfort a sobbing woman. When he asked if there was anything he could do, she replied, 'No. I am crying, but I am so happy, for now I know that all my three sons who have been killed in the war have not died in vain.'[8] Many compared the celebrations to Mafeking Night in 1900, when its relief during the Boer War brought a sense of jubilation out of all proportion to its military importance. Winston Churchill thought the Armistice night celebrations were more muted:

> Then the crowds were untouched by the ravages of war. They rejoiced with the light-hearted frenzy of the spectators of a great sporting event. In 1918 thankfulness and a sense of deliverance overpowered exultation. All bore in their hearts the marks of what they had gone through. There were too many ghosts about the streets after Armageddon.[9]

For soldiers in Britain, the reaction was mixed like at the Front. Plenty of Tommies were in the thick of the revelling, but some were in a more sombre mood. Lieutenant Ernest Parker wrote that:

> Alas, I could not share their high spirits, for the new life which was now beckoning had involved an enormous sacrifice, and would be yet another challenge for those like myself who had the good fortune to survive the perils of the long war. Surrounded by people whose experiences had been so different, I felt myself a stranger and I was lost in thoughts they could not possible share.[10]

Siegfried Sassoon, embittered about the war, described the crowds as 'all waving flags and making fools of themselves … a loathsome ending to the loathsome tragedy of the last four years.'[11] Oswald Mosley, a wounded officer now working for the Ministry of Munitions, was appalled at the partygoers: 'smooth, smug people who had never fought or suffered … laughing on the graves of our companions. I stood aside from the delirious throng, silent and alone, ravaged by memory. Driving purpose had begun; there must be no more war. I declared myself to politics.'[12]

Outside London, local officials were also organising impromptu celebrations. There was usually a street party or a parade, with a few speeches by local dignitaries. Some employers gave the rest of the day off. Those that didn't often experienced widespread absenteeism. Who could concentrate on such a day? Town centres heaved as school children swelled the crowds. 'In Sunderland impromptu fancy-dress parties were soon in full swing; in Blaina in South Wales 'practically every house exhibited a flag.'[13] Like London, there were church services and the bells rang for the first time since the Battle of Cambrai the previous December. There was also plenty of boozing. Soldiers on leave or recovering from wounds usually fared well. Pubs often ran out of beer.

'Today we have seen the greatest event in the history of the world'[14] commented the Lord Mayor of Cardiff with understandable hyperbole. 'The cause of righteousness and justice has prevailed … and the liberty of humanity secured by our valiant and glorious defenders and noble allies.' Boy scouts in Cardiff rode around on bicycles sounding the 'all-clear' with their bugles. The *South Wales Echo* reported that 'a limbless soldier wheeled down St Mary Street, ringing a bell with the vigour of a muffin man', while a young lieutenant 'exhort[ed] the crowd outside the Queen's Hotel to sing Rule Britannia'.[15] In the railway town of Wolverton, a group of apprentices at the Carriage Works ignored the whistle to return to work for the afternoon shift. Having 'organised a scratch band of bugles and drums'[16] they encouraged their older workmates to join them. They then marched on the school and chanted, 'let them out'. The teachers had little choice but to give pupils the rest of the day off. By the late afternoon Wolverton's celebrations had become more official: there were flags, the town band marched and there was a parade by the Scouts and cadets. In Gravesend, Kent, Nell Elston recalled Armistice Day ninety years later. Four at the time, this was her oldest memory: 'The town crier had brought the very welcome news that the Armistice had been signed … Women were out shouting in the streets and waving blankets.' Nell was mainly worried that 'her little brother was out in the street with no trousers on'. Then her mother said, 'Your daddy's coming home.'[17] She had already lost three uncles on the Somme.

Mabel Brown, who worked for a local printer, thought of those who had lost relatives: 'We'd got 1 or 2 girls in the department who, [*sic*] their brothers were not coming back … Give the girls their due … they rejoiced to think it was over and joined in with anything that went on. We thought they were wonderful the one or two that had lost brothers.'[18] Some soldiers, like the poet Robert Graves, were in no mood to celebrate. In North Wales he was 'walking alone along the dyke above the marches of Rhuddlan, cursing and sobbing and thinking of the dead'.[19] Others wanted to finish the war with their comrades. Sergeant Major Arthur Cook was initially pleased to receive a 'Blighty wound' that got him back to England. However, he regretted not celebrating the Armistice at the Front: 'What would I give to be with the battalion now!'[20]

'WE WANT OUR CIVVIE SUITS': DEMOBILISATION

'Send the boys home. Why in the world delay? The war is not officially 'over', but every-one knows that in fact it is over. Munition-making has stopped; motorists can joy ride; the King has had a drink; society has had its victory ball and is settling down.'

The Daily Herald, *7 December 1918*[1]

In the immediate aftermath of the war, no issue proved as controversial with soldiers as demobilisation. The challenge of moving 3.8 million soldiers[2] back into civilian life was enormous, but the original plan proved flawed and provoked serious protests. The Minister of War, Lord Derby, had devised a demobilisa-tion scheme which prioritised men deemed 'pivotal' for the transition from war to peace, like miners and agricultural workers. Policemen were also needed to maintain order; so desperate was the government that any soldier over 6ft could immediately sign up for the force.* Lord Milner, Derby's replacement, believed the 'guiding principle was to demobilise in the way most likely to lead to the steady resumption of industry'.[3] These groups were clearly vital to keeping the country running. What caused rancour was that troops who had jobs already waiting for them were also given priority; all they needed was a 'slip' from their former employer. Those who had volunteered at the start of the war had been out of the job market the longest and were less likely to obtain this slip – they would be punished for their patriotism. Some had joined straight from schools or interrupted university courses. The recent arrivals, mainly conscripts, could find ex-employers more easily. The scheme also lent itself to fraud: someone with

---

* This may be where the nickname 'Old Bill' originated, as so many ex-soldiers became policemen. 'Old Bill' was a popular wartime cartoon character, a wily old Tommy with a prominent moustache.

a friend or family member in business could simply sign one, regardless as to whether the soldier had worked for them or not – 'humbug and jobbery' was Winston Churchill's description of the scheme.[4] Harry Wharton's dad was asked:

> Would he take two ex-officers to train for farming? This was when the war was over, he got this letter. And the old boy was clever enough to reply, he'd be very pleased to have these two boys, provided he could have his two sons home from France to help him. And we were sent home in the February.[5]

This 'last in, first out' principle clearly discriminated against those who had answered the call in 1914 and 1915. It angered veterans of the Somme and Passchendaele that more recent arrivals were going home first. Some had been 'combed out' of well-paid jobs in the final months of the war. Fears that those who returned last would find it most difficult to get work proved all too true.

Field Marshall Haig sensed trouble, believing the scheme was 'based upon the necessity for a rapid reconstruction of the civil and commercial life … without any consideration of length of service overseas'.[6] The reconstruction committees hadn't taken soldiers' feelings into account. In fairness, no one had expected the Armistice to happen so early and officials were simply not ready to start demobilisation in 1918 in sufficient numbers to satisfy the troops. The 4,000 a day demobilised in the first two months of peace still left huge numbers abroad. A fair amount of bureaucratic incompetence made matters worse. Soldiers had to have new work contracts verified by the Ministry of Labour. This could take so long that some men who'd found jobs on leave were shipped back to France before the process was complete. Lloyd George had said during the December general election that the troops would be home in a few weeks, raising impossible expectations. Not for the last time, the government would promise in haste and repent at leisure.

Another problem was the armed forces still had duties to perform. The Rhineland needed policing to ensure compliance with the peace terms; Britain's Empire was increasingly restless. The collapse of the Ottoman Empire left a power vacuum the British and French were anxious to fill, but these new territories had been promised independence if they rose against their Turkish masters. Ireland was descending into violence and, most controversial of all, troops were being sent to intervene in the Russian Civil War.

The British Armed Forces had been remarkably disciplined when there was a war to win but being asked to guard distant oil installations or intervene in far-flung regional conflicts was another matter. They were anxious to get home. In Egypt, there was a mood of a defiance over the slowness of the demobilisation process. 'Men did not trouble to salute officers in the streets and surly acquiescence to orders was a common feature in infantry regiments.'[7] A Soldiers'

Council was formed, which established its own guards. Attempts at tightening discipline didn't help. The army command thought this reversion to pre-war norms was necessary to stop the army from disintegrating. Parades and polishing were the order of the day and the easier relations that had developed between non-commissioned officers (NCOs), privates and even some junior officers were discouraged. But the army now consisted of better-educated, more independent-minded men. The pettiness grated and some were reluctant to put up with it. In Salonika, Colonel Alfred Bundy found that the men 'now showed a degree of independence that was disconcerting'.[8] Believing that strict discipline might be counter-productive he tried to reason with them, but was greeted with 'catcalls and rude noises'. He suspected that they were a minority and it was only when he threatened to have people arrested and their demobilisation delayed that order was restored.

Boredom is a feature of any army, but purposeless boredom is particularly dangerous. The army did try to relieve this with football matches and some lectures but most men just wanted out. Trouble erupted two days after the Armistice, at a base in Shoreham; soldiers took to the streets of Brighton when an officer pushed a soldier into the mud. The army speeded up the demobilisation of the camp. At Folkestone the atmosphere was notably more tense. Men learned that they would be shipped back to France, and rumours circulated that Russia was the final destination, despite official denials. The rebels set up pickets to prevent any ship leaving port with soldiers on board. An officer who claimed to be a relative of Douglas Haig was manhandled. Thousands of men marched into town and held a mass meeting to demand speedier demobilisation. A compromise was reached and more leave was granted so men could look for work. No one was punished for this defiance. Similar demonstrations (and compromises) happened in Dover. It was becoming clear that Lord Derby's plan was unworkable.

In December, men burnt down several depots at Le Havre that had become seriously overcrowded with inadequate food and sanitation. They were demobilised as fast as possible.[9] At Calais in January at least 3,000–4,000[10] mutinied over demobilisation and the appalling living conditions of the camps (some men were sleeping in tents in the middle of winter). Haig contemplated court martials for the ringleaders but was overruled by Churchill.[11] Loyal regiments were ordered to fix bayonets and be ready to go in, but fortunately things quietened down enough for bloodshed to be averted. The authorities built new huts, improved the food and abolished weekend working.[12]

January 1919 was a turbulent month as widespread disobedience broke out. Osterley, Bristol, Kempton Park, Aldershot, Shoreham (again), Edinburgh and Maidstone all experienced trouble. In London, troops refused to board a train when they heard it was going to Russia, despite the earlier assurance that only volunteers would be sent. General Trenchard was beaten up when he tried to persuade men at Southampton docks to call off their strike. As a reprisal, around 100 men were hosed down and then made to stand outside on a cold January day.[13] In February, 3,000 marched on Whitehall in an angry protest. Placards with 'WE WANT OUR CIVVIE SUITS' and 'WE WON THE WAR, GIVE US OUR TICKETS' appeared.

A pattern was emerging. The authorities mixed concessions, like better conditions, extended leave and speedier demobilisation, with the arrest of the ringleaders when they felt sufficiently in control. When they didn't, the ringleaders were often the first to be demobbed to get rid of troublemakers. It needs emphasising that though these acts of defiance were widespread, they still involved a minority of the British Army. The government could call up loyal troops like guards regiments to quell the most violent demonstrations. Guards were moved home, as Charles Carrington wrote many years later:

> … and paraded through London in fighting order, ostensibly to allow the Londoners to welcome their own familiar defenders, and with a secondary motive of warning the seditious that force would be met with force … it was a celebration, and at the same time a warning that there was still a disciplined army.[14]

The new Minister for War, Winston Churchill, faced a dilemma. He was the strongest advocate for intervention in the Russian Civil War and favoured a military solution to Ireland. A passionate believer in an expansive and expanding empire, Churchill knew he needed a large peacetime army to achieve this. He initially considered conscripting a million men but it was becoming clear no government could enforce such a measure. Churchill decided to bow to the inevitable and speeded up the demobilisation process. Priority was now based on the length of service and the number of times a soldier had been wounded. Demobilisation increased to 185,000 per week and by November 1919 the total British Army was less than a million. It took until 1922 for the British Army to return to something like its pre-war numbers of 230,000.[15] Indiscipline diminished, especially as those who had remained had their pay doubled. The crisis was over but the process of returning men to civilian life had been unnecessarily long and bitter.

Some writers have speculated that Britain came close to a revolution in this period. Revolutionary activity had just toppled governments in Russia and in Hungary. In Germany and Italy there were serious outbreaks of political violence, with soldiers taking a leading role. It is true that members of the British Government were rattled, given the international situation. Some descended into hyperbole. Lloyd George told union leaders:

I feel bound to tell you, that in our opinion we are at your mercy. The Army is disaffected and cannot be relied upon. Trouble has occurred already in a number of camps. We have just emerged from a great war and the people are eager for the reward of their sacrifices, and we are in no position to satisfy them. In these circumstances, if you carry out your threat and strike, then you will defeat us.[16]

Churchill said that if only the troops had formed a 'united resolve' then no power 'could have attempted to withstand them'.[17] But there was no united resolve; anger was over specific grievances rather than against the whole system. Once these issues had been dealt with there was little trouble. British soldiers had not shown themselves keen on Bolshevik ideas spreading from Russia, but they had a strong sense of fair play and were sometimes prepared to use violence to achieve it.

4

ARRIVALS

Keep the Home Fires Burning,
While your hearts are yearning,
Though your lads are far away
They dream of home.

Popular First World War song,
Ivor Novello and Lena Guilbert Ford

Soldiers had naturally dreamed of returning home during the war. This is reflected in sentimental trench songs like 'Keep the Home Fires Burning' and 'It's a Long Way to Tipperary', but what did they find on their return? Some things had obviously changed. The cities were dingier as house repairs had virtually stopped, though there was nothing like the physical damage of the Second World War. The food was less varied but Britain had escaped the widespread hunger that Germany and Austria had experienced. Rationing was phased out over the next three years, though a return to pre-war overindulgence (for those who could afford it) never quite resumed. Relative poverty had declined. Full employment and higher wages for unskilled workers meant that 52,490 children were being given free school meals in 1918; in 1915 it was 422,401.[1]

To the annoyance of moralists, some wartime fads, like tea dances, nightclubs, jazz and American cinema, continued. Initially, at least, women were more visible in the workplace for the first time in areas of employment like the police. Their fashion was more daring and more practical for work. The sight of trousers and raised hemlines, as much as 10in from the ground, shocked many, as did the sight of women wearing mascara and smoking in public. The desire for greater personal freedoms pitted against a return to traditional values would be a feature of the interwar years.

After demobilisation, soldiers were given twenty-eight days' pay and a rail pass home. They could keep their army greatcoats or receive £1 instead. Many chose the former and these coats became a common sight on down-and-outs after the war. The troops also received a gratuity – 'blood money', as it was soon labelled – depending on rank, averaging around £40. An army commander was given £30,000 plus a viscounty – Haig pocketed £100,000 and an earldom (he had asked for double that).

The returning soldiers were usually greeted as heroes, though some receptions were grander than others. E.R.M. Fryer of the Grenadiers recalls, 'It was raining … but all the same we got the welcome home which we had looked forward to for years; and the band played "See the Conquering Hero Comes" as we got out of the train; and with uncased Colours and fixed bayonets, we marched through the city'[2] Soldiers who came back on their own or in small groups received a more modest welcome, often from family and friends. Private Robert Renwick remembered his mother embracing him in tears. Some of the village came out because 'I'd been reported killed twice'.[3] Families had to readjust to soldiers who had been away a long time. Myfi Jones recalled when her dad returned from the war her younger brother was terrified of this strange man in uniform; he didn't remember his father at all.[4]

Local communities also honoured the men with street parties (or 'peace teas') and receptions. Private Walter Hare of the West Yorkshire Regiment recalled 'A good meal and a lot of sing songs … it was a happy do.'[5] These street parties became a tradition in Britain for national occasions like jubilees and coronations. The year 1919 provided the template, with long tables, tea, sandwiches, bunting and flags. Florence Cole from Edmonton remembers her party didn't take place until August:

> Money for the party was collected from door to door; games were organised and the street was decorated with bunting … Whole families joined in … I was dressed in the colours of the Belgium flag … The fancy dresses were not elaborate because so little money was available, but a lot of creative ideas went into them.[6]

Not everyone was made to feel welcome. Sapper 'Jack' Martin, on a train back to London, thought other passengers were 'looking on us with suspicion and even shunning us. We were sneaking home – that's all that can be said for it. Evidently the stay-at-homes did not welcome our return. Where were the flags and the banners and the laurel wreaths and trumpets?'[7]

Nationally, 19 July 1919 was declared Peace Day to celebrate the end of the war, with London the focus of a huge victory parade. Almost 15,000 troops took part, with representatives from all the Allied armies, including Generals Pershing and Foch. Crowds started arriving the night before for the biggest parade London had ever seen. In France, disabled soldiers were given pride of place in its parades, but in Britain they were conspicuously absent; they had a view from the stands and a message from the king:

> To these, the sick and wounded who cannot take part in the festival of victory, I send out greetings and bid them good cheer, assuring them that the wounds and scars so honourable in themselves, inspire in the hearts of their fellow countrymen the warmest feelings of gratitude and respect.[8]

Peace Day was a bank holiday, so many towns organised festivities. Generally, these were happy affairs, but there were grumblings that the cost of the celebrations could be better used helping veterans. One angry letter to the *Manchester Evening News* complained that:

> Peace Day will send a cold shiver through the bodies of thousands of 'demobbed' men who are walking about the streets of Manchester looking for a job. Could a term be found that would be more ironical for such men. Perhaps, after the Manchester and Salford Corporations have celebrated this 'Peace' and incidentally will have wasted the thousands of pounds which it will cost, they will devote their spare time to alleviating the 'bitterness' and 'misery' which exist in the body and mind of the unemployed ex-soldier.

The Norwich branch of the radical veterans' group the National Federation of Discharged and Demobilized Sailors and Soldiers declared:

> Our pals died to kill militarism, not to establish that here. We have had militarism burned into us, and we hate it … The Norwich branch of the federation, which consists of nearer 4,000 men than 3,000, has decided that they will take no part in the celebration of this mock peace.[9]

In Luton, the mood turned ugly. Already frustrated at the slow pace of demobilisation, veterans were angered at council plans. A lavish mayor's banquet would be held without any servicemen. Veterans first heckled the official speeches and then broke into the town hall, trashed it, then burnt it to the ground. During the riot, they raided a music shop and dragged pianos into the streets to accompany their singing and dancing. The mayor was lucky to escape unharmed. It once more showed that soldiers in the immediate aftermath of the war were quite prepared to use violence if pushed too far.

Amidst the celebrations, there came a tragedy that marred the first few months of peace. At least 50 million people died from a strain of the H1N1 virus, similar to the bird flu pandemic of 2009. The Spanish Flu killed more people than the Black Death did and considerably more than the First World War. Victims could feel the first shivers at breakfast and be dead by the evening. The effects were described in a letter dated September 1918:

> It starts with what appears to be an ordinary attack of la grippe. When brought to the hospital, [patients] very rapidly develop the most vicious type of pneumonia that has ever been seen. Two hours after admission, they have mahogany spots over the cheek bones, and a few hours later you can begin to see the cyanosis [blueness due to lack of oxygen] extending from their ears and spreading all over the face. It is only a matter of a few hours then until death comes and it is simply a struggle for air until they suffocate. It is horrible.[10]

The 'Spanish Lady', as some called it, hit India the hardest; 17 million lost their lives there. South Africa and the American Midwest also suffered grievously. They were a long way from the battlefields, which begs the question, how much did the war affect the epidemic? This is still debated. The massive movement and crowding of people caused by the war possibly increased the number of fatalities. John Oxford argues that the army's base depot at Étaples[11] was crucial in spreading the flu. One hundred thousand soldiers could be stationed there at one time and its insanitary conditions became a haven for the virus to spread rapidly. The weakening of people's resistance due to wartime privations also contributed to the high death rate. A healthier population might not have succumbed in such numbers. On the other hand, unlike normal influenza outbreaks that disproportionately kill the old, Spanish Flu mostly hit young adults. Many were soldiers. In fact, the large crowds during the Armistice celebrations helped spread the disease, giving the virus a new lease of life in the first six months of peace. 'Funerals seemed to pass the house non-stop,' remembered one Plymouth resident.[12] In Salford, there were 415 deaths alone in November 1918.[13] The functioning of society started to break down. Mail delivery was cancelled and fires were left to burn out on their own, such was the shortage of manpower. Churches, theatres and dance halls closed their doors. People started wearing masks or not turning up for work.

There was something particularly poignant about a man surviving the trenches and then being felled by flu. Wilfred Timilty, a sergeant and winner of the Distinguished Conduct Medal, could be found resting on his crutches at Pendleton tram depot, joking with the tram conductors, before he died of the flu.[14] William Leefe-Robinson VC, the first pilot to shoot down a German airship, died in December 1918 after returning from a POW camp; his weakened state was a contributory factor. Arthur Conan Doyle's son Kingsley was convalescing from wounds when his flu turned to pneumonia; he died two weeks before the war finished. His brother, a brigadier general, also succumbed in February 1919. Conan Doyle turned to spiritualism for consolation. Soldiers sometimes returned home to find members of their family dead or dying. Corporal Flowers heard that his wife had died while celebrating the Armistice at the Front. His officer arranged for him to get home and he had to travel back on a boat full of troops celebrating the peace. He saw a man weeping. It transpired the same thing had happened to him.[15] Sometimes the men brought the virus with them. Frederick Darwin, who spent four years in the Royal Army Medical Corps, contracted the disease in a military hospital. Not only did he die but so did his wife and son.[16]

With a lack of medical knowledge, there wasn't a lot doctors could do. Some expert recommendations included drinking more whisky or port and cutting down on tobacco. People fell back on old superstitions like having rhubarb or vinegar for their supposed medicinal powers.[17] Not much of an improvement on the treatments used during the Black Death. By April 1919 it disappeared as rapidly as it arrived but around 250,000 Britons had died.

POWs were in a particularly bad condition when they returned. Many were severely malnourished through ill treatment and the effectiveness of the British blockade of German ports. This had brought Germany to the brink of starvation but British POWs had suffered too. 'Emaciated' and 'like skeletons' were frequent descriptions; some died later from illnesses like diarrhoea, dysentery and, inevitably, influenza. Officers and NCOs had been excused manual labour but privates were made to do hard physical work. Private Ernest Wilson of the Durham Light Infantry recalled clearing roads, digging reserve trenches and unloading rail trucks on 'meagre rations', mostly turnip soup. He survived despite describing himself as a 'weakling' because he managed not to 'lose his spirits',[18] unlike physically more robust men who gave up hope. Lance Corporal Hunt said he was so thin his father immediately put him on cod liver oil when he got home.[19] Corporal Joe Armstrong's grandmother thought his face was 'less than a baby's'. He only weighed 86lb.[20] The Imperial War Museum's photograph archive shows men like Private Norman Veitch of the 5th Battalion, Yorkshire Regiment who was made to work on the German railways until he grew too sick.[21] His body resembled that of a Holocaust survivor. Like them, returning POWs were stuffed full of food, which caused violent reactions in stomachs unused to a proper diet.

They have received nothing like the attention of the Second World War's POWs yet there was more of them. Over 180,000[22] were captured and at least 3,000 died.[23] Not all camps guards were brutal but many were; POWs complained of random beatings and summary executions. War crime trials were held at Leipzig, with German judges. Only twelve guards were put on trial, seven of whom were charged with mistreating POWs. Of the four found guilty, three were given sentences of less than a year, causing anger in Britain about how few were prosecuted and the leniency of their sentences. The behaviour of Turkish guards was far worse. Around half of the POWs died at their hands and those who came back were in an appalling condition.[24] All men, regardless of rank, had to do hard manual labour in stifling heat with insufficient rations. The forced death march of weakened British soldiers after the Siege of Kut is comparable with Japanese death marches in the Second World War.

The chaos following the Armistice meant many prisoners were simply abandoned by their guards. Percy Williams recalled that 'we didn't realise there was an armistice until about a fortnight afterwards'.[25] They were left to make their own way to the Allied lines or a neutral country, walking for miles, scavenging what they could. It was too much for some. Private Walter Hare remembered one of his friends, Jack, dying on the way, through 'exposure and lack of nourishment'.[26] Arriving in Britain, POWs were taken to dispersal camps and debriefed about their treatment. The policy was to offer the soldiers a £2 gratuity and an immediate rail pass home. If they took the money they waived their rights for a medical examination and, of course, a potential pension. Two pounds seemed a lot of money, so many took it, to their later regret. Sergeant Hawtin Munday was one of them. 'Well just think what you could do with two quid in those days … and this is what makes me mad ever since … I had been wounded three times, been a prisoner of war – and never had a bloody penny: I should have had that examination.'[27]

Many soldiers' families were shocked to see them. POWs often arrived before demobilisation had got under way so they were some of the first men to get home. Families had no idea they were still alive, as they had heard no news for months if not years. Ada Croft's remembered:

> My brother Arthur and my sister Addy's husband were prisoners … and we couldn't hear nothing about them whether they was dead or alive, and we'd come home from church one Sunday evening … and a knock come at the Front door and I don't know whether my Auntie had a premonition that it might be Addy's husband but when she got to the door that's who it was, and he nearly fell in the door, he was so weak, and of course he give us all a turn when he walked in.

However, Addy's husband was also in for a nasty shock:

> In the meantime she'd had her baby, but while she was carrying this baby she was really worried over him because she'd heard that he was a prisoner of war

… so of course when her baby was born she'd fretted so much she lost her baby and that's the first thing he asked for when he got in, he says, 'Where's the baby Addy?' So then of course that upset everybody that did.[28]

There was no more tragic a homecoming than what happened on the Isle of Lewis. Like many rural Scottish communities, the men had volunteered in disproportionate numbers. Consequently, they were particularly badly hit. Out of the 6,200 who joined up, at least 800 had died, perhaps the greatest proportionate loss of any community in Britain.[29] Many of the survivors wanted to get home for New Year but the regular ferry was full, so the navy commandeered a yacht, the *Iolaire*. The boat was packed when she sailed at 9.30 p.m. on 31 December and there were insufficient lifeboats and lifejackets. With hindsight she shouldn't have set off for Stornoway. The captain and crew had never attempted this manoeuvre, which was hazardous even during daylight.[30] The weather deteriorated as a gale started to blow. In poor visibility, the *Iolaire* hit a notoriously rocky outcrop nicknamed 'the Beasts of Holm' in the early hours of New Year's Day. The boat sunk so quickly that most were drowned. One man, John Macleod, managed to reach the shore and set up a safety rope, which helped another twenty-five to escape. Overall 205 men died. They'd come through the war only to then perish within sight of home. Men like Kenneth Macphail, recorded on the island's roll of honour, who:

> Was the sole survivor of a ship torpedoed in the Mediterranean in October 1917. He had a terrible experience before he was rescued having been nearly 36 hours in the sea … pathetic in the extreme it is to think that this powerful seaman after so miraculous an escape in the Mediterranean, perished within a few feet of his native soil.[31]

It was the worst maritime disaster of the twentieth century off British coastal waters. Lewis was devastated. *The Scotsman* reported in January that the 'villages of Lewis are like places of the dead. The homes of the island are full of lamentation – grief that cannot be comforted. Scarcely a family has escaped the loss of a near blood relative. Many have had sorrow heaped upon sorrow.'[32] Some thought its depopulation problems started here. The Admiralty callously tried to sell off the wreck before all the bodies had been recovered. It prompted the local commanding officer to telegram London, 'It has come to my knowledge inhabitants of islands resent wreck being sold while the bodies remain still unrecovered.'[33] The Admiralty abandoned the sale.

PART II

UNFINISHED BUSINESS

5

'OUT OF IRELAND'

Out of Ireland have we come.
Great hatred, little room,
Maimed us at the start.
I carry from my mother's womb
A fanatic heart.

W.B. Yeats[1]

During the summer of 1914, the Ulster Unionist leader Edward Carson wrote, 'I see no hopes of peace; I see nothing at present but darkness and shadows … we shall have once more to assert the manhood of our race.'[2] It was two weeks before the First World War started but Carson wasn't talking about the crisis enveloping Europe. For many in Britain, the Irish situation was more important than any trouble on the Continent.

Ireland was on the verge of Home Rule – a form of devolved government similar to Canada and Australia, where Ireland would control its internal affairs but would still be part of the British Empire. There was a complication: the Protestant community of British settlers, called Loyalists or Unionists, made up the majority of the population in most of the counties of Ulster, the north-east province of Ireland. They were bitterly opposed to joining a devolved Ireland. For them, Home Rule meant 'Rome Rule' – the dominance of the Catholic majority. Often from Scottish Presbyterian stock, anti-Catholicism was part of their communal identity. Loyalist troops cried 'No Popery' as they charged German trenches. An armed militia, the Ulster Volunteers,* was formed in 1912 to maintain Protestant hegemony and oppose Home Rule. The men started drilling

---

* Soon renamed the Ulster Volunteer Force (UVF).

and imported caches of arms. Catholics (sometimes referred to as Nationalists) responded with a smaller paramilitary force: the Irish Volunteers. Only an agreement to postpone the question until the end of the war prevented a descent into sectarian violence.

Fifty-two thousand, three hundred and sixty-five Unionists joined up in 1914. A huge number from such a small community.[3] They were fiercely pro-British, whatever their grievances with the London government. Carson said, 'We do not seek to purchase terms by selling our patriotism.' The Ulster Volunteers merged into the 36th (Ulster) Division and served with distinction, particularly on the Somme. The behaviour of Irish Catholics is more puzzling. Overall, 64,607 Irish Catholics soldiers volunteered, despite their dislike of the British Empire.[4] The reasons were complex. Some signed up out of sympathy with Belgium, a Catholic nation invaded by Protestant-led Germany. Tom Kettle of the Irish Volunteers was in Belgium in 1914 buying arms, but still joined the British Army, as he sympathised with small nations (like Belgium and Serbia) being bullied by larger ones (Germany and Austria Hungary). This is explicit in the Cork War Memorial, which honours those 'fighting for the freedom of small nations'.[5] Another was to show that an independent Ireland could prove itself as a nation. There were fears, well founded as it transpired, that Britain would water down the Home Rule legislation, and war service might pressurise them not to do so. A few Catholics wanted to learn how to be soldiers to prepare for any future conflict. Others were simply looking for a chance to get away from home. Tom Barry, a sergeant in the Royal Field Artillery, wrote in his memoirs:

> In June, in my seventeenth year, I had decided to see what this Great War was like. I cannot plead I went on the advice of John Redmond or any other politician, that if we fought for the British we would secure Home Rule for Ireland, nor can I say I understood what Home Rule meant. I was not influenced by the lurid appeal to fight to save Belgium or small nations. I knew nothing about nations, large or small. I went to the war for no other reason than that I wanted to see what war was like, to get a gun, to see new countries and to feel a grown man. Above all I went because I knew no Irish history and had no national consciousness.[6]

There were Nationalists who hoped the war would bring better relations with Irish Protestants. Tom Kettle, who enlisted as an officer, wrote that 'this tragedy of Europe may be and must be the prologue to the two reconciliations of which all statesmen have dreamed, the reconciliation of Protestant Ulster with Ireland, and the reconciliation of Ireland with Great Britain'.[7] Willie Redmond, brother of the Irish Parliamentary Party leader, hoped the shared experiences of the trenches would reduce sectarianism after the war. Protestants and Catholics did fight side-by-side, notably at Messines Ridge in 1917, with a harmony absent in peacetime. Redmond was killed in that attack and the 36th formed a guard of honour.

But the Easter Rising of 1916 soured relations between the two communities. The Rising was an insurrection organised by ardent Nationalists who declared Ireland an independent republic. The rebellion was swiftly defeated but left a bitter legacy. The British and Loyalists saw it as a treasonous act during wartime. Even some Nationalists didn't approve, particularly the wives and mothers of servicemen fighting on the Western Front, but the British decision to shoot fifteen rebels changed Catholic opinion, as did the occupation and behaviour of British troops in Dublin. Troops had indiscriminately fired on civilians during the suppression of the Easter Rising and continued to treat the Irish as an enemy. Tom Kettle, while against the Rising, realised what these executions would mean for Catholic troops in the British Army: 'These men will go down in history as heroes and martyrs; and I will go down – if I go down at all – as a bloody British officer.' The last poem he wrote, a sonnet to his daughter, explains why he joined up:

> Died not for flag, nor King, nor Emperor
> But for a dream, born in a herdsman's shed
> and for the secret Scripture of the poor.

He was killed on the Somme soon after.

Any comradeship between Unionists and Nationalists had disappeared by the end of the war. After much bloodshed, a compromise settlement was reached in 1921. Ireland would be partitioned on roughly religious lines. The twenty-six Catholic counties that constituted the Irish Free State were given dominion status. Six counties in Ulster, with a Protestant majority, remained part of the United Kingdom. There were religious minorities on both sides of the border. Catholics in Northern Ireland believed the British should not have gone back on their original agreement to give the whole of Ireland Home Rule. Many joined the Irish Republican Party (IRA).

Catholic ex-soldiers in the new Free State were sometimes viewed as traitors who had fought for the hated British. A view not widely held in 1914, but more common in the aftermath of the Easter Rebellion. The IRA shot over 200 veterans between 1919–1922 and unemployment for Irish ex-servicemen stood at 46 per cent a year after the war.[8] Further misery was added when the IRA intimidated Ministry of Pensions officials, which disrupted veterans' medical treatment and financial allowances.[9]

When the British pulled out, many Nationalists thought the agreement was too much of a compromise and civil war broke out in 1922. The new Irish government badly needed soldiers; about half the troops and 20 per cent of the officers of the Free State's National Army had served under the British in the First World War. Emmet Dalton, a major in the Dublin Fusiliers, chose to side with the government despite his former membership of the IRA; some veterans fought on the anti-treaty side like Tom Barry. Men who had served together in the British Army now fired at one another.

In Northern Ireland, tensions between the religious groups soon broke out into violence. Protestant soldiers were greeted as heroes in Ulster. Their bravery became part of Unionist folklore, who were now even less willing to stop being British. As Sir James Craig, Northern Ireland's first prime minister, said on Armistice Day 1922, 'those who passed away have left behind a great message to all of them to stand firm, and to give away none of Ulster's soil'.[10] Protestant ex-servicemen reconstituted the Ulster Volunteer Force to renew their struggle against Catholics in a campaign that bordered on ethnic cleansing. Men like Basil Brooke, a future Northern Ireland prime minister who had been a captain in the 10th Hussars, organised Fermanagh Vigilance to prevent any attacks on the county by the IRA. Wilfred Spender, quartermaster general of the UVF in 1913, who had joined the 36th (Ulster) Division, helped organise the Ulster Special Constabulary – and the notorious 'B-Specials'. Many were former members of Protestant regiments, figures of hate in the Catholic community but for Loyalists a bulwark against the IRA.

Loyalists feared that the Civil War in the Irish Free State would spill into Northern Ireland and were deeply suspicious of Catholics who remained, even those who had fought in the war. J. Bower Bell wrote that Protestants were 'fearful of absorption into a Green, Catholic Ireland and … blindly angered by the presence of heresy and treason in their midst, struck … at the Catholic community … vengeful Catholics struck back with counter-terror'. Unionists' fears increased as Catholics became more radical. Sinn Féin had made huge gains in the 1918 general election, returning seventy-three MPs – with the moderate Irish Parliamentary Party being consigned to the dustbin of history. Many Nationalist leaders like Éamon de Valera refused to recognise the partition of Ireland and the IRA started to supply arms to Catholics north of the border.

From 1920–22 a period of sectarian violence broke out in Northern Ireland that was more intense than the Troubles in the 1960s and '70s. Much of it centred around Belfast, where 465 deaths occurred and over 1,091 people were wounded.[11] Former Loyalist veterans played a significant part in the 'Belfast Pogroms'. The trigger was the killing of a detective inspector in Lisburn by Nationalists in August 1920. Sectarian tensions had already been high with increased competition for jobs. On 21 July, all 5,000 Catholics were forcibly cleared from their jobs in the Belfast shipyards – a fifth were ex-servicemen.[12]

No one was killed, but there was violence: Catholics were thrown in the river and pelted with stones.

Both communities forced their minorities from their homes and businesses. Both sides lost lives (two Unionist MPs were killed, for example). Shops and churches were looted and destroyed as Northern Ireland became more segregated. Neighbours turned on each other. It has been estimated that over £3 million worth of property was destroyed. The worst violence happened in July 1921, when twenty-two people were killed and 200 houses destroyed over a four-day period. It became known as Belfast's Bloody Sunday. Ultimately, the war had not brought the unity Willie Redmond hoped for; if anything it had stoked sectarian hatreds.

> Oh, come out you Black and Tans,
> Come out and fight me like a man
> Show your wife how you won medals down in Flanders
> Tell them how the IRA
> Made you run like hell away,
> From the green and lovely lanes in Killashandra.
>
> 'Come Out Ye Black and Tan'
> Irish rebel song by Dominic Behan

> ' … rough, brutal, abusive and distinctly the worse for liquor.'
> British Labour Party report on the behaviour
> of British veterans in Ireland[13]

In the Irish War of Independence, the IRA waged a campaign against British rule. Fifty-one local policemen were killed and many resigned from the force. In January 1920, the government started recruiting ex-servicemen to be temporary constables in the Royal Irish Constabulary (RIC). Their task was to help pacify Ireland, something they singularly failed to do. The Black and Tans nickname came from their motley uniforms that reminded locals of a pack of Limerick foxhounds. Another group, the Auxiliaries, were recruited from the officer class and was the idea of Winston Churchill, the War Minister. Curiously, the 'Auxies' never achieved the notoriety of the Tans even though the IRA thought they were a deadlier foe. Few names evoke as much hatred in Ireland as the Black and Tans. After a century it can still cause upset. When Ben and Jerry's Ice Cream (innocently) introduced a Black and Tan flavour there were howls of protest, even though this was not commercially available in Ireland.[14]

They have been likened to Germany's Freikorps – right-wing veterans used by the government to put down communist uprisings. The Tans and the Auxies may not have been as consciously political as the Freikorps but they could match them in violence. They showed all the insensitivity of soldiers policing a civilian population, intensified by the animosity many Brits held for the Irish. One English major later admitted, 'I think I regarded all civilians as "Shinners",* and I never had any dealings with any of them.'[15] There was a degree of hypocrisy here. The British Government had condemned the German treatment of French and Belgian civilians during the war, but condoned atrocities on Irish soil.

Why did ex-servicemen sign up? Unemployment was high among veterans and 10 shillings a day was better than the dole. Some men had developed a taste for warfare and with the British peacetime army rapidly shrinking, this was their only outlet. About 7,000 joined the Tans, 1,500 the Auxiliaries.[16] There was also a smattering of British war veterans fighting for Irish independence, like Tom Barry, who used his wartime experience to become a highly able field commander of the West Cork Brigade.

Clearly some of the ex-servicemen had been scarred by the First World War, and without the discipline of the regular army, they descended into vigilantism. They often operated in rural areas in the South West where there was little central control. Their behaviour even forced the resignation of their commander, General Crozier, who said they had been 'used to murder, rob, loot and burn up the innocent because they could not catch the few guilty on the run'.[17] Bert Clark, who had been a private in the Northamptonshire Regiment, had no regrets about using brutal methods on the Irish population: 'in those days it was tit for tat – if they did something to us, we went back and did it to their people.'[18] Towns like Limerick and Balbriggan were ransacked, but perhaps their worst atrocity was the burning of Cork. After an Auxiliary was killed, they destroyed more than 300 buildings in the city centre, and then proceeded to wear burnt corks in their hat as a celebration. This crassness is still remembered in Ireland.

Violence provoked retaliation and both sides committed atrocities. The Tans and Auxies often targeted the Irish economy, resorting to acts of violence like burning down creameries. Sometimes torture was used: Tans would carry out the practice of 'cutting out the tongue of one, the nose of another, the heart of another and battering in the skull of a fourth'.[19] In 1920 they fired into a crowd at a Gaelic football match in Dublin – another Bloody Sunday. This was in reprisal for the assassination of suspected secret service agents by the IRA, but this indiscriminate targeting of civilians drove moderates to the Republican side. As one Nationalist later said, 'What probably drove a peacefully inclined man like myself into rebellion ... was the British attitude towards us, the assumption that the whole lot of us were a pack of murdering corner-boys.'[20] This was a war the British were never going to win. The local population saw them as alien intruders and were more prepared to excuse

---

* A nickname for supporters of Sinn Féin.

the IRA atrocities as justifiable retaliation. The British were militarily quite successful in suppressing trouble but they lost the battle for hearts and minds, helped by Erskine Childers' *Irish Bulletin*, which highlighted British military operations in dramatic terms.

Many British people were distinctly uneasy about what was going on in Ireland. George V hated the idea of the Tans. A pressure group, the Anti-Reprisals Association was formed by prominent writers and politicians. Clementine Churchill, showing her customary good sense, was shocked about the behaviour of the troops and urged caution on her husband – not believing 'hunnish' ways would prevail. Winston Churchill was convinced that ruthlessness would eventually bring victory. Churchill later thought greater violence, along Bolshevik lines, might have worked.[21] It was his way to meet force by force. What made him such an inspired war leader could also make him a liability in peace. Even Lloyd George, more of a realist than Churchill about Ireland, thought the British were on the verge of winning when he said, 'they had murder by the throat'. Eventually the British Government realised they had to find a political solution. After the 1921 Settlement,** Britain withdrew her troops. It was the end of the Auxies and the Tans but many found another military avenue in Palestine.

In Ulster, First World War commemorations were largely a Protestant affair. The Belfast Peace Day celebrations of August 1919 'became a massive display of unionist solidarity'.[22] Thirty-six thousand men and women who had seen war service formed a procession 11 miles long. It was twice the size of London's and took three hours to pass the new Cenotaph at the City Hall. The number of people was also significant: it celebrated the role of the 36th (Ulster) Division. Subsequent Armistice Days had a deep Orange hue,*** despite the contributions from both communities. General Sir William Hickie, president of the British Legion (Southern Ireland Area) thought Loyalists were trying to 'turn the 11th of November into the 12th of July'.****[23] They became a commemoration of the sacrifice of Loyalist soldiers. The 11 November was a chance to display Unionist symbols. The memorials on the Western Front were not free of Unionism either. When the writer Geoffrey Dyer visited the Connaught Cemetery for the Ulster Division in the 1990s, he still read comments in the visitors' book that said 'No surrender' – the old battle-cry of the Unionists before the First World War.[24]

**   This split Ireland into two and caused the Irish Civil War after Britain withdrew.

***   Orange was the colour of the Irish Protestant community, after William of Orange (1650–1702), a Loyalist hero.

****   12 July is when Irish Protestants celebrate their ascendency through the Glorious Revolution (1688) and the Battle of the Boyne (1690).

How was the First World War to be commemorated in the new Irish Free State? Local memorials were constructed, though Nationalist pressure blocked a proposed memorial in Merrion Street, Dublin as being in too prominent a place. In 1925 the *Dublin Times* reported that 12,000 people still turned up on College Green on 11 November for Remembrance Day where a temporary cross had been erected.[25] It wasn't until 1936 that a memorial garden, away from the city centre, was built, using ex-servicemen (Irish and British) for its construction. Clearly some Nationalists found any act of memory provocative, especially when crowds sang the British national anthem.* There was fighting during commemorations between veterans and Nationalists, resulting in the ceremony being moved from College Green to Phoenix Park, considered to be safer as it was less central. In Dublin, Republicans would sometimes beat up poppy sellers or attack poppy depots.[26] This grated on Irish ex-servicemen, who believed they had joined up in 1914 for honourable reasons. John Flynn wrote to *The Cork Examiner* explaining:

> We felt that it was our duty to stand against the threat to civilisation … Had we any doubts about our duty to Christianity and to our country? …We went into the war in the name of Ireland, with clean hands and a pure heart, and we came out with a reputation that did not disgrace the name of Ireland.[27]

Twenty years after the war there was an attempt at reconciliation. The Irish Fianna Fáil government sent a wreath to the London Cenotaph on Remembrance Day, which read 'in memory of the brave.'[28] Ironically, Fianna Fáil was led by Éamon de Valera, one of the men who had taken part in the Easter Rising of 1916. By 1998, with the Good Friday Agreement in place, an Island of Ireland Peace Park at Messines in Belgium was dedicated to both communities. The Unionist politician Glenn Barr and the former Irish Teachta Dála Paddy Harte read out the following:

> From this sacred shrine of remembrance, where soldiers of all nationalities, creeds and political allegiances were united in death, we appeal to all people in Ireland to help build a peaceful and tolerant society. Let us remember the solidarity and trust that developed between Protestant and Catholic soldiers when they served together in these trenches.[29]

---

* There was still a substantial Protestant community in Dublin after the war.

6

THE RUSSIAN EXPEDITION

'I think the day will come when it will be recognized without doubt, not only on one side of the House, but throughout the civilized world, that the strangling of Bolshevism at its birth would have been an untold blessing to the human race.'

Winston Churchill[1]

The toppling of the Czar in February 1917 was greeted with widespread enthusiasm in Britain. It was hoped that Russia's new democratic regime would improve her military performance. It was not to be. Russian Army discipline collapsed and a disastrous summer offensive paved the way for another revolution in October. The little-known Bolshevik Party under Vladimir Lenin seized power. Nothing would ever be quite the same again.

Few believed Lenin would last but they seriously underestimated him. The Bolsheviks quickly made peace with Germany in the Treaty of Brest-Litovsk to concentrate on winning the Russian Civil War. In signing the treaty, they had to give up a quarter of its population and most of its coal, oil and iron. From Britain's perspective, the treaty could tip the balance of the war in favour of the Central Powers. Huge reserves of resources were now available to Germany and her soldiers on the Russian Front could now be used against Britain and France. An immediate concern was that Allied supplies to Russia might fall into German hands. It was decided to dispatch forces to protect them. Another aim of the expedition was to intervene in the civil war. Winston Churchill, then Minister of Munitions, was a particularly strong advocate of preventing the Bolshevik government from getting established.

But who was going to do this? Britain couldn't spare many experienced troops for the expedition. Twenty thousand men[2] were scraped together, including teenage conscripts and recently released POWs who would normally not have been sent abroad. An Admiralty document acknowledged that this partially explained the debacle.[3] Just as the slowness of demobilisation affected discipline, the longer the Russian intervention went on the more difficult it was to maintain order. Most soldiers had no interest in the civil war. The anti-Bolshevik White Army certainly did not inspire confidence. A ragbag of czarists, liberals and socialists, they had little in common except a hatred of the Bolsheviks. Geographically isolated from each other, they rarely coordinated offensives and spent much of the time squabbling. The Whites lacked the determination, unity and the ruthlessness of their opponents. They also had a habit of defecting to the Red Army, taking their British-supplied weapons with them. R.H. Earnshaw of the Royal Army Ordnance Corps commented that it 'cost us a lot of time effort, uniform, rifles'.[4] There were even cases of White Army troops shooting British soldiers. Their most capable leader was General Anton Denikin, who commanded the southern front; his men were trained and supplied by the British. Denikin's army managed to advance to within 250 miles of Moscow but was thrown back by superior forces. After that, the civil war was effectively over. Intervention was ultimately counter-productive. The Allies didn't send enough troops to make a real difference, but enough to give the Red Army a propaganda triumph. The Bolsheviks could claim that at least they didn't rely on foreigners.

Another reason for the British troops' discontent was that they weren't told the purpose of the mission. Some thought they were going to supervise a plebiscite on the Danish-German border; the original reason, to guard supplies against the Germans, was clearly not relevant after the Armistice. Despite Churchill's claims that if 'Russia is to be saved … she must be saved by Russians',[5] the expedition became about regime change. Most troops were sent to Northern Russia. Advancing south from Archangel, they grew increasingly restless. Armistice celebrations were muted affairs – 'Te Deums' rather than a knees-ups. Most just wanted to get home and some even showed Bolshevik sympathies. In February 1919, two sergeants from the Yorkshire Regiment organised a sit-down strike. They were court-martialled and sentenced to death, but this was later commuted to lengthy prison sentences due to pressure from George V. In June, when the Hampshire Regiment refused to continue an engagement with Bolshevik forces, its ringleaders were demobilised. Some in a 'Slavo-British' legion changed sides, shooting their officers before they deserted. The British troops generally performed well against untrained Red Army recruits but the unreliability of the men seriously hampered any effective action. Dave Lamb in *Mutinies 1917–1920* claimed the Bolshevik victory was down to the Allied decision to pull-out, 'largely influenced by the mood of their own soldiers'.[6] The claim is exaggerated but it was certainly a factor in the White Army's defeat.

It hadn't escaped anyone's notice that men were being killed after the Armistice. In August 1919, Guy Warneford Nightingale wrote home to his wife, 'Lost my 2nd. in Command killed early in the attack. Awful bad luck. Had been wounded 6 times in France. I am the only officer in my Coy, who hasn't been hit.'[7] Families were still receiving telegrams months after the war, like the ironically named Mary Pine-Coffin, who 'heard of the death of her husband Tristram, killed in action in Russia September 1919, aged 33'.[8] A letter to Pine-Coffin's mother from a fellow officer read, 'His death came as a terrible shock to us all, for somehow we could not imagine any harm befalling him, he had been through many escapes and always came through laughing. He was one of the bravest.'[9] There is an Imperial War Graves cemetery in Archangel, Siberia*. A memorial to the missing is at the far end of the cemetery. It could be in Belgium or France. Carved on it are the names of soldiers: Private Charles Ainsworth of the King's Liverpool Regiment; Vincent Colledge of the Worcesters; Sapper Eric Simpson of the Royal Engineers[10] – just three of the 221 soldiers whose bodies were never identified.

By the end of 1919, the public was demanding an end to British intervention. Dockworkers in East London and Rosyth prevented ships bound for Russia from leaving. Even the hawkish *Daily Express* wrote that the 'frozen plains of Eastern Europe are not worth the bones of a single grenadier'.[11] The British withdrew in 1920, having failed to displace Lenin's government. The expedition had cost around £50 million. Britain and Russia's relations were affected for years, and Winston Churchill's role as the key advocate of intervention was long remembered by the Soviet leadership, which made cooperation more difficult during the Second World War. Stalin remarked in 1945 that he believed President Roosevelt would stick to his word, but as for Churchill, 'that one might do anything'.[12]

★ Later changed to the Commonwealth War Graves Commission

7

THE SWOLLEN EMPIRE

'The German Emperor is very wise. He wages against all kings. When the war is over, many stories will be printed. In India, the Englishman rules. We had no knowledge of any other king ... In India this is a problem: The people know nothing.'

Sib Singh, a Sikh Prisoner of War[1]

Peace did not mean an end to fighting for those who remained in the armed forces. There were colonies to defend and barely enough troops to defend them. The British Empire stood at her territorial zenith in 1919 but was hopelessly overstretched, causing governments to resort to questionable methods throughout the interwar period. It was increasingly clear this was an empire based on force not 'fair play'.

At the Paris Peace Conference Britain acquired large swathes of land from the defeated powers: Palestine, Transjordan, Iraq, Tanganyika, parts of the Cameroons and Togoland. The empire now comprised around 25 per cent of the world's population, yet Britain had emerged militarily and economically weaker. The Irish situation, demobilisation protests and the British Expeditionary Force's (BEF) lukewarm performance in Russia showed a lack of reliable troops. In light of this, the decision to take more territory was a rash one but the government regarded these mandates* as the spoils of war.

---

* League of Nation mandates were colonies in all but name. The power that controlled the mandate was meant to prepare it for independence, but the timetable for independence was not of the mandate's choosing. The last to be given independence was Namibia in 1990.

Britain and France's carve-up of the Middle East was a particularly cynical act, the consequences of which are still felt today. Arabs had been promised independence if they rose against their Turkish rulers, yet the Sykes-Picot Agreement (1916) secretly divided the Middle East into French and British spheres. The Arabs were bitterly disappointed. Puppet rulers or colonial officials governed territories without regard to ethnicity or religion. The discovery of oil only added complications. The legacy continues. Isis released a video called 'The End of Sykes-Picot', boasting of destroying the border created by the British and French** – 'We are all one country,' they said.

It didn't take long for the British to find out how ungovernable the Middle East was. In Egypt, an attempted revolution in 1919 led to nominal independence three years later. The uprising was partly caused by the conscription of hundreds of thousands of Egyptians into the Labour and Camel Transport Corps of the Egyptian Expeditionary Force during the war. Britain might have taken an early warning about loyalty when three-quarters of Egyptian soldiers at Sollum deserted to the enemy.[2] The stationing of British and Commonwealth forces also upset nationalist feeling, as did the blocking of Egyptian self-government at the Paris Peace Conference. The revolt started with a wave of strikes that were mercilessly put down. The uprising spread and was ultimately pacified with a mix of force and concessions. Britain offered Egypt self-government but maintained her political, maritime and economic interests there. The Suez Canal, the vital artery that linked Britain to India, stayed under western control.

Britain's difficulties in maintaining colonial rule were also demonstrated in Iraq. T.E. Lawrence noted that whereas the Turks had run Iraq with 14,000 local troops, Britain needed 100,000 men to maintain order.[3] The expense of the occupation force meant an increasing reliance on air power. When Iraqis rose against British rule in 1920 the RAF flew missions totalling 4,008 hours and dropped 97 tonnes of bombs.[4] The cost was greater than the financing of the Arab Revolt against the Ottomans in 1917–18. The British retreated to the shadows and placed pliable Iraqis in power while retaining their military bases and oil fields. Costs fell, though the bombing continued, especially when Arthur Harris arrived and ordered 'terror raids' on Iraqi civilians. He would become the controversial 'Bomber Harris' of Dresden during the next war.

The Mandate for Palestine also caused problems. Palestinians were no happier about British rule. Winston Churchill, as Colonial Secretary, thought order might be maintained by sending over Auxiliaries and Black and Tans, fresh from Ireland, as a 'gendarmerie' – at 10 shillings a day they were on a decent wage. He hired an old friend from his Sudan days, Brigadier General Angus McNeill, who had

---

** Syria was the mandate given to France, Iraq to the British. Neither conformed to ethnic or religious realities, with consequences still being felt today.

served in Gallipoli. Churchill wanted a high-profile role for them: 'The spectacle of these men riding about the country is an important element of the whole policy.'[5] These hardened veterans showed the same contempt for Arabs as they'd shown the Irish. Douglas Duff in his memoir wrote, 'Most of us were so infected by the sense of our own superiority over these "lesser breeds" that we scarcely regarded these people as human.'[6] The inevitable brutalities occurred, including the killing of civilians in Jerusalem and the use of labour camps.[7] A full-blown revolt broke out by the resentful Palestinians in 1936, which was put down with maximum force. The gendarmerie again lacked discipline, and within twelve months a quarter had been dismissed for bad conduct or had decided to leave. In Jaffa some went on a drunken rampage. Ultimately, they were disbanded because of cost rather than behaviour. In a letter to Churchill, McNeill put his finger on the dilemma of these ex-servicemen, now surplus to requirements: 'Is there no work for my band of toughs anywhere? ... You must remember that these are fellows who have been at it since 1914; have no trade or profession to go back to, and yet must live.'[8]

He (Caribbean and African man) fought with the white man to save the white man's home and the war was won. Black men all the world over are asking to-day: 'What have we got? What are we going to get out of it all?'
                    Felix Eugene Michael Hercules, Trinidadian writer[9]

They had been disillusioned with the European war, they kept on having fright-ful clashes with English and American soldiers, besides the fact the authorities treated them completely differently from the white soldiers ...
                                        Claude McKay[10]

The First World War also encouraged independence movements in areas that had previously shown loyalty to the empire. Nowhere was this more so than in the Caribbean, where ex-servicemen formed the nucleus of the pro-independence leadership. The racism they experienced fighting for the 'mother country' radical-ised these soldiers, perhaps more than any other troops in the British Army.

In 1914, Britain could call on reserves from the 400 million people in her empire. Increasingly short of manpower, she relied more and more on the colo-nies and dominions as the war progressed. This would prove a mixed blessing. White Canadians, Australians and New Zealanders were seen as acceptable for front-line duty and proved some of the finest soldiers of the war. Black soldiers, largely from Africa and the Caribbean, were regarded as inferior, and the British were reluctant to use them against white enemy troops. They were intended for non-combatant roles like the Labour Corps, though black soldiers still saw action in the Middle East and Africa, where they rarely fought Europeans.

Indian troops occupied a position somewhere in the middle; they were categorised according to their perceived military ability and used accordingly. 'Martial races' like Pashtuns, Sikhs or Muslim Punjabis were fit for front-line service and were deployed on the Western Front, as well as theatres outside Europe. Indians from lowland areas were regarded as little better than black troops and only saw combat in Africa. This was a mistake given the manpower shortage, though overall the contribution of the Indian subcontinent was massive – 1.3 million men served in Europe, Africa and the Middle East.[11]

Initially there was widespread enthusiasm for the war across the empire. Most white settlers in the dominions* (South African Boers were an exception) saw themselves as British. In the colonies, there were also black and Asian men willing to fight, for the chance of adventure or the regular pay the military could provide,** but many volunteered out of a genuine attachment to Britain. George Blackman remembered singing 'Run Kaiser William, run for your life, boy.' He commented: 'We wanted to go. The island government told us the king said all Englishmen must go to join the war. The country called all of us.'[12] The British mistook the rush to volunteer as unqualified loyalty. It wasn't. There was an expectation that things would be different after the war. Indians wanted dominion status. An editorial in *The Bengalee* said Indians' cooperation means 'the complete recognition of their rights as Citizens of the finest State in the world'.[13] What they got was a partial measure called the Government of India Act (1919) where power at the centre still remained in British hands. Indian Nationalists felt their contribution to the First World War deserved more – 53,486 had been killed.[14] Five months after the Armistice, hundreds of Indians were massacred at Amritsar on the orders of Colonel Reginald Dyer – a commander in the Seistan Force during the war – further alienating Indians from the empire. Gandhi had supported the British war effort in 1914: he would not do so the next time round. Another resentment of Indian troops was the way they were treated. 'We were slaves' commented Sujan Singh many years later. They were regularly flogged, denied promotion, segregated and paid less than white troops.[15] What's more, they saw how a free people lived. Matt Singh remembered, 'When we were in France, we felt the French people were so lucky and were enjoying their freedom. So we also felt that India should be free – this war showed us the right path.'[16]

---

* Dominions were parts of the empire given a fair degree of independence to run its own affairs. In 1914 the dominions were Canada, Newfoundland, New Zealand, Australia and South Africa.

** There was high unemployment in the Caribbean after the Panama Canal had been completed and many workers returned home.

The Caribbean did not have a developed nationalist leadership to compare with India but there was still a belief that their services would be rewarded. Jamaican activist Marcus Garvey encouraged fellow West Indians to show loyalty and fight but assert themselves as equals. Over 15,000 soldiers served in the British Army, not just on the Western Front, but also in the Middle East and Africa. Around two-thirds of the troops came from Jamaica,[17] mostly joining the British West Indies Regiment (BWIR).

The BWIR saw combat in the Middle East. General Allenby, Commander of the Egyptian Expeditionary Force, complimented them in a telegram to the Governor of Jamaica:

> I have great pleasure in informing you of the gallant conduct of the machine-gun section of the 1st British West Indies Regiment during two successful raids on the Turkish trenches. All ranks behaved with great gallantry under heavy rifle and shell fire and contributed in no small measure to the success of the operations.[18]

On the Western Front, black troops in the British Army were usually given non-combatant roles. Fighting Europeans might challenge a pillar of white supremacy: military prowess. One British colonel acknowledged a widely held view when he wrote, 'to teach and encourage the use of the rifle by native races may result in trouble if not disaster'.[19] In contrast, white Bermudans were allowed to join the Royal Lincolnshire Regiment as combat troops. This was also the approach of the US Army where segregated black units were largely confined to labour battalions. The BWIR were given tasks like digging trenches, loading ammunition or laying telephone wire, but as this anonymous poem suggests, this still exposed them to danger.

> The Black Soldier's Lament
> Stripped to the waist and sweated chest
> Midday's reprieve brings much-needed rest
> From trenches deep toward the sky.
> Non-fighting troops and yet we die.

George Blackman recalls being involved in trench fighting, despite the official British policy:

> [The] Tommies said: 'Darkie, let them have it.' I made the order: 'Bayonets, fix' and then 'B company, fire'. You know what it is to go and fight somebody hand to hand? You need plenty nerves. You push that bayonet in there and hit with the butt of the gun – if he is dead he is dead, if he lives he live.[20]

His comments expose the racism they endured, though George Blackman thought at least in combat they were equal: 'They called us darkies. But when the battle starts, it didn't make a difference. We were all the same.'[21] By the end of the war, 185 members of the BWIR had lost their lives fighting.[22]

The discrimination that Caribbean troops faced was manifest. Those discharged as unfit were not given pensions nor was there adequate provision for the disabled. Promotion was limited: black soldiers could not become officers. Many were well-educated, often former teachers and clerks, and saw how exploited people were asserting themselves across the world.[23] Black newspapers like *The Crisis* were an inspiration, so was the Easter Rising in Ireland and the Russian Revolution. Closer to home, there was a mutiny in Houston, when African-American troops rioted after local police physically assaulted a black woman. These were men increasingly frustrated at the discrimination they faced. One infamous incident happened in 1916: a contingent of Jamaican troops were diverted to Halifax, Nova Scotia, but, inadequately clothed for the cold climate, around 600 got frostbite or exposure and five died.[24] When people heard about this back home, the number of volunteers dropped off. After Armistice Day, 1918, eleven battalions of the BWIR were stationed at Taranto, Italy waiting to be demobilised. There was already resentment about the manual work they were doing, like unloading the ships, as well as their unequal pay – they hadn't been allowed to take part in the victory parade either. After being ordered to clean the latrines of white soldiers, a number refused to work. During ensuing riots, an NCO killed a mutineer and the officer who gave orders to clean the latrines was assaulted. The mutiny lasted four days. A machine gun corps was ordered in and the 9th BWIR was disbanded. Sixty were tried and one man was executed; most were sentenced to three to five years in prison though one received twenty. The BWIR were given an armed escort back to the Caribbean. Fearing trouble, the British Government sent three Royal Navy cruisers to the West Indies during demobilisation. Some troops were even dumped in Cuba and Venezuela to delay their return.

After the mutiny, sixty NCOs formed the Caribbean League for Independence and Black Rights. There had been Pan-African congresses before the war, attended by a few Caribbean activists calling for an improvement in conditions of black people. Now the war had radicalised a whole generation of soldiers who campaigned for full independence. Their experiences helped unify West Indians who had fought and suffered together. When one sergeant at a meeting said 'the black man should have freedom and govern himself in the West Indies and that if necessary, force and bloodshed should be used to attain that object',[25] he was loudly applauded. BWIR veterans would play prominent roles in Caribbean independence movements. A secret government memo said, 'Nothing we can do will alter the fact that the black man has begun to think and feel himself as good as the white.'[26]

The British authorities were right to sense a change had come over the Caribbean. BWIR veterans were joining a wave of strikes and riots that gripped the colonies in 1919 over low pay and a lack of jobs. Discharged West Indians received little more than 'a few shillings, a cheap suit of clothes and free railway transport to their home'.[27] Some had given up decent jobs to fight. Recruiting officers had promised land to those who would join up but that promise was never fulfilled. There was not even leasing schemes or a land sale programme. The 1920s and '30s saw further trouble. In Grenada, there were bombing campaigns by BWIR veterans called the 'Dynamite Gang' aimed at symbols of colonial rule. In British Honduras, ex-servicemen took over the main administrative buildings until cleared by a Royal Navy cruiser.[28] Strikes were frequent, particularly among plantation workers, and the British Armed Forces were beefed up throughout the West Indies.

When the Great Depression caused widespread unemployment and poverty, many had to emigrate. They'd learnt the hard way that loyalty is rarely reciprocal between the coloniser and colonised. Marcus Garvey proclaimed:

[t]he first dying that is to be done by the black man in the future will be done to make himself free. And then when we are finished, if we have any charity to bestow, we may die for the white man. But as for me, I think I have stopped dying for him.[29]

Many ex-soldiers joined the independence movements that sprang up in Jamaica, Grenada and British Honduras, invoking the 'spirit of Taranto'. Not all were black: former BWIR Captain Arthur Cipriani had French-Corsican ancestry. He'd been impressed by the calibre of the men he'd led and was converted to the cause of self-government for Trinidad and Tobago. He later founded the Trinidad Workingmen's Association and Trinidadian Labour Party. Norman Manley had a mixed-race background and served in the Royal Artillery where he won the Military Medal. He campaigned for Jamaican independence and founded the left-leaning People's National Party. Most of the veterans though were of African ancestry like Buzz Butler, who organised Trinidad's oil workers, and St William Grant, the Jamaican labour activist.

Some Caribbean veterans joined Marcus Garvey's Universal Negro Improvement Association (UNIA) as part of a uniformed guard, the African Legion, for African-American events in the US. In 1920s America, this took courage. They helped drill new recruits in the manner they had learned from their time in the British Army.[30] The spirit of Taranto was present at the 1932 Pan Caribbean Conference that would inspire the British West Indian Federation after the Second World War. Many of the delegates had fought in the First World War. The conference declared:

Our work is to wash out the stains that now besmirch the Union Jack, stains of injustice towards weak nations ... we are British to the core ... But we demand that our flag shall be an emblem of Equality, Fraternity and Fairplay to all peoples over whose head it flies.[31]

The last word goes to George Blackman, the former BWIR veteran, still bitter at 105 years of age, 'I had to come and look for work. The only thing that we had is the clothes and the uniform that we got on. The pants, the jacket and the shirt and the boots ... the English are no good.'[32]

A similar pattern occurred with the Pacific Island of Fiji. At first, many Fijians demonstrated loyalty to the British Empire by wanting to serve in the army. Pressure for manpower allowed the formation of a Fijian Labour Corps, which eventually arrived at Boulogne. David Olusoga writes:

After their epic journey, they employed loading trucks. While in France, they experienced persistent racism where they found many 'whites only' facilities. They were separated from Chinese labourers, who it was feared might undermine the status of Britain in the eyes of the men of Fiji.[33]

Even an educated Fijian like Lala Sukuna, whose father was a tribal chief, could only serve in combat by joining the French Foreign Legion. He had wanted to fight in the British Army for a similar reason to many Irish Nationalists, in order to gain respect for his country. Like many Caribbean war veterans, he went into politics and is regarded as the mentor and inspiration for the Fijian independence movement.

African soldiers also fought in the British Army during the war. The first shot fired by a British soldier on land wasn't in Belgium but in Togoland, by Regimental Sergeant Major Alhaji Grunshi of the British West African Frontier Force.[34] Unlike Caribbean troops, they were not used in Europe but confined to the African continent, nor were they all volunteers. African conscription began in 1915, a year before Britain, under the Native Followers Recruitment Ordinance. Often it was done through the tribal chief, whose loyalty to Britain allowed him to exercise some power over his people. Buganda chief, Samwiri Mukasa, provides an example, when he wrote:

A war against Britain was a war against Buganda, and so, when I was appointed to lead some soldiers, I at once left for Kampala with 5,000 men. There I was told not to go to the battlefield at once, but to wait in my country and do as I was directed. While waiting, these are some of the things I did:

a) I did all I could to recruit men for the armies.
b) I sent in a lot of carriers.
c) I very much encouraged the growing of food.
d) I encouraged further the growing of cotton.
e) Because I very much wanted peace I tried my best to get into contact with the British armies for *I did not want the enemy to get to our city London* [Author's italics].

The men had little idea what they were getting themselves into:

The chief called us and handed us over to a government messenger. I didn't know where we were going, but the chief and the messenger said that the white man had sent for us and we must go. After three days we reached the white man's compound. …

Then he told us we were going to the Great War to help the king's soldiers who were preventing the Germans coming to our country and burning it. We left and marched far into the bush. The government police led the way and allowed no man to stop behind.[35]

Not all soldiers were conscripts, some were attracted to the relatively high army pay. There was also an element of pro-British feeling among middle-class Africans like in the Caribbean, at least initially. They were often used as combatants as they were usually fighting non-Europeans. The King's African Rifles had 30,000 Africans in 1918 (but the 3,000 officers and NCOs were all British). Over 100,000 died in East Africa alone.[36]

Many Africans were unhappy about British actions during the war as their treatment was even worse than Caribbean troops. There were rebellions in Malawi over forced conscription, and in Kenya and Yorubaland over war taxes. Africa had economically suffered during the war years through an end to investment and a disruption to trade. Around a million men were used as carriers. Regarded as little better than slaves, their casualty rates were enormous. No exact figure can be given, as the British were so lacking in concern for the carrier's wellbeing, though one post-war estimate puts the figure at 250,000.[37] Most were not given a proper burial – no Imperial War Graves Commission headstones – but allowed to 'return to nature'.

The sinking of the SS *Mendi* is still remembered with anger in South Africa today. The *Mendi* had sailed from Cape Town with 802 black South African members of the Native Labour Corps. Two miles south of the Isle of Wight, it was accidently struck by a much larger cargo ship, the *Darro*, which did not even send a boat to check the extent of the damage. Six hundred and eighteen black South Africans died, along with nine white officers and thirty-three crew members.[38] South Africans still commemorate 'Mendi Day' on 21 February, the day of the sinking.

The South African National Congress had hoped for greater autonomy but African representation at the Paris Peace Conference was ignored. Instead, new mandates were created in sub-Saharan Africa to the benefit of the Europeans. As the *Sierra Leone Weekly News* noted:

> After Africa's sons had shed their blood on the altar of liberty and after having experienced that terrible plague called the influenza epidemic, are we not the same manna loving people?
>
> … What is Sierra Leone doing? We have been sleeping too long. It is high time we take up the world's cry and work – reconstruction![39]

Partly in response, four Pan-African Congresses were held between the wars, calling for home rule and a better economic deal for Africans. However, compared to the Caribbean, Africa never produced many ex-servicemen ready to challenge colonial authority. That was for the next generation.

8

'THE WATCH AT THE RHINE': THE OCCUPATION OF THE RHINELAND

'Men wearying in trenches used to tell one another sometimes what they fancied the end of the war would be like ... the commonest vision was that of marching down a road to a wide, shining river ... for most men the Rhine was the physical goal of effort, the term of endurance, the symbol of all attainment and rest.'

C.E. Montague, from Disenchantment *(1922)*[1]

'Firm and True stands the Watch, the Watch at the Rhine!'

German patriotic song

One of the thorniest issues during the Peace Conference in Paris was the future of the Rhineland. Bordering France and Belgium, it was a springboard for any German invasion of the West. France wanted to create an independent state to stop future incursions but this was too much for Britain and America.[2] A compromise was reached. The Rhineland would remain German but their military forces or fortifications could not be maintained within 50km east of the River Rhine. Allied armies would occupy the area for fifteen years.*

The British would administer Cologne, the Rhine's main city, and the surrounding area. On 7 December 1918, British troops crossed over the famous Hohenzollern Bridge. The band played 'When We Wind up the Watch on the Rhine' – a joke the local population probably didn't appreciate. Captain Westmacott wrote to his wife, 'The men marched with fixed bayonets, wearing their steel helmets, and carrying their packs. I wish you could have seen them – each man making the most of himself, and full of pride and elan.'[3]

---

* The British in fact started leaving in 1926 as relations improved. A few remained in Wiesbaden until 1930.

The reaction of the Rhinelanders to a military occupation was mixed. Major Fryer of the Grenadier Guards remembered, 'we were received in silence, but not indifference; crowds collected as before, but they just stared vacantly, except the children, who loved the drums and marched along beside them.'[4] Philip Gibbs, the war correspondent, observed the British troops marching into Germany and saw young girls laugh and wave handkerchiefs at the soldiers: 'There was no sense as yet of passing through a hostile country where we were not wanted.'[5]

Fryer found the residents of Cologne to be 'civil', even 'cringing'. The grenadiers made sure they knew who was in control now:

Our methods were firm; salutes were required from anyone in uniform, and civilians, if spoken to, had to remove their hats. When we were on the march anyone failing to comply with these rules was immediately arrested ... [6] An element of pettiness accompanied this ... there was a pretty liberal interpretation of what a uniform was ... I remember one luckless postman in the act of delivering letters being marched off miles from his beat. We enjoyed the game immensely, and it showed the Germans we meant business.[7]

Some British soldiers behaved like soldiers often do. Private Smiler Marshall recalls trashing a café in the first German village they entered: 'We drank everything ... didn't pay for a thing. Then when we'd finished, we lined up all the bottles, and smashed them on the floor.'[8]

Compared to some of the things that went on during the German occupation of Belgium and France this was mild, and milder than when the French troops occupied the Ruhr in 1923, though the British had never suffered as the French had during the war. Relations seem to have remained reasonable with the local population. A threatened strike never materialised. Violet Markham, wife of the chief demobilisation officer, thought the Germans were generally courteous. They were not the cruel automatons of British propaganda (which many of her friends back home believed). She witnessed German girls going out with British troops – and you cannot get more courteous than that.

Some troops enjoyed the Rhineland. Their work was light, mostly route marches, drilling and guard duty. The billets were relatively good and there was plenty of sport, booze and entertainment. Fryer mentions cabarets, opera, 'English Pierrot shows' and pantomimes. A Pathé newsreel of the time[9] captures the easygoing existence of the British soldiers. Two Tommies stand guard by the Rhine with Cologne Cathedral in the background. Soldiers inspect civilian papers. A football match is filmed. Later there's a shot of guards marching through the centre, while young children with hoops and sticks stand around. This was a better posting than Ireland or Russia, though some missed home. There were around 13,000 troops in the British Army of the Rhine in 1920; to relieve veterans, new draftees were brought in and many of the original battalions were effectively broken up as replacements started to arrive. Albert 'Smiler' Marshall got £50 for signing on for a year, which was a lot more than a soldier's pay during the war.[10]

When C.E. Montague visited Cologne, he noticed a difference in British behaviour. Those who hadn't fought were now demanding harsher treatment for the Germans. 'We must show these fellows our power,' was a common cry. Montague describes a civilian who 'drove into Cologne in a car plastered over with Union Jacks, like a minor bookie going to Epsom. It passed the wit of man to make him understand that one does not do these things to defeated peoples.'[11] Another burst into the offices of the *Kolnische Zeitung* and dictated pro-British propaganda to the editor. As a journalist himself, Montague was shocked this could happen to one of Europe's leading newspapers.

Soldiers who hadn't fought at the Front also came up for censure. Montague heard one non-combatant general say, 'I hope to God … that there's going to be no rot about not kicking a man when he's down.'[12] He contrasts this with the behaviour of the front-line veterans, 'Sober or drunk, the decimated troops who held Cologne at the end of that year were contumaciously sportsmen.' He once heard two inebriated Highlanders say to a local, 'Och, dinna tak' it to hairrt, mon. I tell ye that your lads were grond.'[13] We need to be cautious about Montague's account, as it was part of his angry book, *Disenchantment* (1922). He was particularly resentful about how troops like himself were let down by civilians,* but he does echo the sentiments of many veterans who felt less hatred for the Germans than those who hadn't fought. Violet Markham agreed. In Cologne, 'the fighting soldiers are at one and the same time more generous [than civilians] and in the true sense more pacific.'[14] They expected the population to obey orders but realised any brutality would be counter-productive. 'Also they will admit frankly they have found many of the Germans with whom they have had to deal capable and amenable.'[15]

In 1927, as the British were withdrawing from the Rhineland, *The Spectator* wrote of the way the 'British private soldiers, non-commissioned officers and subalterns are capable of living with a beaten enemy. These terms are simple, natural and friendly; they are majestic in the simplicity with which they instinctively avoid continuing an humiliation.'[16] The international situation at that time looked good. Germany had just been allowed to join the League of Nations. British troops had behaved about as well as any occupying force could. Another war seemed inconceivable.

---

* Despite being 47, he had volunteered in 1914, dying his hair black to look younger.

PART III

ADJUSTMENTS

9

'THE CHASM': COPING WITH CIVILIAN LIFE

'… The old men came out again and took our victory to remake in the likeness of the former world they knew.'

T.E. Lawrence[1]

'Every soldier I've spoken to experienced the same thing. We were a race apart for the civilians and you could speak to your comrades and they understood but the civilians, it was just a waste of time.'

Anonymous soldier[2]

A gulf emerged during the war between those who fought and those who hadn't. The historian R.H. Tawney, who was a sergeant in the 22nd Manchester Regiment, wrote about the 'dividing Chasm' that separated the soldier from the civilian: 'There are occasions when I feel like a visitor among strangers whose intentions are kindly, but whose modes of thought I neither altogether understand … between you and us hangs a veil.'[3] Soldiers often became sceptical of civilians in general but certain non-combatants were especially loathed: war profiteers, armchair patriots, anti-war activists and conscientious objectors – unless they volunteered as ambulance drivers and stretcher bearers – and striking workers, whose pay vastly outstripped anything the soldiers earned. Robert Graves thought his men would have happily shot striking munition-workers: 'They think that they're all skrim-shankers.'[4] Even family and friends could be hard to bear. It was difficult to communicate with people who hadn't experienced trench life – much easier just to confine conversation to the mundane. Herbert Read wrote, 'They simply have no conception whatever of what war is really like and don't seem concerned about it at all.'[5] Bernard Martin was once asked, 'When it is too dark to go on fighting – are you free for the evening, can you go to a cinema?'[6] Graves, on leave in London, recalled that 'Despite the number of uniforms in the streets, the general indifference to, and ignorance about, the war surprised me.'[7] Siegfried Sassoon was typically frank when he wrote about 'the callous complacence with which the majority of those at home regard the continuance of agonies which they have not sufficient imagination to realise'.[8] Some men felt relief when they returned to their comrades at the Front. Even soldiers who never saw action were held in contempt: the stay-behind padres who preached about just wars; the 'canaries', yellow armed-banded trainers who barked at the troops about 'cowardice' but never faced enemy fire themselves; the red-tabbed staff officers whose medals seemed inversely proportionate to the dangers they had faced.

This division remained a feature of the interwar period. Vera Brittain, when she returned to Oxford University, detected 'a gulf wider than any decade divides those who experienced the War from their juniors by only a year or two who grew up immediately afterwards'.[9] Ex-servicemen frequently saw the world in binary terms: old verses young, civilian verses soldier, front line verses staff officers. And this could last a lifetime. Harold Macmillan, a captain in the Grenadier Guards, continued to divide his generation into those who had served and those who hadn't. Forty years later, as prime minister, it was the first thing he asked about a man.

Undeniably, some ex-servicemen found peacetime difficult. Some were carrying physical and psychological wounds. Corporal Tommy Keele thought the war changed him in several ways. He was more aggressive and short-tempered. He loved to whistle as a kid but stopped after his experiences in the trenches. Butcher shops reminded him of the bits of men he had to bury.[10] The term 'Lost Generation' is frequently misused to describe the high death toll of the age group who fought in the war. Rather it was coined by the American writer Gertrude Stein, to describe the veterans who couldn't adapt to civilian life, when she heard a garage owner abuse a young mechanic in Paris by shouting, 'You are all a generation lost.'[11] For others, peacetime was an anti-climax. Flight Sergeant Bill Hill was a pilot but after the war he said, 'I had to come down and I merely became a clerk in an office.'[12] It helps explain why ex-servicemen volunteered to fight in Ireland and Palestine. A more controversial opinion is that some men simply enjoyed killing and peacetime deprived them of a pleasurable pursuit. Joanna Bourke called this 'the dirty secret that dared not be uttered after the war if combatants were to settle back to their calm civilian life, unbrutalised'.[13] Bourke mentions Charles Alexander Stewart, a New Zealander who sent a letter after Passchendaele to his cousin saying 'it was with a feeling of fiendish joy that I used that rifle & bayonet'.[14] This view is not universally accepted by psychologists, who argue that training someone to kill without question doesn't mean they enjoy it. Stewart later saved a young German prisoner from being murdered in cold blood after his 'joy'. But it's an awkward fact that some former soldiers perhaps suffered more from nostalgia than nightmares.

Perhaps the most famous example of a man who could never settle in the post-war world is T.E. Lawrence, better known as Lawrence of Arabia. Lawrence has been the subject of numerous biographies, documentaries and films. His military exploits became the stuff of legend. What's less well known is the years afterwards. It's hard to believe that Lawrence's wartime experiences did not play some part in his restlessness after the war. He lost two brothers and numerous friends. He was captured, tortured and possibly raped by Turks, which might explain the brutality he then showed to Turkish prisoners. He took 'nearly suicidal risks' as a commander, once attacking a troop train, despite being so short of weapons some of his men threw rocks.[15] Peace was a let-down. Bitter at the treatment of Arabs at the Paris conferences, he took a fellowship at Oxford where he and Graves agreed not to talk about the war, as 'we were both suffering from its effects … '[16] There was a spell at the Colonial Office but the work bored him. He wrote to Graves, 'I wish I hadn't gone out there: the Arabs are like a page I have turned over; and sequels are rotten things. I'm locked up here: office every day.'[17] He wanted to return to the armed forces but, uncomfortable with his post-war fame, Lawrence enlisted in the RAF anonymously. After a brief spell in the Tank Corps, he seemed at his happiest testing high-performance speed boats in the air force. This love of speed led eventually to his death in a motorcycle accident at the age of 46.

Another veteran who struggled with stability was John Beckett, a politician who joined more political movements than many people have had jobs. Rarely was he not having a row with someone. He moved from the hard left to the hard right, starting out as a firebrand in the National Union of Ex-Servicemen (NUX) and the Independent Labour Party (ILP). He was elected MP for Gateshead and then Peckham. He once grabbed the mace during a debate, which led to his suspension. He was abusive to fellow Labour MPs, who were glad to see the back of him when he joined the British Union of Fascists (BUF). He then fell out with Oswald Mosley and most other leading fascists, even when they were interned together during the war. His attachment to anti-Semitic movements (he joined several after leaving the BUF) is all the more strange considering Beckett was Jewish. His son, the journalist Francis Beckett, said his mother 'had always hoped her husband would settle down to a quiet, normal job and give up politics'.[18] It was not to be. Like Lawrence, the war may have had nothing to do with Beckett's subsequent life, but both men exhibited nothing like their rootlessness and discontent before the war.

The army also encouraged a set of values sometimes absent from civilian life, like a sense of teamwork and mutual obligations rather than competition and individualism. The former chancellor of the exchequer and Second World War veteran, Dennis Healey, thought 'the most valuable legacy of war service was the knowledge that I depended on other people and that other people depended on me. It was this knowledge which created the sense of comradeship so characteristic of wartime and so lacking in peace.'[19] Friendships made in the army had an intensity rarely found in civilian life. It's unsurprising that many soldiers missed this. More would have re-enlisted but for the government cuts called the Geddes Axe*that significantly reduced the size of the armed forces. The reduction in Territorial Army funding, with its much-loved summer camps, was another blow for this type of male bonding. Now they had to face the world, as Charles Douie wrote, 'without the support of either the old comradeship or the old faith'.[20] Trust was also an essential part of trench life; stealing was seen as one of the most despicable crimes, but trust was not held in such high esteem afterwards. Demobilised troops with gratuities in their pockets found themselves prey to crooks. Trooper Sydney Chaplin came across his old major, down-and-out after being conned into buying a fraudulent business. He later met an ex-company sergeant major who was selling lucky charms in the streets and had been tricked out of 5 shillings for some worthless tat. 'Now after a day without anything to eat or drink he was broken-hearted at the thought of going home to his wife without a penny.'[21]

Some ex-soldiers, like Richard Aldington, found it hard to fit into the post-war world:

> There was a devil-take-the-hindmost scramble for money and position in the new world, and an extravagance which seemed incredible to one who had known the old sober England. I stood aghast at this degeneration of my people, visible to me, as it was not to them, because of my long absence.[22]

One way ex-servicemen reduced stress was by smoking. This became a hugely popular pastime after the war. Tobacco consumption was already on the rise since the nineteenth century but the British Army increased this habit by giving soldiers a daily ration of 2oz of tobacco a day. Just four months into the war, 96 per cent of British soldiers were regular smokers.[23] Due to the poor quality of pipe tobacco, cigarette use increased, even becoming a sort of unofficial currency ('two fags

---

*   Named after Sir Eric Geddes, the Chair of the Committee on National Expenditure, who oversaw swinging expenditure cuts in the early '20s.

for a haircut'). Puffing Tommies appeared on postcards or billboard adverts that
linked cigarette smoking with the war effort. Several tobacco funds were set up
to supply soldiers. There was even one to provide the wounded 'with tobacco and
cigarettes in hospitals here and at the Front … and is at the moment sending regular supplies to over 200 hospitals and convalescent homes'.[24] It is not surprising
that so many ex-servicemen smoked for the rest of their lives. Addictive, calming
and then considered harmless, cigarettes were a cheap form of relief and, for the
poorer ex-serviceman, they suppressed his appetite. Lighting a fag was the first
thing Sidney Chaplin did when he woke up sleeping rough, and what he offered
his down-and-out old major. How many veteran's lives were cut short because of
this? Captain Roy Page's grandson remembered him smoking heavily until the
1960s and dying of throat cancer.[25]

Perhaps the most successful thing about the British Legion was its social clubs.
Ex-servicemen could drink together and talk about their experiences with
people who *knew*. Regimental reunions or trips back to the Western Front with
organisations like the Ypres League served a similar function. It was difficult to
explain to those who weren't there what it was like, so some veterans preferred
the company of old comrades. Private Leonard Hewitt said:

> In no circumstances in my opinion can anyone tell you what war is like unless
> they're actually in the front line … unless they've been in the front line they
> cannot tell you. And even if they told you, you cannot grasp the thing, what it is,
> it's impossible to convey by word the actual scene in the trenches.[26]

Regimental reunions, visits to the Western Front, a drink at the Legion club. They
all helped. George Louth thought people weren't interested anyway: 'It would
have been useless telling them and if you did they would have laughed at you, say
it wasn't true.'[27] Many preferred silence. Robert Renwick said that 'neighbours
used to ask me, but my mother used to shake her head and say he'll not talk about
it and I didn't, all through my working life.'[28] Mark Rogers recalls his grandad
Lewis saying, 'If you were there, you wouldn't want to talk about it.'[29] It was
made worse for him by losing a brother then having to tell his mother the details.
George Louth didn't tell his wife, 'even she never heard my story and we were
married seventy years'.[30] Holocaust survivor Aharon Appelfeld described it as
belonging 'to the type of enormous experience which reduces one to silence'.[31]
While the First World War was not as tragic as the Holocaust, it surely qualifies as
such an experience.

The journalist Magnus Linklater also noticed the reluctance of his father to talk about the war. He had joined up underage and was almost killed at Ypres. Linklater thought it was an 'an unbridgeable gap between those who had lived through experiences that we could not even begin to imagine, and those who had suffered them'.[32] When he did talk it was to tell funny stories like the time he was 'marching from one position to another in pouring rain, when his company was given the order to remove kilts and wear them as capes, with the result that ... We said goodbye to Passchendaele with a flutter of grey shirt-tails dancing behind our bums.' Like many veterans, a few stock incidents, preferably amusing, would be a substitute for telling people about more disturbing experiences. Linklater's dad didn't talk about his near escape from death (shot in the back of the head by a machine-gun bullet, which left a permanent dent) and only wrote about it much later. Stoicism might also have been a factor. Linklater believed he was typical of that generation in that he bore 'unimaginable conditions, without complaint'.[33] Ex-servicemen were often reluctant to boast about what they'd done. Robert Graves thought those who attended the local war memorial service were 'modest men: I noticed that though respecting the King's desire to wear their campaign medals on this occasion, they kept them buttoned up inside their coats'.[34] Frank Richards, who had also served with the Royal Welch Fusiliers before 1914, thought that those who hadn't been front-line soldiers were the most likely to display their medals on Armistice Day. These were 'bare-arsed' medals, without bars, given to those who had not seen action. Old soldiers would have been ashamed of wearing them, wrote Richards, 'the only action they were ever in was with some of the charming damsels in the Red Lamps behind the Front.'[35]

It was not only shell-shock victims who continued to be psychologically affected by the war. Graves thought it took him ten years to recover from the frequent visions of the Front – its sights, sounds and smells would invade his normal life.[36] Stanley Casson, the archaeologist, tried to forget about what he had been through by throwing himself into his work. He thought that 'he had put the war into the category of forgotten things'. But he found this impossible, 'The war's baneful influence controlled still all our thoughts and acts, directly or indirectly.'[37] One old soldier recalled on his wedding day that 'even though I was going to be so happy, just as I was crossing the churchyard with its rows of tombstones, I suddenly started to cry. I wept and wept and couldn't stop. It was because of all the others.'[38] A single incident could haunt a man for the rest of his life. Benjamin Clouting, at 97, still remembered a soldier with his right arm blown off leading another who'd been blinded, 'bandages draped across his eyes'. Not an unusual sight in the trenches but Clouting never forgot it.[39]

Recurrent nightmares were particularly common. They often involved a particularly traumatic incident. A number of psychiatrists noted that this contradicted Freud's theory that dreams were a desire for 'wish fulfilment'. Soldiers certainly did not wish to repeat the experiences that haunted their dreams. Freud's explanation of why soldiers had such dreams shows his lack of contact with them when he argued that 'the precondition of war neuroses would seem to be a national [conscript] army; there would be no possibility of their arising in an army of professional soldiers or mercenaries'.[40] But nightmares afflicted all types of soldiers: conscripts, volunteers and seasoned professionals. Rifleman Fred White recalls having restless nights for years due to recurring images of the war. He wasn't alone. 'I've got up and tramped the streets till it came daylight. Walking, walking – anything to get away from your thoughts. And many's the time I've met other fellows that were out there doing exactly the same thing. That went on for years, that did.'[41] A.P. Herbert's nightmares were so bad he would 'throw off the bedclothes and stumble about the room screaming'. His wife 'tied his wrist to hers at bedtime to reduce his alarm'.[42] Graves wrote that, 'shells used to come bursting on my bed at midnight even though Nancy [his wife] shared it with me'.[43] In the more severe cases, nightmarish visions might happen during the day, 'right in the middle of an ordinary conversation when the face of a Boche that I have bayoneted, with its horrible gurgle and grimace, comes sharply into view', said one infantry captain.[44] Survivor's guilt could also play a part in soldier's dreams. Lieutenant Norman Collins dreamt of the dead soldiers he had known walking away while he remained in the trench. This vision, which started at the Armistice, was to haunt him for years to come, though, typically, he never told anyone. It was a 'private matter between my old comrades and myself'.[45] John Laister managed to put the war out of his mind until he was old, but 'things crop up, and I'll see myself in the trenches, which I don't want to do … I get a mental picture, fantastic pictures, and I see every detail exactly as if I'm there'.[46] Reginald St John Battersby died in the 1970s but in his last hours his son remembers him yelling orders to his men shouting, 'The Bosch are coming!' Over fifty years on and his last thoughts were still of the Western Front.[47]

In the terrible ordeal where a man is placed upon a pedestal the greater the number of lives taken by him, it is not easy, indeed it is not sensible, to expect to bring him back to the adequate appreciation of the standard compatible with order and civilisation.

Sheffield Mail, 1920[48]

If you read the popular press after the war you'd be forgiven for thinking veterans were responsible for an epidemic of violent crime. Brutalised by war, these trained killers were running amok. Newspapers dedicated columns to police and court reports about the latest outrage committed by former soldiers. In December 1919, Albert Redfern robbed a bank in Leeds and shot the manager; the previous January, Lieutenant Colonel Norman Rutherford killed Major Seton, who he believed had an evil influence over Rutherford's wife and children. Overall, in 1919, about a third of all murder or suspected murder cases reported in *The Times* and the *News of the World* involved ex-servicemen.[49]

It was not only the newspapers that raised concerns. General Sir Nevil Macready, the commissioner of the Metropolitan Police believed a spate of robberies in 1919 was due to men 'grown callous after four years' experience of killing'.[50] In the same year, former war correspondent Philip Gibbs wrote that a significant minority of men had been changed by their wartime services: 'They were subject to queer moods, queer tempers, fits of profound depression with a restless desire for pleasure. Many of them were easily moved to passion when they lost control of themselves. Many were bitter in their speech, violent in opinion, frightening.'[51] Parliament responded to fears about ex-servicemen committing armed robbery with the Firearms Act (1920), the first restriction on gun ownership in the modern era.

But how representative were these cases? The evidence is inconclusive. Murder rates were higher in 1919 and 1920 than the year before the war, but then fell below the 1913 level from 1921–24. Assaults and rapes (despite reports of sex-crazed soldiers) were lower in the first seven years of peace compared to 1913. The summary level of violent offences was much lower in 1919 (34,479) than 1913 (43,147), rose in 1920 (45,196) then fell again in 1921 (40,596). These figures don't represent an epidemic. Churchill was more accurate when he wrote, 'when "four million trained and successful killers" had come home after the war violence actually declined.'[52] This also fits with Robert Roberts' picture of slum life in Salford during this time. Roberts observed that the troops who returned were more broadminded than when they left:

> Husbands who had driven their wives to despair over what they would or would not eat, would now try anything at dinner time. Children who … had dreaded the return of their soldier parent and the strong discipline that might arrive with him, found instead that he was more inclined to laugh and tolerate, to say, 'boys will be boys'.[53]

Was violence turned inwards? Were ex-servicemen more likely to commit suicide than those who hadn't fought? Many had experienced horrific situations and then found their home life deeply disappointing: perhaps a partner had been unfaithful or they were unable to find a job. One ex-serviceman remembered meeting an old, unemployed comrade in Bristol who told him that after all they had gone through, 'the despair of redundancy and the lack of hope was too much to bear. That same afternoon he went and hanged himself.'[54] There were tragedies like Captain John Walford MC, a veteran of Passchendaele, who suffered from shell shock and shot himself in 1922. A report said:

> [Walford] appeared in his usual health early yesterday morning and talked cheerfully and rationally to a workman on the estate named Ernest Reeve, who shortly afterwards found him lying dead in the orchard adjoining the Court with a six-chambered revolver in his right hand, one of the cartridges having been discharged through his mouth.[55]

Yet, according to the Registrar General, the male suicide rate in 1919 was 'still distinctly low' and below pre-war levels. It had only risen in the over-45 category, a group generally too old for military service.[56] This is similar to other conflicts. Despite being widely misreported, the rates of suicide for the Falklands and Vietnam War* veterans were no higher than their equivalent civilian categories.[57] Obviously the war was a contributing factor in certain cases, but some vulnerable men may still have taken their own lives if they hadn't served. A similar argument could be used to suggest that convicted ex-servicemen were already prone to violence, like Colonel Rutherford, whose wife at his trial told of his 'fiendish' temper before the war.[58]

---

* After the Vietnam War the rate was slightly higher in the first five years but statistically insignificant, and in the long term no higher than equivalent civilian categories.

'YOU HAD A GOOD JOB WHEN YOU LEFT': VETERANS' EMPLOYMENT

'Our main thing in life up to then had been killing Germans.'

James Maxwell Wedderburn[1]

'Left … left … You had a good job when you left … '

Street taunt aimed at unemployed ex-servicemen

One reason why soldiers were frustrated with the slow pace of demobilisation was they suspected the longer they stayed in the army, the more difficult it would be to secure a job. Many did struggle to find regular work. Unemployment remained high throughout the interwar period and disproportionately affected veterans, who had missed years of experience and training. A letter to the *Manchester Evening News* in 1919 complained that 'many Manchester businessmen refuse to employ the ex-soldier on the grounds that he has lost four years of experience in this line or that line of business through being in the army'.[2] Some men had left education directly to join the armed forces and had done nothing except soldiering. Ginger Byrne ruefully noted, 'firing machine guns and looking after them'[3] was not best preparation for civilian life.

Initially, work was fairly easy to get. There was a short post-war boom, partly fuelled by the soldiers' gratuities. Firms needed labour and some employers had promised soldiers their old jobs back when they returned. There was also a view that women who had entered the workforce during the war should now vacate their jobs; numerous British Legion resolutions calling for women to make way were passed at their annual conference. Women's employment rates for those over twenty-five years old were lower in 1931 than they were in 1911.[4] A setback for equality, but it helped soldiers find work.

For some men, jobs guaranteed before they left didn't last long. Frank Gillard returned to the railways at Wollerton and recalled:

> The Railway Company … gave us our jobs and instead of trying to catch up like how you'd expect them to do, to make up for lost time with the things on the Railway that they'd missed, they decided to cut down like they're doing now, and we was on 3 days a week … in June 1921 everything was forgotten and they started sacking us left and right.[5]

Some couldn't even secure their old jobs in the first place. When Private Yarwood contacted his former employers, they wrote saying, 'don't be in a hurry back'.[6] Private Ted Francis also tried, but 'they looked at me like I was a complete stranger. There was hardly anyone I recognised and they almost pushed me out of the door, saying, "We've got no job for you"'.[7] He didn't get regular work for several years.

Neither were those who resumed employment always happy. Lance Corporal William Cowley said, 'I started back at the same firm as before the war – at a very low wage. Admittedly it was a lot more than before the war, but it was still very low.' Inflation had eaten up much of Cowley's wage rise. After his war service, he'd 'expected better treatment'.[8] This was the problem. Soldiers had been told things would be better when they returned. The reality was often different.

Even during the brief boom there were already worrying signs. Unlike other belligerent nations, the British Government's reconstruction plans did not include the compulsory hiring of ex-servicemen. Successive governments saw compulsion as against the dominant free market ideology, preferring to rely on the goodwill of employers. There were few reserved occupations in the public sector, unlike in France, where 65,000 minor government positions had been granted to soldiers in the sixteen years leading up to the First World War.[9] In Austria, a man could claim a job in the police or the postal service after twelve years serving in the army, which could count towards their pension.[10] Australia employed more than 3,000 veterans for the construction of the Great Ocean Road, believing it would 'be a worthy memorial to all Victorian soldiers and a national asset for Victoria'.[11] Programmes in Britain were on a much smaller scale (75 per cent of those employed on public relief work were ex-servicemen), so failed to make a significant difference.

Britain hadn't created a structure for such an influx of soldiers into civilian life. A senior civil servant wrote that before the war, the Treasury was 'never keen in these days, as far as my experience went, to do anything of a specific nature to help the ex-servicemen to get employment'.[12] The annual grant to the National Association, the main pre-war employment agency for ex-servicemen, was only £500. The National Association found veterans unskilled work as 'servants, grooms, coachmen, labourers, ports and messengers'.[13] Voluntary organisations (like the Corps of Commissionaires for security guards) and regimental associations tried to fill the gap left by government. The Veterans Corps and Employment Bureau focused on giving soldiers undemanding work that required some level of trust; typically jobs like caretakers, watchmen and timekeepers.[14] These men were relatively lucky to get work. Over one-third of discharged Boer War veterans were unemployed a year after the conflict had ended. Unemployed soldiers, as the Royal Commission on the Poor Laws (1909) stated, 'furnish the largest contingent of the floating population of the [workhouse] casual wards'.[15]

After the war, the government did set up registers at labour exchanges but it still left the placement of ex-servicemen to the voluntary sector. These organisations were overwhelmed by the number of ex-servicemen needing employment. Nor were they helped by the Treasury, who provided nowhere near enough finances. The National Association's paltry grant was actually cut by half in 1919.

A man o'four-an-twenty that 'asn't
learned a trade
Besides 'Reserve' again' him – 'e'd better be never made.

Rudyard Kipling

The government considered the need for the ex-servicemen's education and training when planning for reconstruction but cutbacks watered down many of these ideas. Not for the last time, the high hopes of 1918 were mugged by fiscal orthodoxy. The major piece of educational legislation, the Education Act (1918), raised the school leaving age to 14. This was too late to benefit veterans, but tertiary education and work-based training would help those whose studies had been disrupted – and here government funds were sadly lacking. The army didn't take responsibility for the education of its troops until after the Armistice, aside from some sporadic lectures a soldier received when out of the line. This reflected pre-war attitudes. Gentlemen officers had independent wealth or a profession while other ranks were regarded as fit for little else but army life. Before 1914, soldiers were even charged for the training courses to prepare them for civilian life.[16]

The unexpected surrender of the Germans in 1918 meant educational and training schemes, like so much of reconstruction, were not ready. Buildings were hastily commandeered and unsuitable facilities were temporarily converted, but demobilisation ensured teachers were among the first groups to leave the army. Lessons were learnt and the Army Education Corps (1920) provided a far more systematic education for soldiers in the Second World War.

Some ex-servicemen benefited from the modest expansion of higher education after the war. Universities like Reading and Swansea were established, and overall student numbers rose from 42,000 in 1924–25 to 50,000 in 1938.[17] Soldiers who had obtained the school matriculation (very few in Edwardian Britain) did receive a university grant, like Private Thomas Hooker of the Machine Gun Corps who got £200 to study at the London School of Economics.[18] Robert Graves resumed his studies at Oxford and was excused some exams on account of his war service.[19] Overall the number of soldiers who went to university remained a tiny percentage of the adult population. Many would have gone there anyway, being predominantly private-school-educated officers. There was nothing comparable to the American GI Bill or the British post-war expansion, which allowed the author's father to train as a teacher after leaving the army. The 'Geddes Axe' meant educational expenditure actually declined from £51.9 million to £41.9 million by 1923–24.[20]

Far more ex-servicemen went to adult education classes, which allowed them to catch up on their studies. Local authorities were particularly active. They made up part of the 2 million people enrolled in English and Welsh technical colleges and evening institutes in 1934, or with organisations like the Workers' Educational Association and university adult classes.[21] Though these were often cut during the Great Depression, some veterans did make good on their lost years and gain higher qualifications, though this involved holding down jobs and studying in their spare time.

The serious skills shortage was partly alleviated by the Interrupted Apprenticeship Scheme, which allowed soldiers to resume where they had left off, though again it was poorly funded. John Obrone resumed his fifth year of his apprenticeship but with a lower wage than when he was a corporal.[22] The government also allocated a limited amount to pay companies to train veterans. However, planned 'continuation schools' for practical education for adults were never implemented, despite being in the original 1918 Education Act. In terms of the training of ex-servicemen, particularly the disabled, Lord Burnham* wrote, 'the State has fallen very far short of its duties ... the scheme for training them both while they have been in the Service and after they have been discharged has largely failed.'[23] In 1925 apprenticeships in the workforce had only increased by 0.06 per cent from twenty years before.[24]

Nor could ex-servicemen expect much help from trade unions. The movement was in a militant mood in 1919 with a series of strikes involving 2.4 million workers – 300,000 more than revolutionary Germany.[25] One key demand was an end to the dilution of skilled labour. The unions had consented to suspend many workplace agreements during the war to increase production. Unskilled workers

---

* Chairman of the Resettlement Committee under the Ministry of Labour.

were allowed to take skilled jobs without the previous training requirements. This agreement* lasted until the end of hostilities. Unions saw shortened training programmes for veterans as a continuation of 'dilution' and blocked them. They feared an influx of soldiers into the job market would provide companies with cheap labour that would undermine hard-won rights gained before the war, but this meant that ex-servicemen without the necessary qualifications, or the chance to acquire them through long apprenticeships, would be debarred from many potential jobs.

> I'm an unemployed Ex-Serviceman
> And don't intend to shirk;
> You can test me if you like sir,
> By finding me honest work.
>
> 'The Unemployed Ex-Serviceman's Appeal', Anon

By the end of 1920 the boomlet was over. Businesses supplying war materials had their contracts cancelled and the adjustment to civilian production was a slow, painful process. Eric Hobsbawm wrote that 'Britain was never the same again after 1918, because the country had ruined its economy by waging a war substantially beyond its resources.'[26] The Geddes Axe sucked further life out of the economy just when it needed stimulating. In December 1920 unemployment stood at 691,000; by June 1921 it was 2,171, 000.[27] It never dropped below 10 per cent of the workforce throughout the decade. Veterans were particularly vulnerable in this tougher climate. One commented it was 'the most difficult thing to realise you're of no commercial value'.[28] By 1921, 600,000 veterans were unemployed.[29] In June the number of unemployed ex-servicemen was greater than the overall jobless figure of the entire workforce in the previous December.[30] Without any legal obligations to hire ex-servicemen, employers preferred more experienced workers. These statistics have human stories behind them. Jim Hooley grew up in a working-class area of Stockport between the wars. On his way to school, he vividly remembered one impoverished family squatting in an abandoned pub. They were evicted of course. The next day a crowd gathered round the pub: the father of the family had hanged himself. Jim Hooley saw three war medals placed on their sideboard that had been left out on the street.[31]

Statutory quotas for veterans in other countries meant their unemployment rate was lower than the general population. The Australian government had

---

* The Treasury Agreement of 1915.

acquired or set apart 24 million acres of land for soldier settlements by 1924.[32] New Zealand gave priority in employment to ex-servicemen. Crown lands were made available to those wanting to farm, with generous grants of up to £4,250. Business loans of £300 were also made available for those seeking self-employment. The RSA, New Zealand's veterans' association, had its own employment agency; over 20,000 soldiers were placed in employment and in the first four years of peace the number of unemployed soldiers looking for work never exceeded 150.[33] In Britain, the ex-servicemen's unemployment rate was higher than average throughout the period.

There were some local government initiatives but this depended on the authority. The future prime minister, Clement Attlee, came from a privileged background but was converted to socialism by the poverty he saw doing charity work in the East End of London. He came to believe that charity only went so far. As Mayor of Stepney in 1920, he wrote:

> In a civilised community, although it may be composed of self-reliant individuals, there will be some persons who will be unable at some periods to look after themselves, and the question of what is to happen to them may be solved in three ways – they may be neglected, they may be cared for by the organised community as of right, or they may be left to the goodwill of individuals in the community.[34]

Attlee certainly included veterans as those who needed caring for by the 'organised community'. He had served in Gallipoli (where he was the last but one off the beach at Suvla Bay), Mesopotamia and France and was well aware of the problems ex-servicemen had finding work. During his time in office, he started schemes in Stepney for returning soldiers but initiatives like these were rare. Few local officials shared Attlee's wartime experiences or political outlook. By 1922 only 382 local authorities out of 2,514 had joined the King's Roll to employ disabled veterans.[35]

Voluntary schemes like the King's Roll for disabled veterans had a limited effect** but many companies were even reluctant to take on able-bodied veterans. Some businesses displayed signs like 'No ex-servicemen need apply'. This frustrated Field Marshall Haig, who thought that if ex-servicemen made up 5 per cent of a company's workforce the problem of unemployment would be solved. He visited the industrial areas of Britain to persuade employees, but in a letter to his cousin admitted:

** See Chapter 12.

In the West Riding 25 per cent of the employers have taken on 9,000 ex-ser-vicemen. There are still 4,000 in that area out of work and 75 per cent of the employers still available to do it. Nearly all of them in that part have made great fortunes, so we are not asking much.[36]

Haig certainly wasn't asking a lot but it was too much for most businesses. Like the government, they found it more convenient to praise returning heroes than help them. One ex-battery commander, writing to *The Times* in 1920, thought businessmen tended to believe they'd already contributed:

I know that many of them worked long hours, even overworked in their country's cause, but they got a reward in experience, in an increase of income, and in good positions. And although the strain of long hours is great, their offices did not admit poison gas, mud, and shells, with the ever present threat of sudden death.[37]

Soldiers (though not officers) had endured a poor reputation before the war as the dregs of society, frequently drunk, violent and unreliable. Their reputation had risen during the First World War, as Britain's new citizens' army drew men from a much wider range of backgrounds, but some of the stigma still stuck. The publicity given to shell shock and the post-war scare about brutalised veterans hardly helped the employment prospects of soldiers; by the late 1920s veterans comprised 80 per cent of the unemployed between the ages of 30 and 34, and 58 per cent of the total unemployed.[38]

The treasury sent a deputation across to me … at which their chief spokesman was in his most insolent mood at my proposed scale for out-of-work benefit, which was 20/- a week for men … He suggested that the treasury might pos-sibly concede up to 14/- for the man. By this time I was in a pugilistic mood and told him that if he were to go to the Tommies in the trenches and tell them he thought 14/- would be enough for them to live on if they could not get a job after demobilisation, he would probably be strung up to the nearest post and would deserve it.

Christopher Addison[39]

S.O.S. Ex-Officer
100% disabled for 3 ½ years
UNABLE to work wants to
RENT today a HOUSE out of London

£35 inclusive or ROOMS to enable

His WIFE + 3 small SONS + SELF

To LEAVE the WORKHOUSE Fulham Rd

> Beggars' placard shortly after the war had finished[40]

The longer an ex-serviceman remained unemployed the more difficult it was finding work. Employers were less likely to take on men who hadn't had a job in months. The National Secretary of the British Legion said that 'they were finding out many cases where the unemployed were degenerating into unemployables. Some of the men had become so despondent that they felt the whole world, including the country for which they had fought, had gone against them.'[41]

There was a frequent pattern of experience for the long-term unemployed. Firstly, a good deal of energy was spent searching for work. This might involve travelling further and further from home or applying for jobs previously considered degrading. Gradually, lethargy and despair took hold as the job seeker started to realise how little work was available. Considerable household economics would have to be made as savings ran out and the claimant moved to transitional welfare payments. Nutrition suffered, as families tended to buy filling rather than healthy food. The levels of poverty varied depending on the number of mouths to feed, the local scales of relief, or if there were any other income earners in the household.

There had been worrying long-term trends in Britain's economy before 1914. Much of Britain's physical exports were made up of the basic staples of the early industrial revolution: coal, iron, steel, textiles and shipbuilding, which were all now in long-term decline. The war exacerbated these problems: due to the glut of ships now being turned to civilian use after the Armistice, two-thirds of the shipyard workers were unemployed by 1921. Britain also faced tough competition from abroad. Many of her overseas markets had been lost during the war: to the US in Latin America and to Japan in Asia. Despite some recovery, exports never reached the pre-war level in the 1920s. Once the 'workshop of the world', Britain now had a significant visible balance of payment deficit. In 1914, she was responsible for 14 per cent of world exports but by 1928 this had fallen to 11 per cent. Invisible earning declined to such an extent that in 1931 Britain was running a current account deficit – something unimaginable before the war.[42] This hit the old industrial regions the hardest and, consequently, the unemployed formed a larger percentage of those in poverty in areas of the Scottish Lowlands, South Wales, Northern Ireland and the North of England. By 1936 these regions accounted for over two-thirds of total unemployment.[43] In York, by no means the worst hit northern city, 72.6 per cent of poverty was caused by joblessness.[44]

What is hard to measure statistically, but is in numerous anecdotes, is the loss of pride suffered by the unemployed. A man was often judged by the job he held.

For the veteran this was a particularly bitter blow, considering the service he had given his country. Private James Brady went back to his native Rochdale and found the economic conditions depressing. Unemployment, temporary jobs or poorly paid ones were what was on offer. He wrote:

> One saw one's friends deteriorate body and soul before one's very eyes under the strain of unrelieved frustration. Many of the lads, raw from the Front, fell for the 'blackmail' of unscrupulous employers offering a serfdom in mills and factories, worse than ever they had suffered before the war-and God knows, that was bad enough at times. Industrial Lancashire was reverting to its pre-war patterns: long hours, hard work and poor pay. And if you were not prepared to 'knuckle under' you could 'push off', get back in the army, or better still-emigrate.[45]

The desperation of ex-servicemen could be gleaned from the adverts newspapers ran regularly: like 'Ex-Captain, 28, seeks WORK. Has wife and child to spur best efforts';[46] 'Commander, R.N. retired, aged 44, married, shortly demobilised, exceptional experience, executive officer of ships for many years, two years in command, total abstainer. WANTS WORK. Moderate Salary.'[47] Both were former officers who previously wouldn't have expected to be unemployed, but the First World War had considerably expanded the officer corps. Two hundred and twenty-nine thousand, three hundred and sixteen combatant commissions[48] had been granted to men from the ranks, widening the social pool from which officers were taken. Oliver Mellors, in D.H. Lawrence's *Lady Chatterley's Lover*, is a fictional representation of the working-class ex-officer. The War Office found that of the officers demobilised, 266 former warehousemen and porters, 638 fishermen and more than 1,000 had been miners.[49] There had always been down-and-out ex-soldiers but impoverished officers were a new phenomenon. George Coppard wrote, 'it was a common sight in London to see ex-officers with barrel-organs.'[50] The Officers' Association set up an employment bureau at Clement's Inn, London, but it struggled. In 1925, its first year, of the 27,000 able-bodied ex-officers who visited the bureau, only 1,000 were placed in jobs.[51] Being an ex-officer was no guarantee of a job. As one remarked, 'We have to wipe this "war record" clear off our minds, drop the "captain" and "lieutenant" off the advertisements, and regard ourselves as fit young civilians who have had a "jolly fine holiday for four years".'[52] The bureau did manage to help some start their own businesses with interest-free loans. One ex-officer later wrote, 'You were courageous enough to advance me the cash to start my business when you could scarcely have known whether it was likely to be a success or not.'[53]

As the situation worsened, beggars and peddlers in greatcoats became a common sight in towns and cities. Trooper Sydney Chaplin remembered sleeping rough on the Victoria Embankment and when he woke the benches and steps were full of ex-servicemen, some of whom were wrapped in old news-papers.[54] T.J. Birrell, secretary of the British Legion's Relief Fund, 'found one ex-servicemen living under deplorable conditions, with two of the youngest children sleeping in boxes on each side of the fire-place. Their bedding con-sisted of green leaves. Another ex-serviceman was found living in an old bell tent in the woods.'[55] J.B. Priestley discovered the plight of his old comrades when he returned to Bradford in 1933. Some wouldn't turn up to a regimental reunion, despite the free admission, because they were too ashamed of the state of their clothes. Priestley wrote caustically:

> I did not like to think then how bad their clothes, their whole circumstances, were; it is not, indeed a pleasant subject. They were with us, swinging along while the women and old men cheered, in that early battalion of Kitchener's New Army, were with us when kings, statesmen, general officers, all reviewed us, when the crowds threw flowers, blessed us, cried over us; and then they stood in the mud and water, scrambled through the broken strands of barbed wire, saw the sky darken and the earth open with red-hot steel, and came back as official heroes and also as young-old workmen wanting to pick up their jobs and their ordinary life again; and now, in 1933, they could not even join us in a tavern because they had not decent coats to their backs. We could drink to the tragedy of the dead; but we could only stare at one another, in pitiful embarrassment, over this tragi-comedy of the living, who had fought for a world that did not want them, who had come back to exchange their uniforms for rags.[56]

Ex-servicemen who returned to rural communities faced a different set of chall-enges. Jobs were relatively easier to obtain, especially as women war workers were usually dismissed. Unemployment was lower than the old industrial areas but conditions remained tough. A worldwide agricultural depression during the 1920s hit wages, which fell from an average of 40 shillings a week in 1919 to 25 shillings in 1923.[57] Agricultural workers did not enjoy the general reduction in working hours and 60-hour weeks were still common in the 1920s. For many in the towns, however, a 40- to 48-hour week, with Saturdays off, was becoming the norm. Nor could veterans always expect a hero's welcome from their employers. A Cheshire man who joined up in 1914 was told he should still receive a boys' wage because he had not completed his apprenticeship. He quit shortly after.[58]

One measure of hardship is the number of charitable organisations that dealt with ex-servicemen in distress. An article in *Legion* calculated there were 500 funds in 1936. The Legion itself played a major role; by 1930 there were 3,000 Legion local relief committees,[59] though even such a well-heeled organisation could only do so much. The relief they offered was usually of a limited and temporary nature, perhaps helping a veteran out between periods when he could receive benefits.

We cannot paint too bleak a picture. Many ex-servicemen did find work, particularly in areas of economic growth. For those who returned to the job they'd left, and continued in it for the rest of their working lives, the war represented a short intermission. The army also helped men develop certain attributes useful to life after the war. Robert Graves clearly suffered after the war but admitted that the army taught him 'endurance: a brutal persistence in seeing things through'.[60] Similarly, Sergeant William Cowley believed that the war, 'made him more responsible. It was marvellous – I felt I could do any job.'[61] Harold Macmillan, who survived when so many of his friends had died, 'felt an obligation to make some decent use of a life that had been spared us'.[62] Roy Page left school in 1914 and joined the Royal Fusiliers (City of London Regiment). He was nicknamed 'Cherub' due to his youthful looks. Permanently injured, and lacking the funds thought necessary to become a stockbroker, he still made a successful career in the City with Montagu Loebl Stanley. He even managed to bail out his father, who ran into trouble as a coal broker during the General Strike. All this before he was 30.[63] Some managed to use contacts they'd made during the war. Cecil Withers found himself unemployed but a chance meeting with his old captain secured him a job in the Ministry of Food, he then stayed in the civil service until he retired in the 1960s.[64]

Another positive impact of the war is that it stimulated Britain to develop industrial products that had previously been imported, like dyestuff, chemicals and rayon. Industry had to become more efficient to meet the demands of the armed forces and, after a slow start, Britain coped well with supplying the necessary armaments for the world's first total war. There was also a good deal of rationalisation, as larger firms were better able to meet government orders and develop mass-production techniques. After the war, these lessons were utilised in sectors like light engineering, electrical generating and car manufacturing, mostly situated in the South East and the Midlands. Where an ex-serviceman lived was a large factor in how well he fared in the jobs market. In 1934, the unemployment rates were 67.8 per cent in Jarrow and 61.9 in Methyr; but in Luton it was only 7.7 per cent and a mere 3.9 per cent in St Albans.[65] By the end of the 1930s, employment in the economically depressed areas improved as rearmament stimulated heavy industry. Overall, the interwar years saw a sharp decline in infant mortality from 108 deaths per 1,000 live births in 1913* to 53 in 1938.[66] This is a reminder of the economic progress Britain made, albeit unevenly. It was the age of the Jarrow Marches but also of the Austin 7, the phenomenally successful small family car that shifted nearly 300,000 vehicles by 1939.

---

*   The figure is for England and Wales, Scotland saw a 36 per cent decline in the same period.

However, for a core of ex-servicemen this came too late. Out of work for years and pretty well unemployable, they got by on a mixture of benefits, pensions and charity. Niall Barr calculated there were about 300,000 unskilled ex-servicemen who were long-term unemployed between the wars.[67] Private Frank Richards admitted that 'I have had a pretty tough time and have had long periods of unemployment and I expect there are thousands of old soldiers who are worse off than I am.' In reference to peacetime, he thought 'the lead-swingers and the dodgers get the best of it'.[68] Private Turner remembered:

> Many's the time I've gone to bed, after a day of 'tramp, tramp' looking for work, on a cup of cocoa and a pennyworth of chips between us; I would lay puzzling why, why, after all we had gone through in the service of our country, we have to suffer such poverty, willing to work at anything but no work to be had. I only had two Christmases at work between 1919 and 1939.'[69]

The British Legion calculated that 35,000 Legion members were in Poor Law institutions in 1924[70] out of a total of 87,000 ex-servicemen who depended on Poor Law assistance. The number would have been higher but for the extension of unemployment benefits during reconstruction. The original 1911 scheme was mainly for the seasonally unemployed and covered just over 2 million workers. The payments lasted only fifteen weeks; after that it was charity or the Poor Law. Though subsidised, it was an insurance scheme not a dole; workers were expected to have contributed a certain amount before they could receive any funds. It smacked of Edwardian self-reliance and a presumption that unemployment was a temporary phenomenon.

The large number of unemployed soldiers forced a government rethink. It would be politically difficult to continue with the pre-war system, as men who had been fighting for their country could hardly be refused help, even if they hadn't paid sufficient contributions. There was also the fear of the radicalisation of veterans. During demobilisation, British troops had shown themselves quite capable of violent protest, while in countries like Italy, Germany, Hungary and, most of all, Russia, discontented soldiers had contributed to serious revolutionary outbreaks. The Home Secretary warned:

> The temper of the men is becoming increasingly bitter … there is much muttering about the ostentation and luxury of the 'idle rich' and agitators have seized upon the real discontent and distress to carry on a ceaseless propaganda of class war.[71]

An out-of-work donation was granted immediately to around 10 per cent of ex-servicemen: in Ireland it was nearer to 45 per cent.[72] In 1920, the Unemployed Insurance Act extended unemployment cover to almost 12 million workers* and benefits were raised to about a third of the average wage.[73] But some of the principles of the original scheme remained. The full benefit of twenty-six weeks was still dependent on contributions already made. The long-term unemployed, of whom ex-servicemen were a disproportionate number, still required assistance, so additional or 'transitional' payments were granted after the time limit ran out. When the act was passed unemployment was still low, so it was thought these people would be few in number, but during the next year the level started its inexorable rise. The costs were greater than anticipated. By 1931 unemployment benefits came to £120 million a year, whereas only £44 million were collected in National Insurance contributions.[74] This created a dilemma. Between the wars, a balanced budget was the goal of every administration but no politician was going to stop all assistance to ex-servicemen. Therefore, benefits were cut in an effort to save money, but not completely so as to prevent outright destitution. At the height of the Great Depression in 1932, when the jobless made up to one worker in six,[75] the unemployed had their benefits cut by 10 per cent to reduce the government's deficit. Transitional payments were even lower and often involved long gaps between payments. This could force unemployed ex-servicemen to depend on the mercies of the local Poor Law Guardians, renamed Public Assistance Committees after 1931. Whatever its name, this was a humiliating experience. The Poor Law wasn't quite the Dickensian regime of yore** but it still carried a good deal of social shame.

The benefits system was a complex one and, like the pension regime, was administered with a degree of petty-mindedness and bureaucracy, the presumption being that the claimant's condition was due to his own fecklessness. Perhaps the most resented element was the means test (1931). The law was introduced by the government as an economy measure. In order to receive transitional payments, claimants had to undergo a visit by the Public Assistance Committee, which could be highly demeaning. Payments were dependent on a man's level of savings, the value of his furniture or the level of war pension he currently received. This could hurt anyone's pride but was especially bitter for a man who had served his country in war and had been promised better times at the end of it. Private G. Kidd had to go before a means test panel:

---

* This was most of the labour force, though some categories were excluded, like domestic servants, farm workers, railway workers, civil servants and the self-employed.
** Much of the help was in the form of outdoor relief rather than in work houses.

There was a very fat lady on the panel, cuddling a Pekinese on her lap. She said, 'We're all got to pull in our belts a hole or two these days.' I was fed up and told her … 'That bloody dog's had more to eat today than I've had.'

There was a row, furniture was knocked over and paperwork sent flying. Kidd got three months in Wormwood Scrubs prison.[76] A land fit for heroes indeed.

11

SEX, MORALITY AND MARRIAGE

'There were well over a hundred and fifty men waiting for opening time, sing-
ing Mademoiselle from Armentiéres and other lusty songs. Right on the dot of 6 PM a
red lamp over the doorway of the brothel was switched on. A roar went up from the troops,
accompanied by a forward lunge towards the entrance.'[1]

George Coppard

When the men returned home, many of them married. Wedding plans that had
been put off when they left for the war could now go ahead. What is more surprising is that marriage rates stayed high throughout the 1920s, despite the toll
the war had taken on Britain's young male population. In terms of births, there
was a brief baby boom (shorter than the one after the Second World War), as the
trend towards smaller families, begun before 1914, continued.

The war had seen a relaxation of morality, but starting a family in interwar
Britain still meant marriage. The peak was reached in 1920 with 20.2 marriages per 1,000 of the population, which resulted in 379,982 weddings. This
was 25 per cent higher than pre-war levels.[2] Though the trend declined slightly,
marriage levels were still higher than Edwardian times throughout the 1920s.
Celibacy rates fell too and the proportion of women married between the ages
of 25 and 34 was 'remarkably stable in the war decade in both England and Wales
and Scotland'.[3] This seems counter-intuitive; surely the war deprived British
women of husbands? Young men were the group most likely to be killed and
most likely to marry. There was a real fear during the war about the potential
consequences. One headmistress told her students:

I have come to tell you a terrible fact. Only one out of ten of you girls can ever
hope to marry. This is not a guess of mine. It is a statistical fact. Nearly all the

men who might have married you have been killed. You will have to make your way in the world as best you can.[4]

She *was* guessing; there was not nearly as many men killed as she thought. War fatalities were less than half of France's and around half of Germany's.* [5] The end of large-scale emigration also helped reduce the gender imbalance, as young men were the group mostly likely to emigrate. Almost 900,000 Britons had left between 1910–13, more than were killed during the war. Add to that the men who returned to Britain to volunteer (there was net immigration of 108,688 in 1914)[6] and the myth of 'surplus women' can start to be explained. J.M. Winter believed that a tendency of women to marry across class and geographical lines also kept marriage rates high. Some showed pragmatism in choosing a partner. Vera Brittain lost her fiancé Roland, then a second soldier she became engaged to was also killed. She did eventually marry after the war but her daughter, the politician Shirley Williams, believes she never got over the loss of Roland. But she still married. Women even placed adverts in newspapers aimed at ex-servicemen:

Lady, fiancé killed, will gladly marry officer totally blinded or otherwise incapacitated by the War.

Spinster, 38, loving disposition, fond of children, entertaining and country life, is anxious to correspond with a wounded officer of cultured tastes, with view to a matrimonial alliance; one with some means.[7]

Others agreed to premarital sex in the hope of marriage afterwards. In response, someone placed a plaque in a well-known London hotel that said, 'To the women who fell here during the First World War.'[8] Ultimately, these social changes helped to break down the rule-based, highly restrictive courtships of Edwardian Britain. Dating became fashionable in the 1920s. Undeniably, some women spent their lives as spinsters. Clive James recalled his London landlady in the 1960s whose fiancé died on the same boat as Rupert Brooke. Still unmarried, her 'connections with the outside world had been broken on the day when her fiancé sailed away to the Middle East'.[9] But she was not representative of her generation.

Not all of these marriages ended happily of course. Just as the marriage rate increased, so did divorce. In 1913 only 577 couples were granted a divorce in England and Wales. The figure rose to 1,654 in 1919 and then the next year to 3,090.[10] Divorce was 'as common as flies in a hot summer', wrote Beatrice Webb. Couples who had wed quickly in the charged wartime atmosphere might find

---

★ Per 1,000 males aged 15–49: Britain 63, Germany 125 and France 133 (JM Winter).

themselves incompatible in peace. Men had sometimes been changed by their experiences and could be difficult to live with. Even those not suffering from shell shock could be susceptible to mood swings and restlessness or retreat into their own world. Corporal Tommy Keele confessed that the war put a strain on his marriage: 'I was bad tempered and my poor wife suffered for it. I would go days without speaking – all this stemmed from the war.'[11] Agnes Greatorex was courting in 1916 before her fiancé went off to war. He was 'nice, kind and very thoughtful', but she recalls that 'when he came back … he was short with people, not like he used to be, I think he resented the war … he'd changed'.[12] But considering the overall number of marriages, divorces were still relatively rare, though this was an age where it was still socially frowned upon and legally difficult. Only in 1923 could a woman divorce a man for adultery (a man could already divorce on adulterous grounds), and it was not until 1935 that drunkenness, insanity and desertion were added to the list of reasons. But social attitudes to divorce cannot entirely account for the long marriages many ex-servicemen enjoyed. Some believed that the war strengthened their relationships. Corporal Charles Templar was glad he served, partly because 'Daisy and I were grateful for the fact that I had survived … All our married life she wanted to be involved with anything that I was doing.'[13]

The birth rate declined during the war, as couples tended to put off having children. After the Armistice, there was a significant increase, peaking in 1920 with almost 958,782 births in England and Wales.[14] Despite the wartime losses, the population had increased in 1921 by 2.4 per cent from its 1914 total.[15] This was a higher figure than any year of the 1940s baby boom, though shorter in duration. Rates then fell throughout the 1920s and '30s.[16] The reasons are still debated. The greater use of contraceptives could be a factor. The army eventually issued sheaths to prevent venereal disease and this habit seems to have continued with ex-servicemen after the war. Previously, condoms had been associated with extra-marital sex and were not seen as respectable for married couples. The introduction of latex condoms in 1929 certainly helped. Women who entered wartime industries had access to greater levels of pro-contraceptive propaganda. A Royal Commission on Population survey found that only 16 per cent of women who married before 1910 used birth control, whereas the figure leapt to 59 per cent of women who married in 1920–24.[17] This meshed with the long-term trend to limit the number of children among families that saw fertility decline in every decade from 1901–31.[18]

Many came back more sexually experienced than if they'd stayed at home.[19] Young men, freed from social convention, naturally experimented with sex, especially when it might be their last, or only, time. Robert Graves wrote that there 'were no restraints in France; these boys had money to spend and they knew they stood a good chance of being killed within a few weeks anyhow. They did not want to die virgins.'[20] Cultural historian Clare Makepeace argues that there was sometimes a direct connection between sex and death: 'Men chose to visit brothels ... either as a reward for surviving battle or as a refuge from an imminent death.' After the war, Captain Harry Siepmann said brothels were a way of escaping 'the "out-of-touch atmosphere" of jingoism and unthinking patriotism in Britain [that] "jarred badly with the grim realities of France".'[21]

And sex was readily available. Cafés often doubled as whorehouses. Corporal George Ashurst recalled:

> We were drinking *vin blanc* in the estaminet ... There were five women in there, and it was five francs to go up the stairs and into the bedrooms with them. The stairs leading up to bedrooms were full; there was a man on every step, waiting his turn to go in with a woman.

Later a padre walked in and reminded the men they had mothers and sisters.[22]

Generally, the army took a pragmatic line over prostitution (it had been a long military tradition after all) and brothels sprang up across the Western Front – *maison tolérées* with red lamps for the men, blue for the officers. Graves wondered whether the officers' prostitutes had particular qualifications for their role.[23] There were estimated to be 137 in thirty-five towns. Le Havre was particularly renowned and attracted 170,000 visitors in 1915 alone.[24] This partly stemmed from the widely held belief that men needed sex regularly for their health. This meant even some clergymen 'excused unfaithfulness to our wives while away from home in the present circumstances'.[25] However, when news about the *maison tolérées* reached home, there was an outcry. Protests led to them being declared out of bounds in 1918.[26] Lord Kitchener had earlier implored his men to 'keep constantly on your guard against any excesses. In this new experience you may find temptations both in wine and women. You must entirely resist both.'[27] The advice was widely ignored. Hospital admission rates for venereal disease went up in the last year of the war.* [28]

There were also temptations at home, as many women were prepared to sleep with soldiers. Pre-marital sex now became more overt. Helena Swanwick, daughter of Oswald Sickert, wrote, 'Sex before marriage was the natural female complement to the male frenzy of killing. If millions of men were to be killed in early manhood, or even boyhood, it behoved every young woman to secure a mate and replenish the population while there was yet time.'[29] Many women were

---

* In 1918, British and Dominion troops rates went up from 2.56 to 3.24 per cent of men serving in France, and 3.19 to 3.34 per cent of men serving in Britain.

attracted to soldiers in what became known as 'Khaki fever'. Edith Sellers wrote, 'I saw some English Tommies, who were being pursued by girls, spring in onto an omnibus for safety. The girls sprung after them.'[30] The women were sometimes from middle-class backgrounds. Laurence Housman wrote that 'a friend of mine in the police tells me … that in his district absolutely 'respectable' and 'virtuous' young women have given themselves day after day to different soldiers as if it were a sort of religious duty.'[31] Mary Agnes Hamilton, the daughter of a professor, wrote, 'Little wonder that the old ideals of chastity and self control in sex were, for many, also lost.'[32] Frances Osborne believed it was one of the few ways such women could be involved in the war.

Pragmatism had its limits in the issuing of condoms. Unlike Germany and France, the army authorities did not initially provide them, fearing the negative publicity if the armed forces aided 'opportunities for unrestrained vice'.[33] In Britain, the image of the soldier was couched in the medieval language of chivalry, where valiant warriors bravely faced the foe – and Sir Galahad certainly wouldn't get the clap. This partly explained why infection rates were seven times higher in the British Army than Germany's.[34] It was only under pressure from the Canadian and New Zealand governments that condoms started to be issued later in the war. This was too late for many: the infection rate went up in each year, reaching over 60,000 in 1918.[35] Unsurprisingly, syphilis and other sexually transmitted diseases became a major concern. An official history described it as causing 'the greatest amount of constant inefficiency in the home commands'.[36] Syphilis was also a matter of deep shame and men who contracted it would have some explaining to do when they arrived home. A man's pay was immediately stopped if he became infected, which would alert his wife that something was wrong. Some preferred to keep it quiet or seek surreptitious treatment from a sympathetic doctor, as it was an offence to conceal the disease.[37] Syphilis also had its attractions. It could be a way out of the firing line and there were cases of men deliberately getting infected.[38] The fact that syphilis was such a painful disease in cure and consequence shows a desperation to leave the front line. Mercury-based cures had been superseded by Salvarsan, but it contained arsenic and had nasty side effects. Doctors even tried 'fever therapy', whereby patients would be infected with malaria to bring on a fever, which was thought to cure syphilis.[39] Soldiers certainly paid a price long after the war. Only when penicillin was introduced during the Second World War was there a safe and effective cure. Overall, there were 416,891 hospital admissions for venereal disease during the war, which was about 5 per cent of the men who enlisted.[40] Treatment of STD led to improvements, with the emergence of a nationwide network of clinics.[41] It was a small step towards a national health service.

Wartime Britain was hardly Sodom and Gomorrah, but there were plenty of moral guardians determined to reduce the serviceman's pleasures. It was a bumper time for the prurient. In 1916, the National Council of Public Morals set up a commission to deal with potentially offensive subjects in films, which included indecorous dancing, men and women in bed together and the realistic depiction of the horrors of war.[42] Women's Patrol Committees and the Women's Police Service often stopped girls (especially working-class ones) from having sex with soldiers – their fields of combat being the park and the cinema. The Assistant Commissioner of Police, when presented with the evidence of such behaviour, commented that 'the conduct of which they complain only constitutes an offence when committed within view of the public'.[43] Nor were the public always on the side of the prudish. 'It is about time,' someone wrote to his local newspaper, 'something was done about ancient spinsters following soldiers about with their flash lights.'[44]

How great were the changes of behaviour brought on by the war? It's difficult to quantify any social change with precision. We know cases of venereal disease increased and the illegitimacy rates doubled from 3 to 6 per cent,[45] but the *overall* number of babies born outside marriage fell due to the declining birth rate. Soldiers, it might be concluded, didn't mind having a good time abroad but were well aware of the consequences of pregnancy at home. Much of the wartime hysteria about wayward soldiers and willing munitionettes was little more than sensationalist newspaper stories. Certainly, men returned with a greater knowledge of sex than if they'd stayed in Britain. It would have been remarkable if they had not, given the length of the war and distance from home. This greater knowledge was augmented by the rise in popularity of the works of Freud, and, beyond intellectual circles, Marie Stopes' huge bestseller *Married Love*, a book that dealt with sex in a remarkably frank way for the era. But its title is worth noting – Stopes was not advocating free love but how married couples could improve their sex lives. It was not a guide to promiscuity.

The evidence suggests that, apart from the greater use of contraception and a less formal approach to dating, any changes were part of trends already present before the war. The rate of extramarital fertility continued to decline, apart from the brief wartime blip, and was a just over a third lower in 1931 than it had been in 1901.[46] Families decreased in size, but they were already doing so before 1914, and the marriage rate stabilised after the hike in the immediate post-war period. There were fewer bachelors.

There was plenty of outrage about declining standards in the 1920s. Some blamed a war that had given the young unprecedented freedoms. Stories in the media abounded of women who dressed provocatively, smoked and drank in pubs and went to jazz dances unchaperoned. 'We all had an awful lot of catching up to do,' said one former member of the Ambulance Corps.[47] This sense of shock was captured by Alfred Noyes in his poem 'The Victory Ball':

The cymbals crash,
And the dancers walk;
With long silk stockings,
And arms of chalk,
Butterfly skirts
And white breasts bare;
And shadows of dead men
Watching 'em there–[48]

The last two lines are important. The frivolity of the Roaring Twenties was often seen as an insult to those who had died in the war. Vera Brittain, on the other hand, thought their behaviour was understandable. In *Testament of Youth* she describes the 'reckless sense of combined release and anti-climax' of her generation after the war, trying to make up for lost time.[49] But there is little evidence for any great changes outside the occasional anecdote. Drunkenness and violence declined, despite press reports about out of control ex-servicemen.* The war unsettled lives but the army also taught self-discipline. It's worth noting that the interwar years had a conservative side. Weaker beer and shorter pubs hours, initially a wartime emergency measure, continued; cannabis, cocaine and opium were restricted as drug laws were tightened. The morality that patrolled parks for copulating couples didn't disappear with the Armistice. This was also the age of Joynson-Hicks, 'the most prudish, puritanical and protestant Home Secretary of the twentieth century',[50] who ordered raids on night clubs and the censoring of D.H. Lawrence and birth control guides. *The Times* refused to publish the announcement that Marie Stopes had given birth to a son in 1924. Nor were hard-partying flappers and 'bright young things' necessarily representative of the war generation – many of the latter group, like Evelyn Waugh, had been too young to fight. They were a privileged minority who had the time and money to behave in the way they did – and the social connections to get away with it. Of course, some ex-servicemen led lives that defied contemporary conventions, but the statistics suggests they were few in number.

Working-class communities were close-knit and overcrowded and little escaped prying eyes. Lower-middle- and middle-class estates had more space and privacy but were bastions of probity. There was no social revolution; instead there were small, incremental changes, such as the Oxbridge colleges that abandoned the rule that unmarried women needed a chaperone when visiting male students' rooms. However, visiting hours were still restricted.

Ex-servicemen were remarkably young, considering what they had been through. A decorated army captain might not yet have reached his twenty-first

---

* See Chapter 9.

birthday. A veteran of the 100 Days could still be in his teens. It's hardly surprising if they were less deferential. They might stand at the bar with their fathers or date girls of their choice. Their clothes and musical tastes could be consciously different. The interwar period was an age of dance bands, Brylcreem and double-breasted suits, sometimes to the chagrin of the older generation.

Rural Britain was slower to change. Pubs were still male-only bastions and elders exercised a greater control over marriages. This could be a frustrating experience for veterans who had seen a lot more of the world than their fathers, though rural Britain wasn't completely immune to modernity. Cheap radio sets and motorbikes (a small two-stroke cost less than a tenner) meant the young could occasionally enjoy outings to the nearest town or listen to jazz or a drama on the BBC. In nonconformist areas like Wales, the strict observance of the Sabbath was never quite as strict as before the war.

12

DISABLED VETERANS

'One evening we were walking along … just as a coach load of soldiers, disabled men, came by. I shall never forget it. Some had got no legs, some were blind, and I remember saying to my husband, "Well, if that's war" … They were young, youngish people, yet they were ruined for life.'[1]

May Brooks

The scale of the conflict and the destructiveness of modern weapons resulted in an unprecedented number of disabled veterans. One million, six hundred and forty thousand British troops were wounded[2] of which 41,050 were amputees.[3] By 1922, an estimated 900,000 ex-servicemen were in receipt of a disability pension.[4] Medical improvements ensured men who would have died in earlier conflicts survived. There were innovations like storing blood rather than transfusing directly from person to person, or the Thomas splint for broken femurs, which improved survival rates from 20 per cent at the start of the war to 80 per cent by 1916.[5] Around 92 per cent of men who were evacuated to medical units lived.[6]

The sheer number of disabled veterans created challenges for cash-strapped governments. Could these men be reintegrated into society, and who would look after those too severely injured to lead independent lives? What kind of training and employment would be suitable and affordable, and what pensions could be offered that would be politically acceptable without adding greatly to government debt? Some politicians and civil servants saw the disabled as a financial burden, but there were also genuine reformers who took seriously the need to care for disabled ex-servicemen. Men like George Barnes, founder of the National Committee of Organised Labour, who campaigned for the introduction of state pensions. As Minister of Pensions (1916–17) he tried to ensure a generous settlement. Then there was Sir Brunel Cohen MP, wheelchair-bound after fighting in the Third Battle of Ypres, who worked tirelessly for disabled veterans, becoming the main spokesman for the British Legion in Parliament.

There was a well of public sympathy for these soldiers, exemplified by the generous donations received by the annual British Legion's Poppy Appeal. In 1921, £106,000 was raised and by 1930 the figure had risen to £524,000.[7] Many were determined not to repeat the scenes of disabled veterans begging in the streets common before the war. Did treatment of disabled soldiers improve? Overall, the answer has to be yes, but considering how poor it had been that's a low hurdle to clear. Before 1915, the government admitted no legal liability for the care of disabled soldiers or the granting of pensions. State provision was threadbare and any assistance a soldier might receive would usually come from charities like the Soldiers and Sailors Help Society. When the Ministry of Pensions was set up in December 1916, part of its remit was the rehabilitation of disabled ex-servicemen.* This included the award of pensions, job training and any necessary medical care.

Preparing disabled soldiers for employment would reduce the government's long-term financial commitments. Most of these veterans were under 30 and might have to rely on public assistance for decades if they were unable to find work. Many had entered the army straight from school and had little to offer an employer. Others had disabilities that would make their previous jobs impossible. Clearly there was a need for suitable training schemes. Holding down work would also boost the veteran's self-esteem in an era where a man was expected to provide for his family, and might mean a veteran would be defined by his job not by his disability. But the unexpectedly early Armistice meant Britain was woefully unprepared for the task.

Belgium, France and Germany already had extensive training schemes and specialist employment exchanges because of their experience of large conscript armies. Britain was also hampered by the Treasury's reluctance to commit funds. A lack of adequate buildings and trainers didn't help either, while the schemes were often badly publicised or unsuitable for what the job market required. The Disabled Society pointed out that getting on a scheme was no easy matter:

> As the Government instructional factories were full, it was often months before a man could get a course, so he had to wait at home doing little or nothing. Such enforced idleness naturally did not improve his mental or physical condition, and made it harder for him to work when the opportunity arrived.[8]

A year after the Armistice, when government cuts began to bite, only 13,000 men were in training.[9] By 1921 the training schemes were wound down completely. The timing couldn't have been worse. Unemployment had risen to over

---

* Disability training was transferred to the Ministry of Labour in February 1919.

20 per cent of the workforce. The next year the British Legion estimated that 100,000 disabled men were unemployed.[10] John Bennett, who was unable to get accepted on an apprentice scheme, spoke for many when he said 'I cannot stand the awful depression much longer; surely I can be of use to someone.'[11]

Without adequate public funding, the government increasingly encouraged the private and voluntary sectors to step in. The most important initiative was the King's National Roll Scheme. Businesses could qualify for the King's Roll if 5 per cent of their workforce was disabled. These companies would receive preferential treatment in government contracts and an official seal for their letterheads. The scheme, benefiting from its royal association, garnered a great deal of publicity. By 1926, 27,592 employers had signed up.[12] Yet they employed fewer than half of disabled veterans. Companies preferred the lightly disabled (someone with a single finger missing for instance) who were easier to integrate; around 15 per cent of the severely disabled became long-term unemployed.[13] One severely disabled man commented, 'I rise in the morning and go out looking for work. A few minutes' interview soon convinces the most optimistic employer that I am of no use.'[14]

The King's Roll was quite relaxed about how a firm qualified. It could include veterans who had recovered and were no longer in receipt of a pension. Nor, once qualified, was a company checked if it continued to employ disabled men. Local authorities set a poor example, as already mentioned, though the civil service had a rather better record.[15] By 1928 nearly 15 per cent of employees in government departments were disabled veterans.[16] This was still far behind the French or Germans, who had long traditions of giving disabled ex-servicemen priority in government posts and counted their years of army service towards civil service pensions.[17]

The King's Roll's main problem was its voluntary nature. Clearly some companies supported the scheme with good intentions but most businesses didn't join. There was a large pool of unemployed so why employ a disabled man when there were plenty of healthy ones looking for work? As George Bernard Shaw remarked, 'No man in his senses will employ a disabled man when he can find a sound one.'[18] Private Francis Sumpter, after being turned down for a number of jobs because of his weakened left arm, was employed as a storekeeper. But when the foreman found out about his arm he was given a week's notice.[19] Once again trade unions feared these men would reduce employment rights or wages. In the Rhondda, the local mining union complained that coal-owners were 'employing Men who had been Disabled in Warfare at Reduced rates.'[20] Another issue was that physically demanding jobs might be unsuitable for disabled veterans. *The Times* posed this question in an article in 1919: 'In disablement the advantage passes to the clerk, who possesses an aptitude that fits him for a dozen callings … But the miner become a cripple cannot so easily adapt himself to sedentary existence; his hands require more discipline than the clerk's mind.'[21]

Some collieries employed men on light duties, like Ebbw Vale Colliery Company where a man with no arms worked as a messenger. However, most mines ignored the scheme. In 1920 there were none on the King's Roll in the North East and only one in Scotland.[22] Nor could men expect sympathetic treatment because of their disability. Fellow workers sometimes complained that they had to do more than their share if a company employed a disabled ex-serviceman. The limits of voluntary schemes were tacitly recognised in 1944 when the government made employment of disabled soldiers compulsory for employers.

In Germany, it was already compulsory for companies of a certain size to employ at least 2 per cent of 'badly incapacitated men'. Consequently, around 90 per cent of severely disabled veterans in Germany remained in employment.[23] Germany had pioneered welfare in Europe through insurance schemes for the sick, unemployed, pensioners and the disabled. Britain only started this just before the war and the spirit of self-reliance and voluntarism was deeply ingrained. Though there was a widespread feeling that something had to be done to help disabled veterans, Britain turned more readily to charitable solutions. As Julie Anderson commented, 'It was not in the British Government's nature to spend money on its citizens.'[24]

Sadly, the government's reluctance to get involved also affected other areas of disabled veterans' lives. The Barlow Committee (1919) found that 55,000 servicemen had contracted TB during the war and the government needed to establish village settlements to treat them.[25] These settlements would provide fresh air, medical help and employment at an estimated cost of £1 million. However, by 1926 parliament had provided only £20,000 and established one settlement, Barrowmore Hall in Chester – but more than 18,000 sufferers had already died.

The Treasury, known sardonically in Whitehall as the Department of Tax and Tears, is often held responsible for putting budgets cuts over the needs of veterans, but they were not solely to blame. The Ministry of Pensions underspent retraining grants by almost a third during 1920–21 and 1921–22, crucial years for ex-servicemen trying to enter the jobs market.[26] The reformers' ideas to help ex-servicemen ultimately depended on public funding. As the economy and finances deteriorated, so did official enthusiasm to support disabled veterans. Charity was their only other option.

> Now, he will spend a few sick years in institutes,
> And do what things the rules consider wise,
> And take whatever pity they may dole.
> Tonight he noticed how the women's eyes
> Passed from him to the strong men that were whole.

'Disabled', Wilfred Owen

In the voluntary sector, a profusion of charities emerged to fill the gaps left by the state. There were still 500 registered in 1936 for ex-servicemen and their dependants.[27] The most prominent were the Star and Garter Homes, St Dunstan's, the War Seals Foundation, the Lords Roberts Memorial Workshops and the Poppy Factories. Music hall impresario Sir Oswald Stoll set up the War Seal Foundation for the severely disabled. He was a man of enormous energy with a genuine commitment to these veterans. His 'Homes for Heroes' fundraising campaign was a huge success, helped by his flair for publicity and ownership of large numbers of music halls and cinemas. The resulting War Seal Mansions in Fulham provided affordable accommodation, purpose-built for disabled ex-servicemen and their families. As Sir Oswald believed:

> It furnishes the kind of housing a disabled man most needs when he leaves the hospital. It foresees his daily disabilities, and gathers his family around him. It makes his pension mean for him happiness or at least contentment in a real home, with necessary treatment at his own door instead, perhaps, of neglect in a slum or misery in an institution.[28]

The Star and Garter, once a fashionable Victorian hotel at the top of Richmond Hill, was turned into a military hospital during the war. It was then rebuilt as a home for the severely disabled. The British Women's Hospital Committee, formerly the Actresses' Franchise League, raised much of the funding. St Dunstan's training centre for the blind was set up in 1915 by Sir Arthur Pearson, founder of the *Daily Express*, who had lost his sight through glaucoma. He wanted servicemen to 'learn to be blind' by developing self-reliance. A man was given a braille watch on arrival as his first step towards independence. They were then taught braille and, if possible, a trade. Veterans were encouraged to walk without guide dogs or sticks, partly to emphasise their independence. This may seem harsh but blind people before the war were associated with begging; the object of pity and a few coins. The centre's aim was 'to assist men to become useful and productive citizens rather than idle and unhappy pensioners, the basic view being that true happiness can only be enjoyed by those who contribute in some way to the work of the world'.[29] Training included typing, telephony and poultry keeping. St Dunstan's helped 95 per cent of the 1,833 blind British ex-servicemen.[30] Sadly, Pearson died from an accident when he knocked himself unconscious in the bath. Ian Fraser, blind from a bullet at the Battle of the Somme and MP for St Pancras North, succeeded him. He proved a redoubtable champion for blind veterans throughout his long career.

The Disabled Society established the Poppy Factory with a grant from the British Legion, which employed mostly disabled ex-servicemen to make the millions of poppies needed for Remembrance Day. Such was its success it had to move to larger premises. Starting with only six staff, it was employing over 350 ten years later.[31] Lord Roberts Memorial Workshops provided eleven sheltered workshops and retraining in various cities across the UK, employing just over 1,000 men to make basket ware, toys, and furniture. Places in sheltered workshops never exceeded more than 2,000,[32] a fraction of the disabled men seeking work. They had the advantage of allowing disabled men to be together, though the work was often repetitive and poorly paid. All these charities provided help when no one else did, but their main problem was raising enough money. The British public's generosity ultimately could not make up for a lack of state funding, as the charities themselves often pointed out. Schemes were usually not as well financed as their continental, state-supported equivalents. Some charities depended on a single benefactor and didn't survive his or her death. Like Bernard Oppenheimer, who set up a diamond factory in Brighton for the disabled with £30,000 of his own money, but after he died unexpectedly in 1921 it lasted only three more years. By the 1930s, funding had started to become a real problem. Memories of the First World War were fading and many older donors had died. Younger people rarely felt the same emotional attachment to the causes these charities championed, though the Poppy Appeal continued to raise prodigious sums.

Did these charitable activities provide an excuse for the government to slough off its obligations? Ethel Shakespear of the Birmingham Local War Pensions Committee thought so. She felt that 'the State … has endeavoured to shrink its responsibilities and to throw them on to the generosity of charitably-minded individuals.'[33] One government handbook even noted that a 'department is expected to fulfil its function largely by stimulating local and private enterprise'.[34] The attitude of the Ministry of Pensions to helping disabled men find work bears this out. It rejected providing directly funded workshops. The ministry would only fund charitable employment schemes when 'organized voluntary work had been exhausted'.[35] Relatively well-endowed organisations like the Lord Roberts Memorial Workshop received an annual £25 capitation grant for each ex-serviceman they employed. Poorer charities could get up to £35. These were miserly sums, particularly as disabled men often needed specially adapted facilities. Overall, there were perhaps 2,000 men receiving such grants at one time[36] – a tiny percentage of those needing employment.

Deborah Cohen argued that though British veterans were materially worse off than their German counterparts, charitable donations made them feel honoured by the rest of society. In Weimar Germany, the crowding out of charities and voluntary organisations by the state had the effect of isolating veterans, making them feel their sacrifice had not been fully appreciated by the public. And there *was* some resentment of veterans' privileges in Germany. They were practically unsackable and were twice as likely to stay in employment during the Great

Depression than the able-bodied.[37] Despite the higher levels of financial support, Cohen believes German veterans were more embittered.

But charity can turn people into supplicants rather than citizens. If men disliked the rules or conditions laid down by sheltered workshops or disabled homes there was little they could do about it. The state would not help and a waiting list of veterans was a reminder they were eminently replaceable. Benefactors often had strong religious and political convictions and this could be reflected in the rules governing behaviour. Drunkenness, for instance, was frowned upon in the War Seal Mansions and the lift was turned off at 10.30 p.m.[38] At the Enham Village Settlement two men were evicted just for forming a branch of the British Legion.[39] If anyone tried to supplement their meagre pensions they were liable to be thrown out. Seth Koven wrote that 'the experience of war bitterly reimposes on wounded male soldiers the dependence, but not the innocence, of childhood.'[40] Charities could sometimes increase this dependence.

The public had expectations about the disabled as well. They looked on them 'with a combination of sympathy and horror'.[41] The closer men were to their original state the more they were accepted. Those with serious facial injuries were more repulsive than the blind, who could wear dark glasses. It's not surprising that facially disfigured veterans chose to live in separate colonies or stay at home. As one doctor wrote, 'The psychological effect on a man who must go through life, an object of horror to himself as well as to others, is beyond description.'[42] Perhaps only the paralysed could elicit as much revulsion. Limbless men found acceptance easier if they wore their artificial limbs. A disabled cricket match between 'Arms' and 'Legs', where men played without their prosthetics, reduced women spectators to tears. The public also liked disabled ex-serviceman to be chirpy and uncomplaining, proud of having sacrificed so much for their country. Newspaper articles regularly featured disabled veterans cheerily making the best of it or a disabled sporting event where Tommy showed the kind of pluck that won the war. The Star and Garter selected patients to meet visitors because of their demeanour and personality. Members of the public were happy to take out residents of St Dunstan's on outings if they met certain criteria, as one patient noted: ' being fairly passable in my uniform with my Military Cross I'm in great demand … whereas old Podds, who's in mufti, and Jimmy, who's disfigured … they never get a chance.'[43]

It wasn't all for show; disabled men often took pride in their stoicism. Many did remain positive throughout their lives, despite all they had to go through. A study of surviving territorials from the Leeds Rifles revealed that even the severely disabled ones did not regret their war service.[44] Reginald St John Battersby was only 15 when he joined up and was perhaps the youngest commissioned officer in the British Army. He lost a leg on the Western Front just after his 17th birthday but still continued to serve with the Royal Engineers until 1920. His loss did not stop him volunteering for the Home Guard and then as a naval chaplain in the Second World War. His son said his father 'did his bit', which is certainly an understatement.[45] Ronald Blythe interviewed George, a disabled veteran in the late 1970s. A bullet bowed and shortened one leg and left him with a rolling gait, yet he built a successful business career and marriage. For George, the war remained the central event of his life; he had no regrets despite everything. 'I never looked upon it as a disability,' he said.[46] Similarly, six of the surgeon Harold Gillies' patients, all with severe facial injuries, wrote essays about their experiences. There was a general consensus 'that it had been worth it'. One of them, Private Best, wrote, 'I cannot say I am sorry I joined the army, as it has broadened my outlook on life … So after all, I lost little, and gained much, through the Great War.'[47]

Herbert Read captures this in his poem 'Kneeshaw goes to War'. Kneeshaw experiences a tough time at the Front, at one point witnessing an officer shooting one of his men who couldn't be rescued from sinking in the mud. Kneeshaw is 'mercifully' wounded but loses a leg. In Britain he finds a sort of peace in nature:

> I stand on this hill and accept
> The flowers at my feet and the deep
> Beauty of the still tarn:
> Chance that gave me a crutch and a view
> Gave me these.

But there was a darker side to disability. Men could drink heavily and quickly spent their pensions in the pub. They could be violent or abusive to each other, their carers or families. Some committed suicide or went into deep depressions. These men contradicted the image of cheerful courage in adversity and were rarely reported in the papers. Many continued to endure pain for decades. St John Battersby's son commented:

> Throughout his life he suffered from phantom pain every time the weather changed. He described this to me 'as if someone was twisting his big toe off'. His stump would also jump uncontrollably. For many years he had to take increasingly strong painkillers, finally having to use Pethadine and morphine and these, I think, shortened his life.[48]

'A man cannot realize that above such shattered bodies there are still human faces in which life goes its daily round.'

All Quiet on the Western Front, Erich Maria Remarque

Henry Tonks, the artist and surgeon, did a series of graphic pastel drawings. They show men without noses or eyes, with faces concave or reduced to mush. They are unflinching portraits of what modern technology can do to a body. Yet advances in medicine could partly mitigate some of these effects. Queen's Hospital, Sidcup, where Tonks worked for a while, pioneered facial reconstruction under the leadership of Harold Gillies – sometimes considered the father of plastic surgery. He was shocked by what he described as 'men burned and maimed to the conditions of animals'.[49] He was a great systemiser, improving existing techniques like removing skin from the rib cartilage to rebuild men's noses. The results were often remarkable. Lieutenant Spreckley was a man who had his nose literally blown off at Ypres. His new nose was hardly aquiline, but it would not pass comment on the street.[50] However, in the world before antibiotics, there was only so much Gillies and his team could do. Observers noted how they tended to shut themselves away from other people, including relatives. Robert Tait McKenzie, a hospital inspector, thought they were the 'most distressing cases' in military surgery.[51]

For those too badly damaged for reconstruction, there was another possibility. Francis Derwent Wood, a private in the RAMC, was a sculptor before the war and realised he could use his talent to fashion masks. He wrote in *The Lancet* that, 'I endeavour by means of the skill I happen to possess as a sculptor to make a man's face as near as possible to what it looked like before he was wounded.'[52] These masks could take up to a month. Eyebrows, moustaches and eyebrows were made from slivered tinfoil like Ancient Greek statues.[53] However, the masks themselves could get battered; they were also fashioned into a youthful appearance, so looked increasingly strange as the men aged.

Frank Chapman had both his hands destroyed by enemy fire in 1915. The army had provided only two leather sockets with hooks as replacements. Mary Eleanor Gwynne Holford visited him one day; clearly depressed he indicated his sockets and said, 'Is this all the country can do for me?'[54] Mrs Gwynne Holford was moved enough to go away and raise money for a hospital and limb-fitting centre at Roehampton, which became known as Queen Mary's, after its patron. It was the world's first hospital dedicated solely to the limbless. The men sometimes called it the Human Repair Factory. Forty-one thousand men during the war received artificial limbs at Queen Mary's. It also provided training in the use of these new limbs and had its own employment bureau. Teams worked replacing heavy wooden legs with lighter and stronger aluminium ones. Artificial fingers replaced hooks. After Frank Chapman received his, he married, worked as a farmer and died aged 74 years old.

One time he liked a blood-smear down his leg,
After the matches carried shoulder-high.
It was after football, when he'd drunk a peg,
He thought he'd better join. He wonders why.
Someone had said he'd look a god in kilts.
That's why; and maybe, too, to please his Meg,
Aye, that was it, to please the giddy jilts

'Disabled', Wilfred Owen

There was a sense in the Edwardian era that the health of young men, particularly the urban working class, was in decline. So how could Britain defend her empire if its young men were increasingly feeble? The number of army recruits who failed to pass medical examination highlighted this: between 1900 and 1905, 31.3 per cent were rejected as unfit; disproportionately they were from the cities.[55] The Eugenics Society, founded in 1907 to maintain 'the calibre of the racial stock',[56] believed the countryside was a place where the healthy thrived.

It's not surprising that reformers saw the rural life as a way for the disabled ex-serviceman to regain some of his health and independence. The Star and Garter opened a branch in Sandgate, Kent that combined sea air and a chicken farm. The charity Village Centres for Curative Treatment and Training bought land in Enham, Hampshire for the treatment and rehabilitation of veterans suffering 'the effects of amputations, neurasthenia, shellshock or fever'. Fortiscue Fox, its driving force, was a strong Quaker who saw Enham as a chance to establish a thriving village community of 'self-governing workshops'. Men would learn rural crafts like basketry, fence-making and farming.[57] Enham aimed to bring 'the next generation back to the purer, saner life of villages'.[58]

The growth of organised sports and physical fitness before the war was also part of this desire to improve the nation's health. Public schools had partly developed the modern versions of football, rugby and cricket for this purpose. These had spread to working-class communities and professional sport had developed as a consequence. Many disabled veterans had been keen sportsman before they were injured. As one amputee said, 'The loss of a leg on the Western Front in 1918 was a considerable loss to me whose chief recreations were swimming and walking.'[59] Sport could be a way to reassert the loss of masculinity many disabled veterans felt. Disabled teams played each other or against able-bodied men or women in variations of football and cricket.[60] The British Legion organised an Imperial Sports Rally for disabled men in 1923. This foreshadowed the Paralympic Movement after the Second World War or the recent Invictus Games. Joanna Bourke wrote that the war-maimed were 'irrevocably re-moulded by their experiences, these men struggled to create new lives that challenged their status as physically disabled'.[61]

Reading through accounts of the lives of disabled ex-servicemen, what comes across is their fortitude. A severely wounded man was usually no braver than other soldiers, just unlucky; but after the war many showed a determination that was heroic, demonstrated in the stories of ex-servicemen who persevered in a world with few wheelchair ramps. Disabled men were not allowed discounts on public transport unless they were blind and even a full war pension meant a life of austerity. Yet they kept going, justifiably complaining at times about their treatment, but keeping going nonetheless.

Memories of the First World War still continued to play a part in helping the disabled long after the war. In 1969, the Labour MP Alf Morris introduced legislation that eventually became the Chronically Sick & Disabled Persons Act (1970), described as 'a Magna Carta for the disabled'. Local authorities were given responsibility for welfare services and housing for the disabled.[62] There was a major installation programme of telephone lines in the homes of the disabled, who now had a legal right to equal access to leisure and educational facilities. Morris's father and father-in-law were badly gassed during the First World War and this spurred him to introduce a private members' bill in the face of stiff opposition. Later, Morris became a pioneering Minister for the Disabled. His father had died young when Morris was only 7, the fate of so many injured men who survived the war. Years later Morris said, 'I know how a whole family's life is affected if one member is disabled.'[63]

These changes would have made life for disabled Tommies in the interwar period considerably better but Britain wasn't ready for such an increase in the powers of the state. Direct public assistance was kept to a minimum and the government shied away from forcing companies to give preferential treatment. Whatever the political rights and wrongs (and it should be remembered this was a period of economic difficulties for Britain), many disabled ex-servicemen consequently struggled more than they needed to have done. The sight of beggars in trench coats sadly continued.

13

'THE CRUELLY INJURED MIND': SHELL SHOCK

'Something had altered in them. They were subject to sudden moods, and queer tempers, fits of profound depression alternating with a restless desire for pleasure. Many were easily moved to passion where they lost control of themselves, many were bitter in their speech, violent in opinion, frightening.'[1]

Philip Gibbs

'Must you carry the bloody horror of combat in your heart forever?'[2]

Homer

Post-traumatic stress disorder is as old as war itself. Herodotus wrote of an Athenian soldier who went blind during a battle, even though he was wounded in another part of his body.[3] In Homer's *Iliad*, Achilles loses control after his friend Patroclus is killed. Harry Hotspur, one of Shakespeare's greatest warriors, is clearly suffering when his wife says, 'Why dost thou bend thine eyes upon earth, And start so often when thou sit'st alone?'[4]

Previous wars had their own descriptions of PTSD, like 'nostalgia', when longing for home was thought to be the cause. During the American Civil War, doctors sometimes put the condition down to 'palpitations of the heart'. 'Shell shock' became the standard term in Britain during the First World War. First publicised by Dr Charles Myers in 1915, the term is memorable, compressed, alliterative – but not accurate. It stems from the belief that it was the physical shock of a nearby explosion that affected the senses. The same argument had been used to explain why passengers were traumatised after railway accidents. Yet it didn't explain why soldiers nowhere near a blast broke down. The German word '*Kreigsneurose*' or 'war neurosis' is medically more exact, if less elegant.

There were British doctors who were unconvinced about physical shock being the cause. Lord Moran, later Winston Churchill's doctor, asserted that 'a man's courage is his capital and he is always spending ... I affirm that men wear out in war like clothes'.[5] Moran observed that a soldier would eventually cease to function the longer he was exposed to danger. Shell shock, rather than being sudden, came gradually. This subverted the notion that the rookie might panic but the hardened veteran would hold his nerve. The length of time in the trenches was a factor but there were others. Certain types of soldiers were more vulnerable – snipers, tank crews, shock troops and machine gunners – perhaps because of the harrowing nature of their work, though no soldier was immune. Dr Myers himself was aware of the term's limitations, which was applied to a whole range of symptoms: recurrent nightmares, hallucinations, amnesia, blindness, deafness, impotence, paralysis, mutism, hysteria, stammers, shakes and tics, strange walks and uncontrollable movements, as well as psychotic syndromes.[6] The neurologist Henry Head called it 'a heterogeneous collection of different nervous affections from concussion to sheer funk which may have merely this in common, that nervous control has finally given way'.[7]

Pre-war treatment of mental illness was affected by the attitudes of the period. Doctors, drawn from prosperous families, generally shared their class's outlook that the poor were more likely to suffer from mental illness, just as they were more prone to criminal behaviour or imbecility. Moral degeneracy and weakness of character were the roots of their condition, whereas well-heeled sufferers were typically labelled 'neurasthenic'. This was a more acceptable word, associated with fatigue, headaches or exhaustion with modern life. Harley Street neurologists charged substantial fees for this diagnosis, and treatment often took place in expensive, converted country houses. The poor were usually sent to grim asylums, resembling the workhouse or prison. Attendance carried a deep stigma for patients and their families. Medical conditions could prove intractable and funds short. For example, asylum ratios were typically one doctor to 400–600 patients.[8] They became places of incarceration as much as treatment.

As soon as the first shell came over, the shell-shock case nearly went mad. He screamed and raved, and it took eight men to hold him down on the stretcher ... The terror is indescribable. The flesh on their faces shakes in fear, and their teeth continually chatter. Shell-shock was brought about in many ways; loss of sleep, continually being under heavy shell fire, the torment of the lice, irregular meals, nerves always on end, and the thought always in the man's mind that the next minute was going to be his last.

Corporal Henry Gregory, 119th Machine Gun Company[9]

The intensity and length of the First World War meant the number of sufferers was unprecedented. In the Russo-Japanese War (1904–05) they represented only 0.5 per cent of all casualties.[10] By 1917, shell shock accounted for one-third of those discharged, excluding wounds.[11] The army was simply unable to cope. Despite an influx of civilian doctors there were never enough trained practitioners. The problem was made worse by the lack of screening at the beginning of the war. Britain needed soldiers and doctors passed too many unsuitable volunteers. Peter Barham found cases of men with a history of mental illness readily accepted into the armed forces. Like Private George Gomm, a resident of Hanwell Lunatic Asylum when war broke out. He was released soon after, joined up and was shipped to France the following year, despite another mental breakdown before he left. In April 1916 he was picked up by the military police in a state of extreme agitation, having deserted his battalion. He might have been shot but was lucky to be examined by the eminent Dr Myers, and after a series of military hospitals was once more institutionalised in Britain.[12] All this was waste of time and resources and did little for the mental wellbeing of poor Private Gomm.

In the army's defence, defining who is mentally ill is difficult at the best of times, but is especially so in times of war. Royal Army Medical Corps (RAMC) doctors faced a dilemma their civilian counterparts did not. They had to consider the interests of their patients while ensuring the army wasn't deprived of manpower. Were they army officers or doctors? They tended to the former and were often suspicious of any soldier claiming to be shell-shocked. Peter Leese wrote in a groundbreaking study that, 'The relationship between doctor and patient was primarily military then, not medical … sickness was tainted with the suspicion of cowardice, dereliction of duty and moral failure'.[13] Phrases like 'malingering', 'scrim-shanking' and 'swinging the lead' peppered medical notes. Pre-war attitudes prevailed in a notoriously hidebound branch of the medical profession. The myth that only women suffered from hysteria had been debunked before the war* but for many in the RAMC breaking down was still unmanly. Civilian doctors who joined the RAMC were frustrated by the pressure to send soldiers back to the Front and the antiquated outlook of the medical hierarchy. The army proved reluctant to abandon the idea that the only legitimate cases of shell shock were physical in origin. A 1915 order stated:

> Shell-shock and shell concussion cases should have the letter 'W' prefixed to the report of the casualty, if it was due to the enemy; in that case the patient would be entitled to rank as 'wounded' and to wear on his arm a 'wound stripe'. If, however, the man's breakdown did not follow a shell explosion, it was not

---

* Most famously by the great French neurologist Jean-Martin Charcot (1825–93).

thought to be 'due to the enemy', and he was to [be] labelled 'Shell-shock' or 'S' (for sickness) and was not entitled to a wound stripe or a pension.*[14]

The worst example of military callousness was the refusal to take shell shock into account during court martials. Though the death penalty was rarely applied, these cases still make painful reading. Private Arthur Earp was executed despite obviously suffering from shell shock. Field Marshall Haig wrote, 'How can we ever win if this plea is allowed.'[15] Bernard McGeehan was accused of desertion, despite being traumatised. At his trial he said:

> Ever since I joined up, all the men have made fun of me and I did not know what I was doing when I went away. Every time I go into the trenches, they throw stones at me and pretend it is shrapnel and they call me all sorts of names. I have been out here 18 months and had no leave.[16]

He was still executed. Questions were asked in the House of Commons about shell-shocked soldiers being tried and shot by court martials. Public antipathy to the severity of army discipline, where Britain had executed 306 men during the war**, led to a considerable narrowing of capital offences by the Second World War. It was not until the Armed Forces Act (2006) that these men received a posthumous pardon.

Officers were more likely to be believed because a 'gentleman' would not fake such an illness, and were sometimes diagnosed euphemistically as suffering from Effort Syndrome or DAH (Disordered Action of the Heart) – the cause being put down to strain rather than weakness of character.[17] They still suffered proportionately higher incidences of shell shock – perhaps four times as much,[18] through the pressures of leadership and a lower chance of survival. Robert Graves thought the 'officers had a less laborious but a more nervous time than the men'.[19] This challenged the link between class and mental illness. The officers, initially from privileged backgrounds, broke down more than working-class rankers. The opposite of what was widely believed before the war.

There was also the dilemma that an army has to address in any prolonged conflict: how to balance the need for front-line soldiers against the dangers a sufferer might pose to his comrades. This was particularly pertinent with officers who had greater responsibilities than their men. Graves observed:

> The unfortunates were officers who had endured two years or more of continuous trench service. In many cases they became dipsomaniacs. I knew three

---

*   Later this was changed, war pensions were also granted for 'S' cases.
** Germany in contrast only executed forty-eight.

or four who had worked up to the point of two bottles of whisky a day before being lucky enough to get wounded or sent home in some other way. A two-bottle company commander of one of our line battalions is still alive who, in three shows running, got his company needlessly destroyed because he was no longer capable of taking clear decisions.[20]

But there were undoubted cases of men deliberately feigning the symptoms of shell shock in order to achieve a way out of the war – and a pension. Even a sympathetic observer like Dr Myers wrote that he had 'seen too many men at base hospital … boasting they were "suffering from shellshock, Sir," when there was nothing appreciable amiss with them save funk'.[21]

No doubt they'll soon get well; the shock and strain
Have caused their stammering, disconnected talk …
Their dreams that drip with murder; and they'll be proud
Of glorious war that shatter'd all their pride …

'Survivors', Siegfried Sassoon

The initial treatment soldiers received was often pragmatic. A few days' rest then back to the Front or a job away from the fighting.[22] Doctors realised the effects of shell shock could wear off if a soldier was removed from combat. But more serious cases demanded more extensive care and this led to a variety of approaches. Many doctors focused on discipline, believing this would result in a swift recovery as well as sorting out possible malingerers.[23] Patients whose mental condition was not organically based were viewed with suspicion. Others, like W.H. Rivers, used more psychological and therapeutic treatments, though few were out-and-out Freudians. Ben Shephard characterises these contrasting methods as the 'hard school' and 'soft school'. In her novel *Regeneration*, Pat Barker compares Rivers' approach with the neurologist Lewis Yealland, who thought 'weakness of will, negativism and hyper-suggestibility'[24] were the causes of his patients' behaviour. In one harrowing scene, a soldier suffering from mutism is given electric shocks until he recovers his voice.*** Rivers, on the other hand, treats the poet Siegfried Sassoon with patience and understanding – 'gentle miracles', as Sassoon later called them. Yealland's claimed impressive results – a failure rate of only 13 per cent[25] – but what he didn't record was how many men relapsed. Only 7 per cent of his patients were assessed as fit for active duty, which point to the limitations of his treatment. The 'hard school' tended to treat the symptoms but not the causes.

*** It should be noted that in reality Yealland only used electricity in rare cases.

An early mistake was putting sufferers in general military hospitals without specialist help, unsegregated from the physically wounded. Many were then dumped in asylums back in Britain. Some festered there, others returned to civilian life as budgets tightened – pensioned but rarely cured. The shell-shocked ex-Tommy became a regular sight after the war – almost a literary staple, like Septimus Smith in *Mrs Dalloway* ('pale-faced, beak-nosed, wearing brown shoes with hazel eyes that had the look of apprehension'),[26] Chris in *The Return of the Soldier* or even Lord Peter Wimsey, whose eccentricities were derived from being 'blown up and buried in a shell-hole near Caudry'.[27]

As the war progressed, doctors began to realise the best chance of recovery was early treatment as near to the Front as possible. Telling a shaken-up soldier he is mentally ill then shipping him off to a mental hospital hardly helped his condition. Many doctors thought the chance to escape an unbearable situation at the Front encouraged a soldier to cling onto his symptoms like a lifebelt, while a pension would serve, however unconsciously, as a reward. Prominent members of the 'soft school' also recognised this. On the eve of the next war, a group of leading psychologists wrote: 'there can be no doubt that in an overwhelming proportion of cases, these patients succumb to shock because they get something out of it.'[28]

A number of advanced neurological centres were established at clearing stations. Though an improvement, it was not until 1917 that each had a trained medical officer. If a patient failed to recover he was usually sent back to Britain. Due to growing public concerns and questions in the House of Commons about soldiers being put in asylums, specialist hospitals were expanded or established to cope with these cases. One of the best was Maghull in Merseyside. It was acquired from the Red Cross and had 500 beds for severe or protracted cases. Maghull could boast a roster of distinguished psychiatrists and neurologists and, unusually for the time, most of the patients were from the ranks. Queen Square, a neurological hospital with an international reputation, announced in February 1915 it was 'arranging to send soldiers suffering from shock to be treated at the Hospital in wards specially set apart for the purpose'.[29] This stress on separation was also important. Given the stigma of mental illness, there was already public disquiet about Tommies being mixed with 'ordinary' mental patients. However, Queen Square could only treat up to forty men at one time.[30] This would continue to be a problem after the war: there simply weren't enough resources, medical personnel or hospital places to meet demand.

As the state struggled to cope, the voluntary sector stepped in. The best known was Lord Knutsford's Hospitals for Officers, which was much needed, but they continued the pre-war class difference in treatment. One resident, Captain Leland, described it as 'a very luxurious establishment ... every officer has a room to himself, closet etc. and about three nurses each. The food is exceptional ... fish, game etc. galore.'[31] In Maghull, patients complained about the overstretched staff and a diet of bread, turnips and rice.[32]

These are men whose minds the Dead have ravished.
Memory fingers in their hair of murders,
Multitudinous murders they once witnessed.

'Mental Cases', Wilfred Owen,

After the war, optimists could point to a number of improvements in the treatment of shell shock. For the first time, the government accepted a legal obligation to look after ex-servicemen. There had been a considerable expansion of facilities: in 1918 there were twenty hospitals for shell shock and a number of 'Homes for Recovery' outpatient facilities.[33] As the flood of publications later attested, many doctors had gained valuable insight into shell shock and its treatment from their experiences. Maghull had proven a particularly useful training ground for psychiatrists, whose intense three-month training course promoted techniques that encouraged 're-experiencing of the repressed memories and emotions of front-line experiences'.[34]

During the 1920s and '30s, there was a growth of psychiatric rather than physical treatment. Occupational therapy, with a stress on rural pursuits and fresh air, became fashionable. Its medical efficacy was disputed but it was more humane than the treatment in pre-war state asylums. The public had also shown a sympathy for soldiers suffering shell shock. Lord Knutsford's successful fundraising for specialist hospitals showed that people were prepared to give generously. Some of the press coverage stressed the heroic nature of these men, portrayed as victims not cowards. This ranged across the political spectrum from the jingoistic *John Bull* to the left-wing *Daily Herald*. There was widespread outrage when some of these men were being put into asylums as 'pauper lunatics'. The government was pressured to allow them to be classed as 'service patients' and given their own clothes and better food. One case reported in *The Manchester Guardian* was Richard Cowan of the Royal Engineers. He had been discharged and sent to Prestwich workhouse asylum as a 'dangerous pauper lunatic'. It was only through pressure from Sir Frederick Milner and the man's father that he was given a pension and classified as a private patient. Mr Cowan believed the treatment of soldiers, like his son, was 'a poor return on the services they have rendered to their country and the sufferings they have undergone'.[35]

However, this sunny picture should not be taken too far. The expanded facilities were never enough to keep up with the numbers needing treatment. Budgetary cuts after 1921 stretched an already underfunded sector. Ex-Services'

Welfare Society (ESWS)* estimated that there was up to 6,000 veterans living in mental asylums in the 1920s.[36] General standards of medical care remained poor. Some doctors had certainly gained insights but traditional attitudes often prevailed among medical authorities, as Pension Review Boards' decisions testified.** This ambiguity is highlighted by the findings of the War Office Committee of Enquiry (1922). Set up as a result of public concern over the treatment of ex-servicemen, the majority of the committee was made up of senior medical men from government departments and branches of the military. Despite the committee's makeup, it recognised that some pre-war attitudes to mental illness were no longer tenable. The final report, while rejecting the term shell shock, admitted it was a genuine condition. However, they were still conscious of PTSD's threat to manpower in future wars. One of its recommendations was:

> No soldier should be allowed to think that loss of nervous or mental control provides an honourable avenue of escape from the battlefield, and every endeavour should be made to prevent slight cases leaving the battalion or divisional area, where treatment should be confined to provision of rest and comfort for those who need it and to heartening them for return to the front line.[37]

It wholly rejected Freudian psycho-analysis but conceded the need for some form of psychotherapy, as well as old-fashioned physical treatment:

> Good results will be obtained in the majority [of cases] by the simplest forms of psycho-therapy, i.e., explanation, persuasion and suggestion, aided by such physical methods as baths, electricity and massage. Rest of mind and body is essential in all cases.[38]

Bogacz argued that this would place the doctor in 'a position somewhere between sympathetic counsellor and military policeman, with emphasis on the latter role'.[39] The committee also accepted that anyone could suffer from shell shock regardless of background, despite eugenicist and hereditarian Sir Frederick Mott being one of the dominant figures. Yet most of the witnesses from the RAMC or the military were unsympathetic to shell shock, believing it an excuse for malingerers not to fight. Ex-servicemen often faced these suspicions when standing in front of a sceptical pension board or trying to get treatment for a condition that simply would not go away.

Similarly, the public's acceptance of sufferers only went so far. They elicited nothing like the degree of compassion – or charitable donations – that disabled veterans experienced, whose visible injuries could not be questioned. As one

---

* Now known as Combat Stress.
** See Chapter 14.

serving officer wrote, 'it is just as much a sacrifice to lose one's nerve in the trenches as to lose an arm, in fact I'm not sure that it's not more so, allied to which when you get back people are in no way inclined to sympathize with you.'[40] Pre-war notions of masculinity and 'character' could not be entirely erased. Many who had lost relatives in the war found it difficult to feel pity for men who had broken down but survived. The ESWS, the leading shell-shock charity, found direct financial appeals to the public did not raise anything like the sums needed, so it tended to rely on large donations from sympathetic, wealthy individuals. The charity's attempts to support ex-servicemen in care homes only raised £4,000 in 1921 and provided accommodation for just twenty men.[41] The ESWS highlighted the difficulties in fundraising in a BBC broadcast by an anonymous soldier in 1935:

> You have been most generous to the poor fellows who have been blinded and maimed. God forbid that I should deprive them of the sympathy and help which they richly deserve! But what of the thousands whose minds gave way under the stress of War? Many of them performed feats of heroism. They are now suffering from an invisible wound and their sufferings are, perhaps, far worse and far more difficult to help, than those who receive bodily injuries — grave though they may be.[42]

The widespread medical disagreements were a reflection on the limits of contemporary psychiatry and neurology, both in treatment and understanding. There was public confusion about why men still continued to suffer from shell shock when the war was over. Surely a cure was now a simple matter? Lord Knutsford spoke in Parliament about the people who had written to him with all sorts of ideas for cures that he felt trivialised the condition:

> One lady wrote to me to say that when she played upon her guitar it had a most soothing effect – would I try it? I said it had been tried by David without great success when he played before Saul. Another man wrote to me to say that neurasthenia was a gas that was escaping from people, and that he was a mechanician [sic] and could at once stop the escape of the gas by means of a machine which he had patented and he was prepared to sell it at a reasonable price; he could stop the leak. Another man had actually a colony started for allowing these men to go and live in the woods in a state of nature with no clothes on and enjoy baths in the morning dew.[43]

By the mid 1920s it was becoming clear that a hardcore of sufferers was showing no signs of improvement, despite the variety of methods used. Baths, bromide and basket weaving were not having their desired effects, nor was psychoanalysis able to offer any medical breakthroughs. In 1925–26, the Ministry of Pensions investigated the likelihood of improvement for neurasthenic ex-servicemen. At Saltash Hospital they estimated that only 6 per cent of patients might possibly become 'effective citizens' and a further 28 per cent might possibly improve. At Harrowby, the estimate was 15 per cent.[44] Conscious of a long-term drain on budgets, the ministry switched from treating ex-servicemen in institutions to rehabilitation in the community. In 1939 there were still 187 outpatient clinics in the United Kingdom,[45] but this was no more successful than institutional care.

Some men only broke down after the war was over, like Rowland Luther who 'cracked up' after the Armistice when he found himself 'unable to eat, deliriously re-living his experiences of combat'.[46] There were also troops whose conditions had remained untreated, as their commanding or regimental medical officer had refused to recognise them as genuine. Others had done their best to keep their self-control while the fighting continued. It was an age that placed a high value on such behaviour, but once the war was over, keeping the demons at bay proved too much. A humdrum incident might trigger off a repressed memory. This made claiming a pension more difficult, as a man had to prove his condition was due to the war rather than other circumstances. It also explains why the official number of shell-shock victims – around 80,000 – underestimated the real figure. Edgar Jones believes that at least 250,000 men suffered from PTSD due to the war.[47]

Some veterans suffered from survivor guilt: a feeling that living was wrong when so many of their comrades had died. It is now regarded as a manifestation of PTSD.* There is something of this in the nightmares that afflicted Norman Collins in Chapter 9 or the determination of ex-servicemen to stay on the Western Front after the war.** Another facet is the belief that the cream of their generation was sacrificed. Ex-Sapper Will Leonard showed this when he wrote that 'the best men having died and left us second-raters to carry on the jobs'.[48] This is a natural reaction but a questionable one. An artillery shell does not discriminate between a hero or a man just wanting to get through in one piece. Those who took the greatest risks in combat were certainly brave, but that does not mean they would have led more productive lives in peacetime. The war certainly cut short lives of tremendous promise, like Henry Moseley, the gifted young physicist whose death forced the government to review its policies on who was eligible to fight, or Herbert Asquith's son Raymond, a scholar and barrister who is often described as the most brilliant man people had ever met. The class structure ensured that the middle and upper classes were statistically more likely to get killed, as they tended to become junior officers; for instance, only

---

* See, for example, Herbert Hendin and Ann Pollinger (1991), (Am J. Psychiatry 1991; 148, pp. 586–91).
** Discussed in Chapter 17.

3 per cent of Balliol men went into the ranks.[49] But that is not the same as saying the better men died, only the most privileged.

Most shell-shock victims were able to lead relatively normal lives after the war. Many of those suffering, especially from hysterical symptoms like blindness, needed no treatment, as they recovered by themselves. The end of the war was the cure. Some who received timely and appropriate treatment also had a reasonable chance of recovery. Then there were people with more serious cases whose condition was not considered severe enough for full-time institutional care but who struggled in the post-war world. Adaption to even the most normal of tasks could prove difficult for a sufferer. Arthur Hubbard's symptoms occurred 'right in the middle of an ordinary conversation' when 'the face of a [German] that I have bayoneted, with its horrible gurgle and grimace, comes sharply into view'.[50] Hubbard blamed his condition on being ordered to slaughter Germans who were trying to surrender. With support from their family or an understanding employer it might be possible to navigate civilian life, but demanding jobs might be beyond them and relapses could occur for years to come. The most common level of pension was a 50 per cent rating: the equivalent of an amputee below the knee.[51] This was about a pound a week by the 1930s.[52] Its insufficiency meant veterans who couldn't hold down permanent work were dependent on charity.

Finally, there were those who had no hope of ever returning to life outside an institution: the 'post-war inefficients'. By 1935 there were only 370 ex-servicemen being treated in Ministry of Pensions hospitals.[53] Many more were in state asylums as 'service patients'. They often had prior psychological issues. The most famous being the poet and composer Ivor Gurney who had a mental breakdown before the war but was still passed for active duty. After another breakdown in the spring of 1918, he was discharged with 'deferred shell shock'. He initially seemed to have made some sort of recovery and wrote and composed prolifically, but by 1922 he was certified insane and spent the last fifteen years of his life institutionalised, still imagining that the war was on.

14

PENSIONS

'I believe that the war pensioner is in a safer position and that the pension system is sounder here than in any other country.'[1]

Major George Tryon, Minister of Pensions

With so few employment opportunities available to a disabled ex-serviceman, war pensions became essential for his survival, but they were never intended to be enough to recover his pre-war standard of living. Even a full pension for the severely disabled was set below the level of an unskilled female worker, whereas in Germany it was equivalent to a skilled man. Historians have disagreed about the British Government's performance in this field. Deborah Stone, Deborah Cohen and Joanna Bourke are all critical of the interwar pension system and its level of payment and implementation, while Bettinson and Kowalsky are more positive about Britain's record.[2]

Meaghan Kowalsky argues that Britain was faced with an unprecedented number of claims. The war left around 750,000 men with disabilities. Despite this, Britain managed to improve its pension provision. The fact that a Ministry of Pensions was created in 1916 indicates the seriousness with which the government took its responsibilities. Before the war, disability pensions were not a statutory right, which made any legal appeals difficult. Levels were set low and not adjusted for changes in the cost of living. In 1914 the maximum pension was 10s 6d a week,[3] unchanged since the Boer War, and not enough to cover even a modest food budget. Disabled veterans were often reduced to charity and beggary, as Kipling's Boer War poem 'The Absent-Minded Beggar' captures:

He's an absent-minded beggar, and his weaknesses are great—
But we and Paul must take him as we find him—

He is out on active service, wiping something off a slate
And he's left a lot of little things behind him![4]

The government accepted a statutory duty to provide pensions during the war, confirmed in the Great Pensions Act of 1921. The maximum level that year was 42s 6d,* an improvement even with wartime inflation.** Pensions were set according to rank and the level of disability, judged by the Local War Pensions Boards (LWPB) following Ministry of Pensions guidelines; by 1921 the ministry had granted nearly 40,000 totally disabled pensions.[5] Claimants unhappy with a decision could go to a Pension Appeals Tribunal within a year of the initial judgement. As the level of disability might fluctuate, pension payments would be reviewed until the claimant's condition was deemed to have stabilised and a 'final award' would be made. There was a possible review if the claimant's condition deteriorated after that. However, as payments were now based on the severity of the illness, boards did not consider a man's profession and the impact on his income the injury might entail. The loss of a finger might be crucial to a skilled man like Private Raynor Taylor, who only received a one-off £30 payment.[6]

Kowalsky argues that given the amount of appeals (sometimes medical boards interviewed over 1,000 men a week),[7] inevitable delays occurred, but both the Ministry of Pensions and the LWPBs strove to implement these policies fairly. Sometimes delays were due to the complexity of measuring the extent of a disability. Assessing a PTSD sufferer was particularly difficult. A man who might seem fully recovered could break down again, necessitating another medical examination. As the government accepted conditions that had been 'aggravated' by war, a tribunal would have to determine how much a disability like arthritis or TB was due to the trenches and how ill the claimant was before joining up. Medical records from many years ago might need consulting, assuming they were available. Frank Richards thought this patently unfair. He could not prove his rheumatism had been aggravated by war so his pension was stopped, but if:

a man had only done four week's service in England and had been admitted to hospital for a few days he would have a better chance of being awarded a disability pension than a man who had done four years in the firing line and whose medical history sheet was clean.[8]

---

* This was only for higher ranks; privates, for instance, only received 27s 6d even if there degree of disablement was 100 per cent.

** This was still less than a woman cotton weaver (72s 6d) and a coal-mining labourer (99s 6d). See Deborah Cohen, *The War Come Home*, p. 49.

Even relatively straightforward awards for disabilities like amputations were not always so simple. Pension levels were determined by the extent of the injury: an 80 per cent award was for an amputation of the leg at the hip and a 60 per cent award for one above or through the knee. However, 40,000 men had been re-amputated by 1920 which meant another forty to fifty reassessments per month.[9]

The decisions were not always fair. Gunner William Towers was cheated out of his rightful pension, as they measured the flesh rather than the bone after the amputation of his leg, which gave him a 60 per cent rather than 70 per cent award. Despite two doctors independently verifying his claim, the Ministry of Pensions refused to budge. Forty-two years later, they finally agreed to the original 70 per cent but he had lost thousands of pounds as a consequence.[10] Roy Page was severely injured by a gunshot wound to the abdomen. He suffered from recurring pains, which gave him sleepless nights and stubborn constipation. He never fully recovered yet his final award was only 10 per cent with a £15 gratuity.[11] The Local War Pension Boards could be cold and officious, as George Coppard discovered. He had been severely wounded in the leg at the Battle of Cambrai:

> My leg had shrunk a bit and I was given pension of twenty-five shillings per week for six months. The pension dropped to nine shillings a week for a year and then ceased altogether. At my last medical board in 1920, one of the members, repeating my replies to questions, drawled, 'Says femoral artery has been severed.'[12]

One regular complaint was that the tribunals were often too conscious of sparing the public purse. Dr Wilson, head of the Cardiff Pension Board thought 'Promiscuous granting of pensions will inevitably bring its curse [...] It saps self-respect'.[13] Suspicions that claimants were 'malingerers' were common. H. W. Bayley, an RAMC surgeon, criticised the appeals process in a letter to the *Morning Post*. He found 'that the pensioner [was] regarded as a criminal in the dock' and the burden of proof lay with the claimant.[14] Private George Grunwell believed 'the whole objective of the medical boards was to get you off their backs, with regard to money, as soon as they could'.[15] Human tragedies abound, like the case of Herbert Walker Long whose appeal was rejected despite complaining of being in constant pain and unable to work.[16] Boards were particularly suspicious of a PTSD sufferer who had no visible wound. As discussed, many in the medical profession still thought 'shell shock' was a cover for cowardice. There was also a lack of understanding of psychological complaints. Albert James Castleman had his pension reduced from 50 to 1–5 per cent despite complaining he had no feeling in his left arm.[17]

The British Legion calculated that 34,202 of the 64,383 pension appeals had been overturned, a testament to the harshness of the original LWPB judgements.[18] Even if the claimant won, the initial rejection could be traumatic as well as financially hard. Appeals and reassessment often meant a great deal of travel. Muddle and delay might follow a successful award in a ministry that was understaffed. Local volunteers on boards were more appreciated – they could be a 'human bulwark between the disabled man on the one hand and Departmentality on the other.'[19]

The government didn't always lack generosity, though it sometimes had to be pressurised into doing the right thing. When deflation occurred in the 1920s, the Ministry of Pensions did not reduce the level of pensions, giving disabled ex-servicemen an effective increase. During the Great Depression, Britain was the only belligerent nation not to reduce its compensation to war victims. War pension expenditure always remained over 5 per cent of the national budget and rose to above 8 per cent in 1924–25 and 1925–26.[20] By 1930 war pensions were costing the government £70 million a year – over £4 billion in 2018 prices. John Hodge, the Minister of Pensions (1917–19), called the work of his department 'a great step forward'.[21] It was certainly an improvement. Britain's small pre-war volunteer army was notoriously bad at looking after its rankers and the public would not have tolerated a continuation of the old pension arrangements. The government was aware of this and could be flexible in the face of a press or British Legion campaign, public letter writing or the actions of independent-minded MPs. The granting of 'aggravated' pensions at the full rate, the inclusion of the psychologically damaged for pensions and the decision not to cut pensions in the 1920s are examples of the government changing its mind after the mobilisation of public opinion.

But rates were never as high as countries like Canada, New Zealand and Australia. True, these nations were not as badly affected economically by the war, but Germany was and it still managed a more generous settlement. The German government spent around 20 per cent of its overall budget even in the midst of the Great Depression, which hit Germany more severely. Britain actually managed to *reduce* its pensions provision in the 1920s.[22] For cost-conscious officials this represented a triumph. J. A. Flynn, the Ministry of Pensions first financial officer, saw the pension payment policies as 'indefensible expenditure'.[23] In 1934–35, a full pension was £104 a year without family allowances; better than 1921, but still less than the average unskilled wage of £129.[24] This pension was for a fully disabled man, typically someone who had lost two or more limbs or both feet, a total loss of sight or was permanently bed-ridden. He had little chance of making a living and would also need to meet the extra costs his disability would incur, not all of which was provided by the ministry. To add insult to injury, the unemployment means test took disability pensions into consideration and reduced other household benefits accordingly. Pensions were low enough to force men to live in charitable institutions like Star and Garter homes.

In 1915, the *Morning Post* commented that in regard to pensions the government's role was to 'discover how little the State can do without incurring popular odium'.[25] The government made improvements only after considerable public pressure and, as in the field of disability employment, the provision of pensions lagged behind other belligerent nations.

15

'HOMES FOR HEROES': VETERANS' HOUSING

'To let them [the troops] come home from horrible, water-logged trenches to something little better than a pigsty here would, indeed, be criminal … and a negation of all we have said during the war … we can never repay those men for what they have done for us.'[1]
Walter Long, President of the Board of Trade

One of Lloyd George's pledges during the 1918 general election was to provide 'homes fit for heroes'. It was the most ambitious part of the government's reconstruction programme and perhaps its greatest challenge. Britain faced a housing crisis. Its stock was in a dreadful state, as few homes had been built for four years. The scale of the task was apparent to those working for the new Ministry of Reconstruction. In 1918, they estimated that 300,000 houses were needed immediately and 500,000 in the next three years. This did not include the clearance of existing slums, which contained some appalling dwellings.

The First World War had exposed the poor state of health of the nation's young men. This was partly blamed on the poor condition of pre-war housing. As one wartime poster said, 'you cannot expect to get an A1 population out of C3 homes'. J.M. Winter pointed out that respiratory infections actually increased while there was a general decline in other diseases – poor housing being a major factor for this.[2] A Royal Commission into the state of Scottish housing found:

> unspeakably filthy privy-middens in many of the mining areas, badly constructed incurably damp labourers' cottages on farms, whole townships unfit for human occupation in the crofting counties and islands … gross overcrowding and the huddling of sexes together in our industrial villages and towns … groups of lightless and unventilated houses in the older burghs, clotted masses of slums in the great cities.[3]

Rent controls hadn't helped improve the quality of the rented sector (and 90 per cent of the country still rented). Some landlords were raising rents exorbitantly due to wartime demand, but a rent strike in Glasgow led by a redoubtable mother, Mrs Barbour, forced the government to pass the Rent Act (1915). This stopped rent rises for the duration of the war and prevented social unrest but left no incentive for landlords to carry out improvements.

It was broadly agreed that the state must assume the financial burden and responsibility for a housing programme. The war had left the private sector short of capital and unlikely to invest in homes with no guaranteed profit. But should this mean central government or local authorities? The former had the ability to provide the finance but the latter had the experience of building public housing.* Ultimately it was decided that central government should pay most of the initial cost, but the schemes should be run by local councils. Another question was should the emphasis be on quality or quantity? The 'homes for heroes' implied both – decent houses for the millions of returning servicemen, but tight budgets and limited time meant there had to be a trade-off. This was the same dilemma facing ministers of housing after the Second World War. The costs were higher than reformers hoped, as housing depended upon the price of labour and materials and there was a shortage of both. Many experienced builders had been killed and the unions didn't want an influx of cheap labour. Costs might fall after a few years, as Britain switched to a peacetime economy, yet this would delay tackling the immediate housing shortage.

During the war, the government had cautiously dipped its toe in the water with schemes for workers near munitions factories like Rosyth Docks, but what was now needed was far bigger in scale: the construction of numerous high-quality council houses. The Tudor Walters Committee (1918) was set up to review housing conditions and make recommendations for working-class homes. It drew inspiration from Ebenezer Howard and Raymond Unwin, leaders of the town and garden movement. Model garden cities had already started in Letchworth, Hertfordshire and would continue with Welwyn Garden City. These were places that 'planned for industry and healthy living; of a size that makes possible a full measure of social life, but not larger; surrounded by a permanent belt of rural land; the whole of the land being in public ownership or held in trust for the community'.[4]

The committee recommended decent-sized 'cottages' (three bedrooms) on small estates, set well apart (at least 70ft from each other) in a green setting away from the city centre. They should be varied in design to prevent monotony. If the subsequent houses didn't live up to this dream, they were significantly better than most existing working-class dwellings. Front or back gardens, indoor plumbing,

---

* Council houses still constituted less than 1 per cent of housing stock by 1911.

gas and electricity – these were all luxuries before the war, with just 2 per cent of the population having electricity at the turn of the century.[5] One Lancaster man recalled, 'It had a bathroom that was another luxury … and what my mother particularly enjoyed was hot water from the boiler, just open the tap and that was it, smashing. And there was an open space at the back and a garden to sit in'[6] But due to the slow pace of delivery, demand was great and queues long.

The London County Council was particularly active, with huge council estates on former farmland like Becontree. With over 100,000 people, it was the largest in the world but took until the mid 1930s to complete. Provincial cities also expanded their stock of public housing in areas like Kirkby (Liverpool) and Wythenshawe (Manchester). The problem wasn't just an insufficient quantity of new houses but rent averaged 14 shillings a week – beyond the reach of most working people. It was, for instance, 40 per cent of an agricultural worker's wage.[7]

The responsibility for housing nationally went to Christopher Addison, one of the most committed reformers in the government. He headed the Ministry of Reconstruction from 1916 with powers to improve transport, housing, demobilisation, labour, education, health and child welfare. Addison planned for 800,000 council houses but by 1921 only 213,800 were built – though of a decent quality.[8] Construction costs were far more than had been estimated (four times higher than before the war), and with a government debt of £9,300 million he was forced to scale back. The economic recession that started in 1920 and the subsequent government cutbacks effectively curtailed Addison's plans.

There was also political resistance. After the 1918 general election, the House of Commons was dominated by Conservatives, 'a lot of hard-faced men who look as if they have done very well out of the war', in Stanley Baldwin's classic phrase. They bore a particular animus to Addison, believing him a free-spending socialist, and rejoiced when he resigned from government in 1921 after his housing scheme was halted. He was perhaps ahead of his time. In his ambitions in housing and health, he was closer to the reconstruction that took place after the Second World War.

The minutiae of the various Housing Acts between the wars is for another book but a brief summary is important. The Addison Act (1919) gave local authorities the task of planning new council houses according to housing needs. The costs beyond the local authority's penny rate would be borne by the Treasury. It was an important landmark as it established the state's responsibility for social housing. Conservative housing ministers preferred subsidising private builders to construct working-class homes (like the Chamberlain Act, 1923). They also reduced quality requirements in order to boost numbers and encouraged the building of flats in cities. Labour preferred to give subsidies to local authorities (the Wheatley Act, 1924), which produced almost half a million homes and controlled the amount of rent local government could charge by linking it to household income.

Were these homes for heroes? They might not have been architecturally daring or aesthetically elegant but they were an improvement, even when quality controls were reduced. On the whole, councils were better landlords than the private sector, having to consider that tenants were also voters. But the 1½ million new council houses were out of reach of the poorest sections of the working class. Council house rents, even when controlled, were still higher than the privately rented dwellings for workers. John Boyd Orr, the nutritionist, summed up the state of working-class housing in 1936. He estimated that one-third of workers lived well in new houses, another third in older but still sanitary accommodation and the other third in slums.[9] This was exacerbated by the lack of slum clearance: only 245,000 houses were demolished between the wars.[10]

So desperate was the housing situation after the war that old railway carriages were converted into homes, like 250 of them in Pagham, West Sussex. Ex-army huts also provided accommodation, as did self-assembly bungalows of wood and asbestos. One such temporary settlement was Peacehaven on the Sussex coast, originally intended as a settlement for ex-servicemen to recover. More permanent structures began to appear, as Londoners were attracted by the low cost of starting a home by the sea, but not all of them were ex-servicemen, defeating the original purpose of the settlement. The most famous resident was Felix Lloyd Powell, former staff sergeant and co-writer of *Pack Up Your Troubles in Your Old Kit Bag*. The war had shattered his nerves so he moved to Peacehaven, where he ran the local theatre. But he experienced financial difficulties and, sadly, committed suicide while serving in the Peacehaven Home Guard during the Second World War. A terrible irony considering the theme of the song.

Of the 4 million new homes built between the wars, 70 per cent of them were private. The growth of new industries in the South and Midlands led to a demand for new workers. Selling cheap houses was more profitable than building for rent. It was a golden opportunity for the construction industry. Relatively low wages, lax planning rules, low interest rates and a decline in the cost of building materials all helped to keep prices down. Cheap land was often purchased near arterial roads or new underground stations which also provided good transport links. In 1935, the peak year, 275,299 private homes were built.[11] The typical starting price was £500, affordable for the lower middle class and upper working class but out of reach for most working-class families. By 1939, about 10 per cent of workers owned their own homes, about 20 per cent lived in council houses and 70 per cent rented. The owner–occupier rate could rise significantly in boom towns like Oxford and Coventry.[12] For the more prosperous, £1,000 could buy a detached property and half an acre. Widespread home-ownership was probably the greatest change in housing between the wars. In 1931, 32 per cent of the population owned their own homes, more than three times the 1914 figure.[13]

These houses were unplanned versions of the garden cities: low-density housing with a decent sized garden but sometimes miles from a pub, village hall or shops. Their style was a distant descendant of the Arts and Crafts movement that encouraged a return to pre-industrial workmanship with mock Tudor beams and pebble dash. At their worst, 'a host of architectural gimmick[s] were offered to mask a multitude of sins that came with poor quality materials, shortcuts, and shoddy workmanship'.[14] They rarely had much of an involvement from an architect, though these houses were no worse than the utopian projects that followed the Second World War. They might have lacked the innovation and drama favoured by planners but it was what people wanted. In a wide-ranging survey taken just before the Second World War, only 5 per cent of people preferred a flat. The majority favoured a small house and a garden.[15] Finn Jensen contended that 'for many, a mythological Elizabethan age and the Tudor past represented an age of stability and secure living ... [producing] a house that at least gave the outward impression of unshakeable stability'.[16]

The quality of houses for ex-servicemen depended on what part of the economic ladder they were on. Few local authorities gave ex-servicemen priority (Oldham was an exception), as there was no national obligation to do this. Some charities provided accommodation for disabled soldiers, like the Douglas Haig Memorial Homes and Westfield War Memorial Village. Places like Peacehaven were rare and not exclusively for veterans. The new council estates and private housing developments tended to be inhabited by skilled workers and the middle class respectively. Some would have been veterans but ex-servicemen would have been disproportionately excluded due to the years sacrificed fighting the war. Many returned to decrepit rural hovels or overcrowded tenements of the type George Orwell found when he visited Lancashire in 1936, 'little brick houses blackened by smoke, festering in planless chaos round miry alleys and little cindered yards where they are stinking dust-bins and lines of grimy washing and half-ruinous w.c.s'.[17]

A seriously disabled British soldier working in a laboratory. He was one of the lucky ones; most struggled to find work.

Mat weaving at St Dunstan's, the charity that did so much for blind veterans after the war.

Lawrence of Arabia never found peacetime easy and was always uncomfortable with his new-found fame.

Tons of rusted armaments are still found on the Western Front. These are from Bapaume-Albert near the Somme.

A shell-shock victim at King George V's military hospital. At least 80,000 servicemen suffered from this condition.

Siegfried Sassoon's long literary career was spent largely writing about the war; in a sense, he never left the trenches.

Ypres became a symbol of the destructive power of modern warfare, and a place of pilgrimage for many ex-servicemen.

- NOTICE -
THIS IS HOLY GROUND
NO STONE OF THIS FABRIC MAY BE TAKEN AWAY
IT IS A HERITAGE FOR ALL CIVILISED PEOPLES
BY ORDER
TOWN MAJOR YPRES

'Yanks and Tommies' at the Armistice celebrations.

WOUNDED BRITISH SOLDIERS BY THE HUNDRED RECEIVING WHAT SLIGHT AID CAN BE GIVEN THEM BEFORE THE
AMBULANCES COME TO TAKE THEM BACK TO THE BASE HOSPITAL.
(© British Official Photo.)

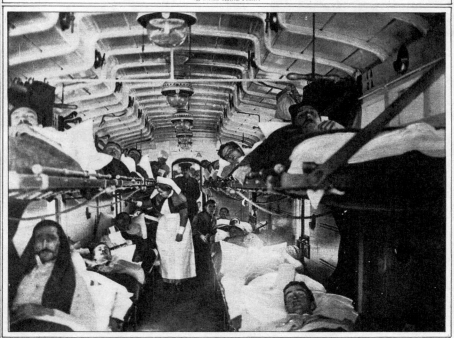

HOSPITAL EXPRESS TRAIN OF THE BRITISH RED CROSS PROVIDED WITH NURSES, DOCTORS, AND EVERY COM-
FORT, SPEEDING TOWARD THE COAST WHERE THE WOUNDED WERE TO BE TAKEN TO ENGLAND.
(© British Official Photo, from Underwood & Underwood.)

Improved methods of treatment meant more wounded men would survive than ever before.

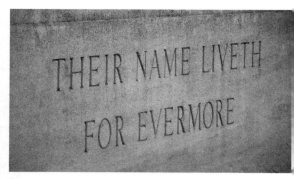

This quote from the King James Bible is on every Stone of Remembrance.

Lutyens' simple but moving design for a British and Commonwealth war grave.

Harry Patch, the longest-surviving British soldier of the First World War.

BACK TO THE LAND: RESETTLING EX-SERVICEMEN

What has the rather primose to do with old rags and bones on barbed wire? ... Everything.'

H. M. Tomlinson[1]

As Britain rapidly urbanised during the nineteenth century, the appeal of rural life became increasingly attractive. Rural Britain was seen as the keeper of traditional values, in contrast to cities – where mobs formed and riots took place. Many were also shocked by the physical state of working-class recruits for the Boer War. This led liberals to the National Efficiency movement to improve the fitness of the nation through social reforms like basic healthcare and welfare. Conservatives were drawn to organisations like the Scouts which encouraged loyalty to the Empire and taught the skills needed for an outdoor life. On the left, socialists like William Morris bemoaned the loss of autonomy caused by factory-production techniques, which were destroying rural communities and the traditional handicrafts that went with them.

The First World War only seemed to enhance Britain's love of the countryside. Paul Fussell remarked how British soldiers treasured the bucolic, even if it was a brief glimpse of flora among the devastated landscape of the Western Front.[2] This contrast between beautiful nature and the ugliness of modern warfare is a familiar theme of wartime literature: Wilfred Owen's 'Anthem for Doomed Youth', D.H. Lawrence's 'Bombardment' or, most famously, John McCrae's 'In Flanders Field'. Many dreamt of a quiet rural life after the war. Taking just the war poets as examples, Wilfred Owen thought about keeping pigs before his life was tragically cut short; Robert Graves moved to rural Boar's Hill in Oxfordshire near Edmund Blunden ('a harmless young shepherd in a soldier's coat');[3] Robert Nichols and John Masefield, 'wrote in a hut in his garden, surrounded by tall gorse bushes'.[4] Graves 'knew it would be years before I could face anything but a quiet country life'.[5] The novelist Henry Williamson retreated to a hut in Devon to write *Tarka the Otter*. He eventually acquired a Norfolk farm in the 1930s. Many non-literary veterans felt the same. Reginald St John Battersby, brought up in Manchester, became a vicar of the quiet country parish of Chittoe in Wiltshire. His son thought it was because he 'wanted to have somewhere that was safe, calm and assured'.[6]

The government was initially keen to encourage ex-servicemen to take up smallholdings as a way of reviving rural Britain: disabled veterans would gain a sense of self-worth and shell-shock sufferers might find peace in the country-side. However, the wartime agricultural boom had made the cost of acquiring farmland prohibitive. The government's fund of £20 million for veteran's land settlement was nowhere near enough. Compulsory state purchases were rejected as too radical and by September 1920 the allocations had been entirely used up, with only 19,000 men acquiring smallholdings.[7]

Land ownership for ex-serviceman was particularly contentious in the Scottish Highlands. There has been a strained relationship between aristocratic land owners and the local crofters for decades, with its roots in the Highland Clearances of the eighteenth century. After the defeat of the Jacobites in 1745, the Highlands were cleared for sheep farming and deer hunting. In contrast to the vast noble estates, the crofters owned tiny plots or no land at all and became squatters. A crofters' movement started in the 1880s organising rent strikes and land raids to occupy parts of the nobles' land – they even put up parliamentary candidates. This pressure secured some rights over the land they already owned and the control of rent. But the main issue, the need for more land, wasn't addressed.

Many of the crofters served in the armed forces during the war and came back expecting change. Politically, promises of better times ahead were made: the government's 1918 manifesto stated the intention to 'acquire land on simple economical bases for men who had served in the war'.[8] The results were the Land Settlement Acts (1919) for Scotland, England and Wales. Priority was given to ex-servicemen* though finance was always inadequate, especially as land prices were high in 1919–20, and funds were used up five months after the act.[9] Of the 7,220 ex-servicemen who applied, only 1,284 could be satisfied with the money available.[10] Landless veterans decided to take matters into their own hands and land raids resumed. Public opinion, and the press, was largely behind their actions, to such an extent that the local authorities refrained from using troops to suppress dissent as they had done before the war. These men had served their country and were only asking for a chance to make a modest living in the area of their birth. They often achieved the desired results: land settlement schemes were set up in

---

*   This rule was ended by 1926.

places like Eoligarry, Scarista and North Uist. Sometimes the link between military service and political action was made explicit:'With flags flying and pipes
playing ex-servicemen drove their stock on to farmland promised to them as
smallholdings by the Duke of Sutherland in protest at government inaction.They
were persuaded to leave pending negotiations with the owner.'[11] It took another
thirteen years but eventually these crofts were established. Crofting was a hard life.
Winters were tougher than England and land more barren, necessitating bigger
holdings than England, yet the failure rate was an impressive 2 per cent in legal
settlements between the wars.[12] However, ex-servicemen formed a disproportionate share of the failed crofts.A Department of Agriculture report blamed the
hurried training and the fall in agricultural prices in the 1920s,[13] a pattern that
would be repeated overseas.

Not all landlords fitted the stereotype of the hunting, shooting and fishing aristocracy. One such was Lord Leverhulme, who had made a fortune manufacturing
soap. He established a model community for his workers at Port Sunlight on the
Wirral, but he was a man of contradictions. He could be arbitrary and domineer-
ing, yet his workforce was well-treated. In 1918, he moved to the Isle of Lewis
because he thought the fish stocks could be the basis of a thriving economy. Still
reeling from the *Iolaire* disaster, the locals saw this as a threat to their traditional
way of life and would end any chance of land ownership.Veterans started land
raids and Leverhulme peremptorily stopped his planned investment. Before he
died his philanthropic side once more emerged and he left a large part of the
island to the locals in the form of the Stornoway Trust.

There was also enthusiasm for settling ex-servicemen overseas. Such schemes
had existed before the First World War and the government was keen to
assist men who wanted to move to different parts of the Empire.The Murray
Committee in 1915 recommended that assistance should be given to servicemen both for 'home colonisation' and settlement overseas.[14] There was a strong
racial motive. Some politicians wanted to encourage white emigration to the
dominions to strengthen the bonds with the mother country, particularly
after the cooperation shown during the war. The most prominent booster was
Colonial Secretary Lord Milner, who told the Imperial Conference in 1921
'the challenge was that "of distributing the white population of the Empire in
the manner most conducive to the development, stability and strength of the
whole"'.[15] British Legion leader Colonel Crosfield thought it could also reduce
the large pool of unemployed ex-servicemen:'in emigration lies the solution of
dealing with our overpopulation.'[16]

The dominions did have large amounts of uncultivated land in countries and generally welcomed men of 'British stock'. Emigration had previously been left to private and voluntary organisations but as the level of veterans' unemployment rose the government saw this was something it needed to facilitate. The Free Passage Scheme (1919) planned to help settle 405,000 in the dominions but a lack of funding meant only 86,027 were settled by 1923 when the scheme ended.[17]

Canada, New Zealand and Australia certainly needed labour for their vast rural expanses, as many young people before the war had moved to the cities for an easier life. The prevailing view was to encourage Britons, who they thought would acclimatise better than other nationalities. However, the quality of many pre-war British emigrants had left much to be desired. They had been largely from industrial areas, in poor health and lacked any experience of rural life. The dominions now wanted skilled, physically fit Britons, rather than the 'residuum' of the cities. Canada insisted they should be 'morally upstanding, possessed an honourable discharge and could provide a deposit of £200 as a surety before sailing'.[18] They also were required to pay 20 per cent for the land, livestock and farm machinery. To help with this, the Empire Settlement Act (1922) provided assisted passages, allowances and training.[19] The Ministry of Labour set up Barham House in Claydon, Suffolk to train men in farming techniques for future emigration – other centres followed. The courses lasted twelve weeks and were supposed to weed out the unfit. As ever, budgets were tight – the average spent on a single man was only £18.[20] These measures provided too high a hurdle for some ex-servicemen whose health had been ruined by the war. The British Legion Annual Conference in 1925 passed a resolution demanding lower medical standards for emigrants and a relaxation of the upper age limit. Major Gilbert Cohen, who had spent twelve years in Australia, told them that 'CIII men could not do the work of AI men … to make good a man wanted good health and a mighty heart'.[21]

Those who qualified discovered the dominions weren't quite the promised lands. Canada was going through a post-war recession with high veteran unemployment of its own. Many British ex-servicemen could not provide the capital and deposit needed for farmland and found jobs in the cities scarce. The *Vancouver World* newspaper estimated there were 3,000 British ex-servicemen in penury by January 1920: 'Arriving here in flocks without any properly authorised persons to advise them, these men are unable to take up land as they intended, some are stranded, others fit for charity … '[22] Many Canadians came to regard British veterans as poor workers and settlers and their government responded by tightening restrictions on immigration. There was also an unwillingness for many ex-veterans to take up agriculture. Some had only used the scheme to get to Canada and, on arrival, preferred to take their chances in the city. This was perhaps understandable: most of Canada's best agricultural land was already being farmed or had been bought by speculators and with a worldwide agricultural depression, the failure rate for veterans' farms was 57 per cent.[23] Some of the veterans were sent to Canada because it was convenient. Jack Page, brother of Captain Roy Page, continued to suffer from PTSD. Unable to adapt to normal life his family arranged for him to emigrate, but he struggled. At one point they lost contact with him and contacted the Mounties to track him down.

Fewer veterans emigrated to South Africa. There was less land available; on some farms, soldiers had to battle malaria and tsetse fly. South Africa quickly gained a poor reputation for emigration and received the lowest number of applications under the free passage scheme – only 6,064.[24] The British Government provided grants throughout the 1920s but these were never enough to make much difference. South Africa's Dutch settlers, the Afrikaners, were afraid of being swamped by British ex-servicemen who might tip the racial balance in elections – as political parties were divided largely on racial lines. In 1924, the Afrikaner National Party won the general election and chose to prioritise poor Afrikaners with land settlement rather than incoming British ex-servicemen. British soldiers who settled later were helped by private organisations like the 1820 Memorial Settlers' Association.* They were aimed at former officers with capital and agricultural experience so, though their numbers were small, settlers tended to have a lower failure rate than Canada.

Australia proved the most popular destination for British ex-servicemen and their families, making up 34,750 of the overall total.[25] In Australia, British veterans faced similar problems to Canada. Farming conditions were harsh, with back-breaking work needed to cultivate poor-quality farms. The ex-servicemen who arrived were often unsuited to this kind of labour or lacked experience in sheep and arable farming. There was little financial help from the national or state governments, who favoured their own veterans. Nor was the city always a better option, as Britons found themselves in competition with Australian ex-servicemen for jobs. One Australian official warned the British Colonial office that 'many of the men you have sent out are wandering the streets here workless and destitute'.[26]

New Zealand was probably the most pro-British of the dominions and the government was sympathetic to settling British ex-servicemen. The problem was that there was simply not enough Crown land to go around. New Zealand veterans had been promised generous terms in acquiring their own farms. The agricultural depression of the 1920s and the fall in wool and mutton prices effectively killed the expansion of soldier settlements.

★ 1820 being the year when 3,500 Britons settled in the Eastern Cape.

Overall, settling British veterans in the dominions as a way of reducing unemployment and solidifying racial bonds has to be considered a failure. The economic conditions were not propitious and the financial help insufficient to purchase suitable land. E.K. Fedorowich estimates that no more than 3,000 settled in South Africa, Australia, New Zealand and Canada as a result of government or philanthropic schemes.* [27] What was politically desirable to men like Lord Milner was never economically feasible in the harsh post-war climate.

---

* This figure does not include those who settled independently.

'SILENCE AND THISTLES'[1]: RETURNING TO THE WESTERN FRONT

The ground which was secured at great expense
The Company keeps absolutely untouched,
And in that dug-out (genuine) we provide
Refreshments at a reasonable rate.
You are requested not to leave about
Paper, or ginger-beer bottles, or orange-peel,
There are waste-paper baskets at the gate.

Lieutenant John Stanley

The former Scots Guardsman Stephen Graham feared that there 'must come a time when no more visit the burial-places of the great war than visit now the cemeteries in Crimea'.[2] He need not have worried; people have flocked to the Western Front ever since. Between the wars, major sites like Vimy Ridge could receive 10,000 tourists a day at the height of summer. Michelin had already published a battlefield guide before peace was declared. Not everyone was happy about this: R.H. Mottram, the writer and a corporal in the 4th Norfolks, felt the Western Front had become trivialised. Volker Rolf Berghahn later wrote the Western Front became filled with 'souvenir stands, carefully preserved trenches that could be visited for a fee, and comfortable hotels in the Salient where hundreds of thousands had died.'[3] Despite all this, many ex-servicemen found it worthwhile returning to the Front.

Talbot House called their visitors' manual *The Pilgrim's Guide to the Ypres Salient* (1920), which is an appropriate description as many regarded the trip as a religious act. There was even a Pilgrim's Hall in St George's, the Anglican Memorial Church in Ypres, while the St Barnabas organisation was formed to help the 'many Pilgrims miles from their hostels, vaguely wandering about in search of cemeteries and with no signposts to guide them thereto'.[4] When Stephen Graham visited Ypres in 1920 a sign simply said, 'THIS IS HOLY GROUND.'[5] Meanwhile, Winston Churchill thought that 'a more sacred place for the British race does not exist in the world.'[6] Veterans could sometimes be seen dressed in funeral mourning walking along the old front line.

When ex-servicemen returned to the Western Front there was a mixed reaction from the locals. The French and Belgians were not always friendly to 'outsiders' and even blamed the British for intruding on their land in the first place. This 'each army was as bad as the other' attitude annoyed veterans who had liberated them from German occupation. Other locals enthusiastically greeted the *bon soldats* and would show them the photos and postcards that old soldiers had sent from England. Tommies could return to cafés and estaminets they had known during the war and receive a hero's welcome. Further thanks could be found on church plaques or town square memorials dedicated to the British, or in street names like Place Kensington in Souchez and Rue Lloyd George in Châtelineau.

The trip, up to twelve hours from Victoria in the 1920s, could be expensive. Some travel agents charged more than £30 – six weeks' wages for the average worker. Accommodation ranged from the upmarket Grand Place Hotel in Ypres to places reminiscent of wartime billets. Organisations like the British Legion, the Ypres League and the St Barnabas Society ran cheaper tours – by 1923 the latter had lowered its prices to £4.[7] There was the added bonus of being able to visit with old comrades. Many veterans returned to see battle sites or the unveiling of their regimental memorial. There are around 1,000 First World War cemeteries and memorials on the Western Front, most of them completed in the first ten years after the war. The two massive monuments to the missing – Thiepval on the Somme and the Menin Gate in Ypres – attracted particularly large crowds. During 1937, 60,000 visited the Menin Gate,[8] many of them ex-servicemen. General Herbert Plumer put the case for such memorials at the unveiling of the Menin Gate in 1927. In a place where thousands of British troops had died, he told the huge crowd of relatives and veterans:

> One of the most tragic features of the Great War was the number of casualties reported as 'Missing, believed killed'. To their relatives there must have been added to their grief a tinge of bitterness and a feeling that everything possible had not been done to recover their loved ones' bodies and give them reverent burial. It was resolved that here at Ypres, where so many of the 'Missing' are known to have fallen, there should be erected a memorial worthy of them which should give expression to the nation's gratitude for their sacrifice and its sympathy with those who mourned them. A memorial has been erected which, in its simple grandeur, fulfils this object, and now it can be said of each one in whose honour we are assembled here today: 'He is not missing; he is here.'[9]

Sassoon was characteristically dismissive in his poem 'On Passing the New Menin Gate':

> Who will remember, passing through this Gate,
> The unheroic Dead who fed the guns?...
> Paid are its dim defenders by this pomp;
> Paid, with a pile of peace-complacent stone

And then concluding:

> Well might the Dead who struggled in the slime
> Rise and deride this sepulchre of crime.[10]

'A sepulchre of crime' is a memorable phrase but Sassoon's views were not necessarily representative of the ordinary soldier. There was an ambiguity among veterans about memorials. Many attended their unveilings, at home or abroad, and sometimes played a prominent part in the ceremonies. The memorials caught the mood of the times with their emphasis on sacrifice and their lack of triumphalism. Some found visits to these memorials an intensely moving experience. The sheer number – at least 60,000 in Britain alone – were physical reminders of what soldiers had been through and a tribute to dead comrades. George V hoped they would serve a positive function that the 'existence of these memorials will, eventually, serve to draw all peoples together in sanity and self-control'. As time passed, they became engulfed by traffic and taller buildings in Britain's cities. In villages they were more central – a reminder of how many young men small communities lost – and rural areas raised proportionately more funds for memorials than urban ones.[11] In France and Belgium, they usually retained their prominence due to where they were situated. There were veterans who thought them a waste of money, particularly when so many veterans were facing hardship. The National Executive of Scotland complained that the expenditure of £150,000 in 'dead stone and lime'[12] for the Scottish National War Memorial would not help ex-servicemen nor the dependents of the dead. 'Honour the dead but serve the living' was only partially being fulfilled. Some of the funds raised were for memorials with a more practical use like a hospital ward or village hall. In Salford 'surplus funds left over from the public's over-subscription towards a borough war memorial' went to supply food parcels for struggling veterans.[13]

Particularly visible on the Western Front are the Imperial War Graves Commission cemeteries – Major General Ernest Swinton called them the Silent Cities.[14] Immaculate, white and sometimes visible for miles, the graves have a uniformity that echoes an ideal parade ground. Henry Williamson thought them too neat, but perhaps that's what makes them so moving. Their deliberate monotony stresses an equality that was never achieved in life: name, rank, unit, regimental insignia, age and date of death, and a cross or appropriate religious symbol. 'Where high and low are one,' Kipling wrote.

Relatives could write short, heartfelt messages:

A LITTLE CROSS OF BRONZE
THE CROSS HE WON
BUT NEVER WORE
MY SON

FORGET ABOUT ME
SAVE SERJEANT DEATON.

HE IS NOT DEAD,
FOR SUCH A MAN AS MY HUSBAND WAS
CAN NEVER DIE

Unidentified soldiers were marked with a simple inscription:

AN UNKNOWN SOLDIER OF THE GREAT WAR
KNOWN UNTO GOD

Even before the war finished, the decision was taken not to bury soldiers in Britain. By January 1918 the Imperial War Graves Commission declared that there would be no repatriation, since all soldiers should 'lie together in their last resting place, facing the line they gave their lives to maintain'. The cost would have been prohibitive but this did present problems. Some families wanted to have them reburied in their local graveyards, but sheer numbers meant the Imperial War Grave Cemeteries remained abroad. It was a considerable improvement on previous overseas conflicts where soldiers were buried where they fell, lucky to get a wooden cross. One million three hundred thousand names were carved on headstones and memorials of the Western Front.[15]

Britain was then still largely Christian in outlook, as the cemeteries showed. The crosses were put on the memorial stones at public insistence against Edwin Lutyens' original intention. He did not want to make the headstones specifically Christian in nature due to his interest in theosophy, which 'sought to distil the wisdom of the ages – from all known religions'.[16] As well as crosses (Muslims and Jews had their own symbols) suitable passages from the Bible were often carved on the stone. Kipling's suggestion, 'Their Name Liveth For Evermore' from

Ecclesiasticus, appeared on every Stone of Remembrance. A Cross of Sacrifice was put into every Imperial cemetery with more than forty graves.

Edmund Blunden wrote, 'At that period above all … The idea that these battle fields would themselves ever again become pasture-lands … would have appeared sheer fantasy.'[17] Yet parts of the Front recovered quickly. Concrete and iron were soon drowned in green. Shell holes were grassed over, trenches filled in. Farmers ploughed fields along the Western Front as if the war had never happened. John Masefield, a hospital orderly during the war, had predicted, 'the ruins will be rebuilt and the field full of death will grow food, and all this frontier of trouble will be forgotten … In a few years' time, when this war is a romance in memory, the soldier looking for his battlefield will find his marks gone.'[18] By the mid 1920s, some prominent landmarks could be found only with a map. Places fought over were surprisingly close together: Ypres to Passchendaele, which took four months of slog during the battle in 1917, is a twenty-minute drive. It was easy to wonder how a small wood or nondescript farm had such importance, or a particularly dangerous part of no-man's-land was now a hop field.

Not all veterans approved. When the landscape returned to silence and thistles it was possible to imagine there had never been a war, but in so doing it became easier to forget. Gunner H.A. Coulter wrote to his wife during a visit in 1927:

> It has been a terrible disappointment … What we last saw as a vast desert of shell holes, bare tree stumps, mud, filth smashed guns and tanks and dead men, is all wavering cornfield, pretty gardens, brand new villages, noisy estaminets, charabancs, quarrelling children and flighty girls. It makes one's heart thump. The only things left to remind one that memories once were immense realities are the cemeteries and the poppies.[19]

Two ex-servicemen, Harold Arpthorp and Bernard Newman, visited the Front in 1934 and wrote the poem 'The Road to La Bassée' afterwards. No one would claim it reached the heights of Rosenberg or Owen but it captures many of the emotions of those who returned.

In the poem, an old soldier visits an area where he'd seen action during the war. The locals are friendly:

> The folks gave me a welcome, and lots to eat and drink,
> Saying, 'Allo, Tommee, back again? 'Ow do you do? In ze pink?'

While the land has recovered to a surprising degree:

> Some of the sights seemed more than strange as I kept marching on.
> The Somme's a blooming garden, and there are roses in Peronne.

But there are always reminders of what had happened:

> You'd never think there'd been a war – ah, yet you would, I know,
> You can't forget those rows of headstones every mile or so.

He finds it difficult to leave his wartime experiences behind:

> I sat at Shrapnel Corner and I tried to take it in,
> It all seemed much too quiet, I missed the war-time din.
> I felt inclined to bob down quick – Jerry sniper in that trench!
> A minnie coming over! God, what a hellish stench!

What affects him the most was a bus route:

> But the one thing that amazed me, most shocked me, I should say
> – There's buses running now from Bethune to La Bassée!

It now takes half an hour to travel a route that took over four years of hard slog and many deaths. What would those who never made it to La Bassée think, now that a bus rattles over the 'sacred, holy ground' they had fought over?

The poem ends on a hopeful note. His dead comrades would say:

> 'Carry on! That's why we died!' I could almost hear them say,
> To keep those buses always running from Bethune to La Bassée!'

They had given their lives to restore normality, which is what the local population also wanted. This tension between development and preservation is still around today. A new road or an industrial estate has to contend with a long process of identifying any remains or protests from historical groups keen to keep the site intact. Here are just two of the many examples:

> Archaeologists in the Alsace region in north eastern France recently discovered the bodies of 21 German soldiers from the First World War in an underground shelter that has not been touched since it was destroyed in a French attack in March 1918. The site was first discovered in October 2010 during excavation work for a road building project (2011)[20]

Here, at Cement House Cemetery near the village of Langemark, the day starts with the burial of three unknown soldiers, whose remains were found by the *Boesinghe Diggers* in an industrial zone near the canal at nearby Boesinghe … The industrial zone is expanding and the diggers excavate sites where soon factories will be built. (2005)[21]

The recovery was sporadic. A road might dip or a building split due to an old tunnel collapsing. Rail tracks could suddenly warp. Army signs re-emerged from under fresh paint. Walls were still marked by shrapnel or soldiers' graffiti, and blasted stumps mingled with the growth of new trees. A decade on, there were mounds from churned earth or land where railheads used to be and, at certain times of the year, the Front's demarcation could be determined – especially in the chalky soil of the Somme where white lines in farmers' fields would show where the old trenches were. A visitor could be walking through normal countryside and then step into a waterlogged crater full of rusted cap badges, water bottles, gas masks or bayonets that looked so old they could have been from another century. Thirteen years after the war, the writer Will Bird, who'd served with the Canadian Expeditionary Force, found a trench mortar, rifle, steel helmet, a Mills bomb and 'a rotting mass of khaki' in a single sap.[22] Dressing stations and bunkers sometimes remained too inaccessible to clear up, while the corrugated iron supports could keep trenches visible for years, unless filled in by the farmers. When Henry Williamson returned in 1924 he still saw 'rifles stood on thinning bayonets in places all over the battlefield.'[23] Military debris stacked on the sides of fields was common.

The locals called this the 'iron harvest'. Farmers reinforced their tractors with metal protection in case they hit a shell. Souvenir hunters or builders could still become casualties of war. In March 2014, two Belgium construction workers were killed trying to dig up a shell. The problem was that roughly 30 per cent never exploded, which left millions of tons of explosives still lethal. In 2009, the Ypres bomb disposal squad 'were called out no fewer than 3,027 times – that's more than eight times a day – to pick up unexploded ordnance from the First World War'.[24] Each year, Dovo, the Belgium bomb disposal unit, recovers 150–200 tons of unexploded ordinance every year.[25] Around 600 people, some of them veterans, have died in the Ypres Salient since the First World War. Piet Chielens, head of the In Flanders Fields Museum in Ypres, said the salient is 'like the laboratory of war'.[26]

The scale of destruction in Belgium and northern France was immense: 300,000 houses had been destroyed in France alone, though no town was more symbolic of the devastation of the First World War than the Belgium city of Ypres. It was the closest the First World War came to a Hiroshima.* In the immediate aftermath, Ypres was full of hastily constructed shacks rather than permanent buildings. It was grim and makeshift – a good place to commit suicide, commented Henry Williamson – but due to the efforts of the local population, the town recovered quickly. By the mid 1920s Ypres had been almost entirely rebuilt except for the Cloth Hall. 'Belgians worked with a purpose to rebuild their shattered towns,' noted Stephen Graham. 'New houses have sprung up overnight. There are thousands of piles of bricks. Every Belgian has learned bricklaying.'[27] Some towns were built in the former styles, others in modern form. The new 'old buildings' had a dream-like quality, familiar, yet strange. A returning soldier could revisit a building he had seen destroyed but was now more pristine than before. The new houses were bright red compared to the older ones, blackened by industrial pollution. The concrete fronts, sometimes built for speed and economy, mixed uneasily with the older red brick. They would take years to blend.

Reconstruction didn't happen at the same speed across the Western Front. Will Bird wrote that the area between Cambrai and Arras was particularly slow in rebuilding – villages like Éterpigny were hardly changed in 1931, where he counted fifty ruins in only two streets.[28] Châteaux remained neglected, as they were the last to get compensation, so they lay in ruins after more modest dwellings had been restored.

The locals made the best of what was left over. Pillboxes became tool sheds, latrines refuges for lovers. Chicken pens were made from salvaged corrugated iron or duckboards. Farmers created ponds from shell craters. R.H. Royle, a former Salford Pal, saw:

> Within a mile of poor devastated Thiepval, shell holes have been filled in, barbed wire removed, and trenches blocked up. Already the French peasants were reaping their harvest, back once more in their own part of their beloved France, living like foxes in holes in the ground, old Nissen huts, trench shelters – anywhere, but full of joy at being home again after nearly five years of exile. At Pozieres a little child was playing on a swing on top of our old battalion H.Q.[29]

Some army huts became cafés. Barbed wire returned to its original purpose. It was a compensation for people whose land had been used as a battleground for four years. Farmers had purchased whole farms salvaging debris; some made $20 per day, a large sum in those days.[30] German rifles were particularly prized, fetching 10 cents more than a British Lee-Enfield.[31] There was also a lucrative trade in war memorabilia and, for the less scrupulous, wedding rings and wrist watches.

---

* In fact, it is twinned with Hiroshima.

Williamson noted that the locals often ended up with better houses and farms than before the war.

Some old soldiers decided to remain in France and Belgium, marrying local girls and becoming part of the community. Typically, they might open a café for visiting ex-servicemen or work as a gardener or driver for the Imperial War Graves Commission – the biggest employer of ex-servicemen. Others sold postcards and souvenirs from war debris. Tour guiding was a popular occupation, especially for ex-officers. A typical advert was:

> TOURS – Ready end January, bachelor, late thirties, refined tastes, fluent French, fair German, recently toured whole front, France, Belgium, would CONDUCT PARTY owning good car over battlefields … [32]

Less pleasant work could be found clearing the land, a huge task that kept people occupied for years. Some constructions like concrete pillboxes and bunkers were hard to destroy. There were hundreds sticking out like mushrooms along the Front. Ironically, veterans were being employed to demolish structures they had built in the first place. The work could be dangerous, filling in craters or souvenir-digging could result in instant death if a spade went through a stick bomb or unexploded shell. Another Herculean task was the recovery of the missing, a job that still hasn't been completed today. Stephen Graham spoke to a couple of old Tommies digging for bodies: 'It's jolly hard work. But it 'as its better side. Some fellers the other day came on a dug-out with three officers in it, and they picked up five thousand francs between 'em.'[33] Unlike the premium for German rifles, more money was paid for a British corpse. Bodies sometimes returned by themselves, washed up by a heavy downpour or the movement of the soil. Stephen Graham saw an angry skull sticking out of the ground when he returned to the Front.[34] A few old soldiers had reasons not to return to Britain: they had deserted or committed crimes while in the army. For others, returning home seemed unthinkable, such was the draw of the Western Front. Some wanted to die with their comrades and were prepared to live a hand-to-mouth existence to do so. In 1914, Frederick Osborne joined the Royal Fusiliers with five of his friends. At the end of the war he was the sole survivor and stayed in Belgium tending the cemeteries of Ploegstraat. 'In 1962 he retired after a lifetime of looking after the dead of his youth'.[35] There was sufficient employment around Ypres to maintain a small British community between the wars, with its own church and school – perhaps 600 living there in the 1930s, many of them veterans. They celebrated

Empire Day and held cricket matches. As the next war loomed, families returned to Britain, effectively ending the community there.

The war is still inescapable in many of the towns and villages along the old front line with their memorials, souvenir shops and the streams of visitors, which British Government grants for school visits has only increased. One of the most moving parts of a visit to the Ypres Salient are the poppies and messages in the German Langemarck Cemetery. Written by British school children, they are often about the need for reconciliation between their two nations; that in itself is a suitable memorial.

PART IV

LEGACIES

RADICALS AND REACTIONARIES: THE POLITICS OF THE SOLDIERS

'Above all [soldiers] will take vigorous action to right any real or supposed wrong! All this seems to me to make for trouble unless our government is alert and tactful.'

Field Marshal Douglas Haig[1]

Many troops were radicalised by the First World War. In Italy, Germany and Russia this paved the way for totalitarian dictatorships but constitutional government was never really threatened in Britain, as few British soldiers adopted extreme ideologies. Discontent was channelled through peaceful protest or mainstream political organisations. Violence was rare and tended to be about specific problems like demobilisation, rather than a desire to change the system.

Some historians have portrayed Britain as on the verge of an insurrection in 1919 by citing the numerous examples of protest, but there was never any threat of revolution. The country had come out of the war relatively unscathed and its suffering, though considerable, wasn't as great as the states who experienced revolutionary outbreaks. Germany, for example, had attempted revolutions from the left (the Spartacists in Berlin (1918–19), the Bavarian Soviet Republic (1919) and the Ruhr Uprising (1920)) and from the right (the Kapp Putsch (1920) and Hitler's Beer Hall Putsch (1923)). But it had lost far more people on the battlefield or through the British naval blockade. One study put the blockade's death toll at 424,000,[2] which continued for eight months after the war to ensure compliance with the Armistice. This prolonged misery helped fuel discontent. Britain's naval dominance allowed for sufficient food imports and rationing ensured that people ate reasonably well; J.M. Winter pointed out that poorer British families' diets actually improved during the war.[3]

Defeat was also a massive psychological blow for the Germans. A nation forged by war with a reverence for the army, it explains the acceptance of the 'stab in the back myth' that Germany had only lost through revolutionary action at home. Ex-servicemen continued to play a violent role in Germany's shaky new democracy. Some joined left-wing groups like the Communist Red Front Fighters but more were found on the radical right. Hitler is the obvious example, and many other Nazis like Ernst Roehm and Hermann Goering took the violent resentments of a defeated army into the political arena. Britain had no such national trauma. In 1918 the overwhelming majority of soldiers believed in the rightness of the cause. The main British war aims – the liberation of Belgium and the defeat of German militarism – had been fulfilled and victory was a vindication of the 'British values' of constitutionalism and individualism; her citizens' army had overcome 'Prussian efficiency'. Why question a system that had prevailed over autocratic rivals? Discontentment with the peace would come later.

Revolutionary activity immediately after the war was confined to the losing nations: Germany, Hungary and Russia.* The exception was Italy, who felt cheated by the small territorial gains received for such huge sacrifices. There was a wave of popular anger, dubbed the 'mutilated victory'. Right-wing nationalists, many of them ex-servicemen, seized the port of Fiume that had been awarded to Yugoslavia rather than Italy. They were led by Gabriele D'Annunzio, the poet and former fighter pilot, and dressed in intimidating black uniforms. They eventually left but had provided a template for Benito Mussolini, another war veteran looking for political opportunities. His Fascist Party contained a huge number of ex-servicemen: 57 per cent of early Fascist members were First World War veterans.[4] Stanley Weintraub called the First World War the 'matrix of fascism'.

If anything, Britain had received too much territory. This partly explains why Britain never developed a comparable fascist movement. There was little fuel to light the nationalist fires. It also lacked a charismatic leader until Oswald Mosley formed the British Union of Fascists (BUF) in 1932. He was a restless maverick who claimed his war experiences formed his politics. He had served with the 16th Lancers and the Royal Flying Corps, and afterwards asserted, 'in the case of the First World War, a single idea existed for me: always to do my utmost in all circumstances to prevent it ever happening again.'[5] Mosley often referred to the war's victims to justify his politics: he talked of the 'need to conceive a nobler world in memory of those who died'.[6] He believed he possessed a 'modern mind' that was a 'hard, realistic type, hammered into existence on the anvil of great ordeal'. Opponents possessed a 'pre-war mind' that was a product of a 'static' age.[7] Like many ex-servicemen, he often divided the population into those who had fought and those who had not. Mosley started life as a Conservative MP, defected to Labour but became exasperated by their financial orthodoxy during the Great

---

*   Though Russia was allied to Britain and France she surrendered to Germany and accepted a humiliating peace treaty in March 1918.

Depression. He launched the New Party, which failed to make a breakthrough in the 1931 elections. A visit to Mussolini's Italy convinced him of the virtues of fascism. His party attracted some support from prominent ex-servicemen like J.F.C. Fuller, the brilliant Chief of Staff of the Tank Corps, John Beckett and the writer Henry Williamson, with a smattering of retired senior military men like Brigadier General Robert Byron Drury Blakeney. The BUF's emphasis on discipline and order, its love of uniforms and violent nationalism had an appeal for a few veterans. Sometimes it used explicit First World War imagery like in the marching song 'Comrades the Voices':

> Comrades, the voices of the dead battalions,
> Of those who fell that Britain might be great,
> Join in our song, for they still march in spirit with us,
> And urge us on to gain the fascist state!
> Join in our song, for they still march in spirit with us,
> And urge us on to gain the fascist state![8]

The BUF attracted publicity but never enough followers to be more than an irritant. At its height in the early 1930s, the BUF claimed 50,000 members (MI5 put the total at 35,000–40,000)[9] but as the Nazi menace increased, membership dropped to little more than 1,000 in 1939. This was only a tiny proportion of the number of ex-servicemen, especially as many recruits were unemployed young men, who would not have been old enough to have fought in the war.

Britain never developed revolutionary left-wing movements of any significance either. Russia was the only successful left-wing revolutionary country at the time and that was through exceptional circumstances. It was too remote and large for foreign armies to stop. Hungary, the only other country where Communists seized the national government, was crushed by invading Romanian forces after 133 days. Russia's internal problems were far more serious than Britain's. The Provisional Government that replaced the czar at the beginning of 1917 was inexperienced and badly led. People were starving and tired of the war, which the new government insisting on continuing. If this wasn't enough, numerous minorities now wanted to leave the Russian Empire, notably (but not exclusively) the Finns, Poles, Ukrainians, Latvians, Estonians and Lithuanians. The Russian Empire, what Lenin had called a 'prison house of nations', had many Irelands. By the end of the year, a ruthless and determined revolutionary party had seized power.

The differences between Britain and Russia were stark. The suffering of the Russian people was even greater than that of the Germans. Russian experience of constitutional government was negligible and never had time to put down roots before Lenin's seizure of power. Britain's biggest protests were about demobilisation. Some of them were angry and violent (the worst case involved Canadian troops at Kinmel Park, North Wales) but after a slow start, the government dealt with them effectively. The motives of the protesting soldiers were not to bring about a change in the political order but to get home quicker. These were men who believed they had done their bit and were frustrated at the slow pace of demobilisation. The cry of 'We want our civvie suits' was not a cry for revolution.

Examples of protesting soldiers abound in the first months of peace. Disabled veterans held up a banner during the Luton Peace Day protests saying 'don't pity us, give us work'. Unemployed ex-servicemen also demonstrated in Sheffield in July 1919. The following spring, there was a protest of between 10,000 and 50,000 in Hyde Park over the way police had brutally broken up an unemployed veterans' march on Downing Street.[10] These actions tended to show that many ex-servicemen could be truculent and even violent. However, the overwhelming picture is of men with specific grievances but not revolutionary attitudes.

These were turbulent times and it is easy to mistake any show of defiance as a possible sign of revolution. Some soldiers and sailors were genuine converts, but for most, using revolutionary symbols and language was part of the spirit of the era. For example, during a naval mutiny at Milford Haven, HMS *Kilbride* hoisted a red flag. Soldiers' Councils, formed during the demobilisation crisis, were sometimes called Soviets. When Robert Graves returned to Oxford University, undergraduate ex-servicemen at St John's had formed a 'College Soviet' to demand improved catering.[11] All these were signs of assertiveness but Oxford was not about to embrace Bolshevism.

There were also enough loyal troops prepared to act against rioting soldiers and civilians. This had already been shown during the British mutiny at Étaples (1917), which was successfully contained by the Honourable Artillery Company and the Machine Gun Corps. The army authorities were usually wise enough to grant concessions. Dave Lamb wrote that one 'question dominated the Government: "Could the troops be relied on, in the event of revolution or serious civil disturbance in England?"'[12] The answer in light of what happened is yes. When General Trenchard was manhandled at Southampton by striking soldiers,* he returned with 250 armed men and military police. The strikers surrendered when they saw that the authorities were quite prepared to shoot. In 'Red Glasgow' there was a series of strikes at the beginning of 1919, which spilled over into widespread rioting in George Square. Ten thousand troops were then moved into the city, the largest deployment of soldiers on British soil in the twentieth century.[13] Peace was restored. Time and again, the government could still rely on large numbers of loyal soldiers. This was shown in February 1919, when 3,000 troops marched on Whitehall over the pace of demobilisation, but there were enough reliable units from the Grenadiers to defuse the situation.[14]

---

* See Chapter 3.

There is also a temptation by historians to conflate the actions of trade unions with ex-servicemen. Both were involved in protests immediately after the war but wanted different things. Unions, whose membership and confidence had grown considerably, wanted better working conditions and pay or the restoration of rights temporarily suspended during the war. The Glasgow riots originally stemmed from a demand for a forty-hour week. The soldiers' protests of 1919 were about getting out of the army, back home and a decent job. Some soldiers sympathised with the strikers; the British Army was large enough to contain the whole spectrum of political opinions. But from the letters and diaries of soldiers there was a strong dislike for strikes during the war. War workers' demands for more pay cut little ice with men who were risking their lives in the trenches on far less money. In 1919, the War Office issued a circular among officers to ascertain the views of their men. In their attitude to industrial action it was found that:

Troops may be relied on to assist the civil power to preserve the public peace and to protect persons and property. They resent unofficial strikes … and realise their duty as citizens in repressing disorderly persons.

But it continued:

They deprecate being used in 'strike breaking' and the general feeling is that it would not be fair to ask troops to do what they themselves would consider 'blackleg' work.[15]

This indicates that soldiers would be unlikely to assist in 'unofficial actions', often the result of more left-wing local officials encouraging strikes against their national leadership's advice. However, they would not be strike breakers; a fear on the left at the time was the army would be used against the working-classes. Troops would avoid going to either extreme.

The years 1917–19 were a time of genuine fear among governments that communism would spread, which accounts for some of the hyperbolic language of politicians, partly fed by reports from the Director of Intelligence, Sir Basil Thomson, who saw reds under many beds. During the police strike of August 1918 Lloyd George said, 'This country was nearer to Bolshevism that day than at any time since.'[16] This was simply untrue: policemen, like the soldiers, had specific demands, in this case better pay and conditions. Not all the behaviour of the troops could be described as left wing either. During 1919, there were race riots in a number of British cities: London, Glasgow, Liverpool, Cardiff, Salford, Hull, South Shields, Newport and Barry. Competition for jobs in seaports and a shortage of housing were the main engines of discontent. On 30 May 1919 it was reported that in a seamen's home in West India Dock Road, 'any coloured man who appeared was greeted with abuse and had to be escorted by the police. It was necessary at times to bar the doors of the Home.'[17] Returning troops sometimes targeted black and Asian workers and sailors. Charles Wootton, who'd served in the navy, was drowned by a mob in Liverpool on 5 June. *The Times* on 14 June wrote that in Cardiff there were 'a number of young soldiers in khaki and many ex-soldiers' involved in racial incidents.

This reflects wartime currents of prejudice that ran through Britain: jingoistic rabble rousers like Pemberton Billing and Horatio Bottomley thrived; prominent Jews were made to sign 'Loyalty Letters'; Britons with a German background (or even tastes) were forced from public life; and not only pacifists but those advocating a compromise peace were also hounded. Soldiers on leave had been prominent at breaking up anti-war meetings during the war: the offices of the pacifist *Cambridge Magazine* were trashed by members of the Flying Corps. This spirit continued into the December 1918 elections when Labour MPs who were thought insufficiently patriotic, like Ramsay MacDonald, Philip Snowden and Arthur Henderson, lost their seats. Even the former Liberal prime minister Herbert Asquith was defeated at East Fife. Churchill described him as 'having a very rough time in East Fife ... and is being subjected to abominable baiting by a gang of discharged soldiers'.[18]

Britain was a long way from a revolution in the aftermath of the war and the far left was as unsuccessful as the far right in attracting veterans. Some ex-soldiers became involved in the radical National Union of Ex-Servicemen (NUX) but this organisation was attached to the Independent Labour Party rather than being actively Marxist. The International Union of Ex-Servicemen (IUX) was more sympathetic to communism but its membership was tiny. The largest Marxist group, the Communist Party of Great Britain (CPGB), was even smaller than the BUF. In 1926 they peaked at 12,000,[19] partly through their active work supporting the strike in mining districts. Thereafter it fell back. CPGB picked up again in the late 1930s with the fear of fascist aggression overseas but was still less than 18,000 before war broke out.[20] As it was concentrated in certain areas it did better in parliamentary elections than the BUF. Glasgow and the mining districts around Fife (which elected Willie Gallacher as the West Fife MP in 1935) and parts of London (they captured Battersea North in 1922) were communist strongholds. Very few of the leaders were veterans. Most had either opposed the war or worked in reserved occupations where there was some communist influence amongst unions. J.S. Snooks, ex-lieutenant and DCM winner, was an exception. The party dominated the National Unemployed Workers' Movement and many ex-servicemen took part in their hunger marches – 75 per cent of the men from Manchester in the 1922 march were veterans.[21] But this never translated into active support for the CPGB; anger about the plight of ex-servicemen was not the same as wanting a Marxist revolution.

Another reason for the comparative moderacy of ex-servicemen is Britain's long parliamentary tradition. The British were always uneasy about extra-parliamentary activity. Before the war, the tactics of Irish Nationalists, striking workers and militant suffragettes had upset people as much as their aims had. Soldiers traditionally kept out of politics, unlike the USA with its tradition of generals running for office, or in Germany where the military believed they represented the nation better than civilian politicians. This allowed General Ludendorff to accumulate huge amounts of political as well as military power during the war. Intrigues and alliances with politicians were practised by French High Command during the war, which would have been unthinkable in Britain. Only two prominent military figures had made it to cabinet level: the Duke of Wellington and Lord Kitchener.

Even the terms right-wing and left-wing were still alien to most Britons in 1918. The two main pre-war parties, Conservatives and Liberals, represented interests not ideologies. Both were wedded to parliamentary traditions, although they could interpret the role and powers of Parliament differently, as was seen over the crisis in the House of Lords. The rising Labour Party was far more cautious than its Continental socialist counterparts, as the brief tenures in office between the wars proved. Its origins were Methodist rather than Marxist. Syndicalism had been in vogue among some union members but these were always a minority of the working class. As Labour made steady progress up to 1929, this became less appealing when it seemed possible that socialism could be achieved through parliamentary means. The failure of the General Strike in 1926 showed the limits of union power.

This dislike of the extremes spared Britain the horrors of Nazi Germany or the Soviet Union, but the general faith in parliament meant ex-servicemen were dependent on the willingness of government to help veterans. Sadly, they were let down by all three parties in the interwar years.

SPEAKING UP: VETERANS' ORGANISATIONS AFTER THE WAR

'[The British Legion] was a product of the First World War and the combination of altruism towards, and fear of, the working class ... '

Mark Garnett and Richard Weight[1]

Who would represent veterans after the war? Britain's tiny pre-war army meant there was no equivalent to the American Legion – a pressure group that had extracted huge concessions from governments since the Civil War. So when the settlement for ex-servicemen was being decided in the immediate aftermath, British veterans were effectively leaderless.

The first organisation to speak for ex-servicemen was a small group called the National Association of Discharged Sailors and Soldiers (NADSS) set up in 1916. Despite its name, it wasn't national; NADSS' roots were firmly in the Labour movement, formed by working-class ex-soldiers in Blackburn. Then came the National Federation of Discharged and Demobilised Sailors and Soldiers (NFDDSS) in the following year. Again, it represented only a section of the armed forces. The NFDDSS, whose slogan was 'Justice before Charity', had strong connections with the Liberal Party. It did not allow officers to join unless they were commissioned from the ranks.

Unlike the right-wing American Legion, both of these organisations were on the left and, in the febrile political atmosphere of 1917, this worried the British Government. The Russian Revolution was becoming more radical, partly led by socialist troops, and the government saw a need for conservative soldiers' associations to counterbalance anything similar in Britain. Sir John Norton Griffiths, a Tory MP and Lieutenant Colonel, was the guiding force for the Comrades of the Great War. It soon garnered heavyweight support. The Earl of Derby, Secretary of State for War, asked local lord lieutenants and chairmen of the

Territorial Force Associations for help. *The Times, Daily Mail and Daily Express* gave the Comrades of the Great War a great deal of publicity, which helped raise £35,000[2] in its opening meeting.

Even more prosperous was the Officers' Association (OA), partly set up at the instigation of Douglas Haig – it raised over £637,000 in 1920 alone.[3] The OA received the support of Admiral of the Fleet Earl Beatty and Air Marshall Sir Hugh Trenchard.[4] It was clear that both the OA and Comrades of the Great War could gain more funds than the NADSS and NFDDSS. The financial pressure for a merger was increased when wartime canteen profits, some £7 million pounds,[5] became available for ex-servicemen, but only if the different groups merged. This provided the financial incentive to form a single organisation. In May 1921 the British Legion was born, though by this time the main elements of post-war reconstruction had already been decided.

The Legion's first Chairman was T.F. Lister from the NFDDSS but its leadership was Conservative in sympathies. Its President was Douglas Haig, who dismissed even Lloyd George's moderate post-war reforms as 'Bolshevik'. Years later, Haig said the Legion 'saved this country from bloodshed during the critical years since the Armistice', and 'I got these organisations into the British Legion, and the Bolshevist organisations were broken up'.[6] Establishment credentials were further burnished by a Royal Charter in 1925 when the Prince of Wales became its patron. The Duke of Connaught, during the Charter presentation, praised the Legion for its 'steadying influence'.[7] Its National Executive Council was disproportionately made up of former officers – men less likely to question government decisions. Britain has been generally lucky to have had little military involvement in politics, but in this case veterans did not benefit from a leadership who wouldn't push government hard. General Sir Frederick Maurice, the Legion's next president, said that it would not be 'a body of agitators to set out to rob the public treasury for our own advantage'.[8]

The Legion's constitution also discouraged radicalism. It called for the 'promotion of unity between classes', which Niall Barr argues perpetuated the existing social order.[9] It wanted 'to inculcate a sense of loyalty to the Crown, Community and Nation' but ministers used this against the Legion, pointing out that loyalty to the Crown could also mean loyalty to the king's minsters. Royal endorsement was also a double-edged sword. It was excellent for fundraising, but it tended to blunt political protest. Politicians and civil servants reminded the Legion on several occasions that it was 'intolerable that direct political action should be taken by a body which is under Royal patronage'.[10] The Legion generally backed down.

At a local level, Conservatives usually ran the Legion in rural areas and small towns. The Legion, like the Women's Institute, the Chamber of Commerce and the National Farmers' Union, could be the Tory Party at play. Hamilton and Ball wrote that by the end of the 1930s the Legion 'differed hardly in any respect from a collection of Conservative working men's clubs'.[11] Often the local elite took prominent roles: in the Leebotwood branch the chairman was the squire, Major Trevor Corbett; in Oxfordshire the local president was the Duke of Marlborough; in Somerset the Duke of Somerset.[12]

This was not true of all branches, particularly in big cities and industrial areas. Here they were not so hierarchical or dominated by upper-class ex-officers. The attitudes to Britain's General Strike illustrated this divide. In 1926 the TUC called out its members to support the miners who were in a bitter industrial dispute with mine owners. The Legion declared itself neutral in the dispute and then showed a distinct lack of neutrality. It issued a statement saying members should 'support such steps as are taken to ensure the interests of the community'. This rather bland statement was then followed up by a press release saying that ex-servicemen should 'come forward once more and offer their services in any way that might be needed by the authorities'. This crossed the line for many – urban branches like Paddington and Stoke Newington lost members and areas with strong union representation[13] saw Legion members help struggling families of strikers with soup kitchens and food supplies.

The Legion's political intervention during the General Strike was a rarity. It generally steered clear of overt party politics. It did issue a questionnaire in the 1922 general election on ex-servicemen's issues with a view to backing sympathetic candidates. This action was never repeated, as candidates promised much and then failed to deliver once elected. The Legion then chose quiet persuasion rather than open endorsement. This had advantages when looking at the experience of Germany where veterans' associations were overtly political, particularly the extreme right-wing Stahlhelm, who could boast over half a million members by 1930. The Stahlhelm barred Jewish veterans and during the Great Depression campaigned violently for an end to democracy. It adopted close links to Fascist Italy and one of its founding members, Franz Seldte, served in Hitler's cabinet. After the Nazis came to power the Stahlhelm was merged with the Nazi's Stormtroopers to become a single organisation. The bromide of the Legion helped make Britain a calmer place.

The Legion used its national status to draw attention to servicemen's issues. Respectability gained them press coverage and access to government ministers. This resulted in a number of successes: it secured priority for ex-servicemen in filling 75 per cent of government-aided work schemes, the continuation of a separate Ministry of Pensions, and the maintenance of pension rates when the cost of living fell.[14] However, the political caution of the Legion's leadership meant that this influence was never fully exploited. It's fair to say that the Legion often seemed more intent on not upsetting the government than campaigning for soldiers' rights. The government felt safe in refusing Legion demands for a National Work Scheme in 1923 to provide jobs for the rapidly growing army of unemployed ex-servicemen. The same year it refused Legion demands to remove the seven-year time limit on war pension claims and a year later to compel employers to accept a quota of disabled veterans,[15] despite this being a legal requirement in many countries. During the 1930s the Legion achieved no significant changes in policy. This seemed to satisfy the leadership of the Legion, who believed the settlement for ex-servicemen was now adequate. The chairman, Major Fetherston-Godley, in a telephone conversation with the Ministry of Pensions, said that the Legion 'has no fault to find with the war Pensions system, which they regard as satisfactory'. Rank-and-file members were unhappy and called for a change to the Legion charter at the 1926 Annual Conference, so it could engage in more political activities. Haig consulted with Prime Minister Stanley Baldwin and the proposal was quietly blocked.[16] This caution frustrated the grass roots. At the 1924 Annual Conference the leadership was criticised for 'not sufficient push' and 'too much education and not enough action'. [17] There were resolutions on a yearly basis calling for a more aggressive approach to improving war pensions. When the government refused to revisit this issue at the height of the Great Depression in 1933, the fissure between the leadership and ordinary members took a very public turn. A new editor of the *Legion*, C.E. Carroll, took Ministry of Pensions to task over government parsimony and that more than half of pension appeals had been upheld against the Ministry's initial ruling.[18] Instead of backing Carroll, the Legion obsequiously apologised to the government on two occasions. During a dinner attended by the Minister of Pensions, Major Tryon, former Legion Chairman Colonel Crosfield said that the *Legion* editor 'wrote things which were most unfair to the Ministry of Pensions and to our good friend, Major Tryon, whom we are delighted to see here this evening'.[19] Incensed, the membership voted unanimously at the next Annual Conference for the National Executive Committee to retract the apology. The motion was ignored, an indication of how little power ordinary members had. The leadership dismissively described these debates as 'blowing-off sessions'. Carroll was sacked later in the year.

Another problem for the Legion was its relatively small membership. Even after several recruitment drives it was just over 300,000 out of 5 million veterans who survived the war.[20] This made it difficult to present themselves as representative of ex-servicemen. Contrast this with the Royal New Zealand Returned and Services' Association (RSA), New Zealand's equivalent veterans' organisation. It could claim 70 per cent[21] of all servicemen *during* the war. This made it a hugely powerful advocate from the start and the RSA used this power to pressure the government into a generous settlement. It showed no fear of upsetting the establishment nor did it rely on public charity. It demanded and received rights that it believed was the soldiers' due. As discussed in Chapter 10, priority was given in employment to ex-servicemen. For the disabled, there were well-funded hospitals and a weekly pension of £3 10*s* 4*d* and, unlike Britain, married men were given a larger settlement. The wages of the able-bodied were supplemented for those learning new trades, free education was given to all veterans whose studies had been disrupted during the war and End of Service gratuities were three times higher than the UK.[22] All this was impressive and a marked contrast to how the British soldier fared. However, the leadership remained unmoved. Fetherston-Godley remarked, 'A great country like our own, which is admittedly beginning to solve its economic difficulties, should not have to learn from her colonies and dominions how to treat men disabled in fighting her battles.'[23] Many ex-servicemen disagreed. Viscount Castlerosse, a disabled veteran, wrote in The *Sunday Express*, 'The Americans, who never went through anything like we did, are on a much better basis. Instead of demanding our rights we went hat in hand asking for charity. We ought to have gone bayonet in hand demanding our rights.'[24]

The British Legion charity work was more successful than its political activities. The Legion's fundraising abilities were impressive, built around the Poppy Appeal every November. It's possibly the single most successful charitable venture in British history. The idea didn't originate with the Legion but they made it their own.[*] Poppies went on sale in Britain in 1921. The next year the Legion was selling 30 million; by the end of the 1930s the sales exceeded half a million pounds a year.[25] These impressive figures enabled the Legion to finance a number of ventures. The Poppy Factory provided work for disabled veterans and funds were made available to take over the running of the Preston Hall Colony, in Kent, for ex-servicemen suffering from TB[26] – without the Legion, the centre would have closed. Ex-servicemen in distress were helped through Employment and Relief Committees. They certainly made a difference to many ex-servicemen and their families between the wars but the work of the Legion could never make up for the neglect of veterans by successive governments.

On the social side, the Legion opened a large number of clubs throughout the country – 2,600 by 1925.[27] They were a place to meet fellow veterans. One ex-servicemen said the reason he joined was a desire 'to perpetuate that wonderful spirit of comradeship forged in the service and especially on the battlefield, where ALL men were real chums and gave real service, friendship, shared joys and sorrows, work and play, and even their rations'.[28] He particularly wanted to help 'disabled chums' who he felt 'nobody seems to want' any more. Disabled veterans joined in disproportionate numbers because of the empathy Legion members

---

[*] The sale of poppies was inspired by Canadian officer John McCrae's poem 'In Flanders Fields', first in America and then in France.

often showed. Going to the Legion club could have a therapeutic value for men still disturbed by their war experiences. Many found it hard to discuss these with their families, so having a few drinks with other veterans could be a blessed relief. Special nights were held, such as 'Dug-out parties', which sought to recreate the atmosphere of the Front with trench songs, army rations and a sprinkling of barbed wire. These clubs also organised outings, formed brass bands and staged sporting contests – like the Maurice Cup for branch football teams. Some of the many unemployed veterans joined because 'it was a place where you could get together and socialise, and it was some small compensation for not being at work – and you could commiserate with others in the same situation'.[29] The clubs were not to everyone's taste, as the small percentage of veterans who attended them suggests.

Another organisation that wanted to continue the spirit of comradeship was Toc H (or Talbot House**). Toc H was set up by an army chaplain, Philip 'Tubby' Clayton. It was a converted hop merchant's house in Poperinge, Belgium, where men could grab a few hours of peace before returning to the Front. Toc H was Christian, but non-denominational, and made no attempt to convert those who stayed, rather emphasising the importance of friendship – a 'haven in hell'. The values of Toc H stayed with Clayton after the war, and he built up an organisation dedicated to fellowship, service, fairmindedness and the Kingdom of God. Perhaps this can be defined in a note from a soldier in 1917:

> Will you pray very earnestly for me that I may have strength given to me to do that which is right and to make an effort to help others; not so much by what I say, but by my whole life. I have wandered away very far, but I want to put things right; and the prayers of Talbot House will mean much to me.[30]

The core of the original post-war group were ex-servicemen, though it was not exclusive for them. Indeed, hundreds of branches were established in Britain and the Dominions; Toc H were particularly associated with LEPRA and the National Blood Transfusion Service.[31]

There were some radical alternatives to the Legion like the National Union of Ex-Servicemen (NUX). They claimed up to 300,000 members, often ex-Federation men, but the figure was probably a third of that number.[32] In the rather jittery atmosphere of the period they were labelled Bolshevik. Winston Churchill

---

** Toc was signaller's speak for T. Talbot was the name of the brother of Tubby Clayton's senior chaplain, Neville Talbot, who had been killed in the war; the original house was dedicated to him.

referred to them when he said there were those who wanted 'to provoke an out-break in the form of a mutiny or general strike, or preferably both together, in the hope that a general smash and overthrow of society may result … to make a general overthrow on the Russian model'.[33] Some of NUX's rhetoric seemed to suggest this. Ernest Mander, ex-Royal Artillery and NUX's first General Secretary, said, 'No one should join the union unless he is joining for a fight,'[34] but in truth it was closer to the left-wing of the Labour than the Communists. They called for direct action, but within the peaceful traditions of British socialism, which pre-ferred mass meetings* to Lee-Enfields in Belgravia. Their call for nationalisation, help for unemployed ex-servicemen and better pension provisions hardly made them Britain's answer to Russia's Red Guards.

Some in NUX were not immune from the fears that the Russian Revolution had caused – but from a left-wing standpoint. They believed the other ex-ser-vicemen's organisations would be used as strike breakers or a 'White Guard' against the working class. David Englander, NUX's main historian, points out that when this did not materialise it was the beginning of the end for NUX. By 1920, as the political atmosphere had calmed down, it pointedly refused to amalgamate with the British Legion and often merged with Independent Labour Party** branches instead.

The British Limbless Ex-Servicemen's Association (BLESMA) was set up in 1932 to represent disabled veterans, partly out of frustration with the Legion's caution. BLESMA campaigned for disabled veterans at a time when the Great Depression was at its height. Most could not find work and were reliant on inadequate pensions and charity. BLESMA commissioned a study of their plight which garnered widespread publicity but no remedial action from the Ministry of Pensions. BLESMA numbers were small, with fewer than 2,000 members,[35] and it was established too late to make an impact on the settlement for disabled veterans. It would have more success after the Second World War.

Another veteran's organisation that was prepared to campaign aggressively for veterans was the ESWS, the first organisation to speak exclusively for veterans suffering from PTSD. As a charity, the ESWS did good work but it also wanted to draw attention to the plight of many shell-shocked ex-servicemen. The ESWS incurred the ire of the government by pointing to the 5,000 veterans stuck in asylums as pauper lunatics and receiving no special treatment. This was despite official assurances that any soldier suffering from shell shock would be treated separately and, if soldiers did end up in regular state mental institutions, they would be given privileges like wearing their own clothes and receiving a financial

---

* There were 47,000 meetings alone, according to David Englander.
** The ILP were a left-wing group affiliated to the British Labour Party.

allowance. The first Minister of Reconstruction, Dr Christopher Addison, had stated it is 'vital that this class of men should escape the stigma and disabilities of being classed as lunatics'.[36] Their campaign gained publicity. In the *Daily Herald* the ESWS argued that a mentally ill ex-serviceman 'in lucid moments realises bitterly that he will have to spend the rest of his life among these unfortunate pauper lunatics'. The Ministry of Pensions countered that these ex-servicemen were classed as private patients in county asylums.[37] Even when the ESWS was raising money for their recuperation home at Eden Manor they managed to highlight the government's neglect, stating that housing soldiers in pauper lunatic asylums was not only 'a serious slight to our defenders, but … a hindrance to their recovery and a stigma handicapping their return to honourable employment'.[38]

The government's response, and how the ESWS dealt with it, illustrates the difficulties ex-servicemen organisations faced in campaigning for veterans' rights. Articles were published in pro-government newspapers like *The Morning Post* not only rebutting ESWS allegations but also attacking the charity itself, which was accused of taking money from veterans in asylums[39] and misusing funds. Prominent Conservative MPs like General Hunter Weston and Major William Colfox joined the assault. In 1924, Prince George withdrew his name as a patron and Buckingham Palace complained about an ESWS pamphlet that attacked the government's treatment of shell-shocked veterans, which also claimed the king as a donor.[40] Finally, the Legion waded in on the side of the establishment. Previously it had worked closely with the ESWS but now the Legion expressed its satisfaction with how shell-shocked veterans were being treated. The ESWS caved in. Box collections and membership fees were not enough to sustain its activities so it was reliant on individual, large donations from wealthy people. These might dry up if the charity gained a reputation for radicalism. At the time, the ESWS was trying to get on the Ministry of Pensions approved list of homes[41] so couldn't afford to upset the authorities. The ESWS withdrew the offending pamphlet and focused on charitable activities rather than campaigning. It continued to do valuable work in this field but shell-shock sufferers now had no one to speak on their behalf.

This sadly illustrates the problems of veterans' associations after the war. They were not as big as their equivalents in other countries and lacked funding and political muscle as a consequence. Too dependent on the goodwill of donors and easily pressured by the government, as charities they achieved much but as campaigning organisations they were limited.

20

ARTISTS' RIFLES: THE WAR AND CULTURE

Wherever war is spoken of
I find
The war that was called Great invades the mind … '

Vernon Scannell, 'The Great War'

The First World War was bound to affect the creative artists and writers who fought in it. Such was its horror and heroism that many ex-servicemen produced their best work: from the surrealist landscapes of Paul Nash to the modernist poetry of David Jones. Some experimented with new ways of expression; others found traditional forms more suitable for what they had experienced.

The war poets have received the most attention. Poetry is the perfect medium for conveying immediate experience and emotion – the 'spontaneous overflow of powerful feelings' as Wordsworth put it. With such short life expectancies, soldiers did not have the time for longer works; the best British war novels were produced years later. Britain also had a stronger literary tradition than artistic. Paul Fussell outlined just how well read the front-line generation was in his seminal book *The Great War and Modern Memory:* 'the belief in the educative powers of classical and English literature was extremely strong … the appeal of popular education and "self-improvement" was at its peak.'[1]

Yet the Edwardian era was hardly a golden age for poetry. Henry Newbolt estimated there were 1,000 active poets before the war, most of whom could be described as part of the 'Georgian' movement.[2] These included talented writers, like Walter de la Mare and Rupert Brooke, but much of the verse was derivative and mediocre. They abandoned the high-flown diction of Victorian poets but Georgians were essentially a backward-looking movement, taking the earlier Romantics and their interest in nature for inspiration. But their 'crocus-crowded lyrics', in Sassoon's words, rarely conveyed the power of the natural world and the emotions it invoked in the way Wordsworth's and Keats' did. At its worst, the poetry was like a suburban couple hiring a country cottage for the weekend to 'get back to nature'.

Not surprisingly, Georgian habits were present in early war poems, notably in Rupert Brooke's five war sonnets. Tremendously popular, running to twenty-four impressions by June 1918, the sonnets eschewed any modernist developments in language or structure (they're sonnets after all) and captured the patriotic optimism at the start of the war in the famous lines:

> If I should die, think only this of me:
> That there's some corner of a foreign field
> That is for ever England.

Brooke has been criticised for his naivety but he was killed before he saw action, dying from sepsis on the way to Gallipoli. If he had lived to see Passchendaele and the Somme would he have still written lines like:

> Now, God be thanked Who has matched us with His hour,
> And caught our youth, and wakened us from sleeping,
> With hand made sure, clear eye, and sharpened power,
> To turn, as swimmers into cleanness leaping.
>
> War Sonnet 1: Peace

Siegfried Sassoon and Wilfred Owen didn't become bitter realists straight away, even after spells in the trenches. As late as 1916 Sassoon was writing verses little different from, though inferior to, Brooke:

> You and the winds ride out together;
> Your company the world's great weather,
> The clouds your plume, the glittering sky
> A host of swords in harmony,
> With the whole loveliness of light flung forth to lead you through the fight.

But by the next year he published his anti-war collection *The Old Huntsman and Other Poems*, which included verses like:

> I'd like to see a Tank come down the stalls,
> Lurching to rag-time tunes, or 'Home, sweet Home',
> And there'd be no more jokes in Music-halls
> To mock the riddled corpses round Bapaume.
>
> 'Blighters'

Safe with his wound, a citizen of life.

He hobbled blithely through the garden gate,

And thought: 'Thank God they had to amputate!'

'The One-Legged Man'

The diction had become harder. There's no pseudo-medieval notions of chivalry and honour. By all accounts Sassoon was an outstanding subaltern, brave to the point of recklessness (he was nicknamed 'Mad Jack'), but the horrors of the Western Front and the death of close friends left him angry and disillusioned – a feeling that did not disappear for the rest of his long life. Brooke thought the war could act as a sort of moral purification for the youth of Britain, but in Sassoon's *Base Details* it's the old who are the lucky ones, as the 'scarlet Major' who 'when the war was done and youth stone dead/I'd toddle safely home and die — in bed'.

Owen still had elements of Romanticism in his later poems – one reason W.B. Yeats excluded him from the *Oxford Book of Modern Verse 1892–1935*. Yet, the war rapidly changed Owen from a sub-Keatsian dabbler to a mature poet before he died.* At Sassoon's suggestion, he purged his poems of elevated diction or used it as an ironic device. Like in 'Dulce et Decorum Est' after his description of a gas attack:

My friend, you would not tell with such high zest

To children ardent for some desperate glory,

The old Lie: Dulce et decorum est

Pro patria mori.

Owen experimented with pararhyme in poems like 'Strange Meeting' '(And by his smile, I knew that sullen hall/By his dead smile I knew we stood in Hell)', but like most British war poets, he largely kept to traditional forms. The realism of 'Anthem for Doomed Youth' can hide its use of iambic pentameter. Unlike art, British literature had seen little experimentation before the war. One of the few moderns was T.E. Hulme, whose 'Trenches: St Eloi' is decidedly imagist:**

The Germans have rockets. The English have no rockets.

Behind the line, cannon, hidden, lying back miles.

Beyond the line, chaos.

---

* Yeats had a dim view of Owen. In a letter to Dorothy Wellesley, he thought him 'unworthy of the poets' corner of a country newspaper'.

** Imagists were Anglo-American modernist poets focusing on precise imagery.

Similarly, Herbert Read's forensic descriptions in free verse were clearly influenced by imagism.

Hulme did not survive the war, nor did Rosenberg and Owen. Add Charles Sorley, killed at Loos, and Edward Thomas, shot through the chest at Arras in 1917, and the war poets seem an unlucky lot. Partly this was due to their social background: most were middle to upper class*** and so became officers, exposing themselves to greater danger in the process. Writers who survived naturally wrote to make sense of what they had lived through. It was the dominant theme in Sassoon's long literary career. Though he turned to religion as a subject after converting to Catholicism, his best poetry still reflected on the war and its aftermath. He attacked the sanitisation of the war ('On Passing the New Menin Gate') or the tendency to forget its unpleasantness ('Aftermath').**** Sassoon needed some distance to form a 'coherent picture'[3] to start his major post-war project. In 1928 he published *Memoirs of a Fox-Hunting Man*, a semi-autobiographical account of George Sherston, a privileged young man's life in Edwardian England. His outdoor sporting life (cricket was a passion) and material comfort clearly mirror Sassoon's youth. This seemed an odd departure for an anti-war poet. Was this an escape? The next book in the series showed not. *Memoirs of an Infantry Officer* (1930) deals with Sherston's experiences in the war, which again partly parallel Sassoon's. The first book's purpose is clear, to contrast Sherston's awful war with the idyllic, but shattered, Edwardian world. The final part of the trilogy deals with Sherston's stay in Craiglockhart mental hospital. It is a theme that writers turned to again and again, that a pre-war arcadia was destroyed by the first mechanised war, with the principal victims being those who had served at the Front. Some critics rate this trilogy as better than his poetry. Howard Spring, in the *Evening Standard*, called it 'the most satisfying piece of autobiography to be published in our time'. Perhaps more than any other writer in this chapter, the war gave Sassoon's life definition and helped him produce his best work.

It's hard to escape the notion that the war also elevated some minor writers like Frederick Manning, an Australian who served with the British Army and fought on the Somme, and who would have faded into obscurity but for *Her Privates We* (1930). Hemingway described it as 'The finest and noblest book of men in war'. The novel's quiet brilliance lies as much in the details of a Tommy's life when not fighting, as it does in the combat scenes. Richard Aldington's literary reputation is not confined to his war novel *Death of a Hero* (1929) but it's

---

***   Rosenberg was an exception. From an impoverished Jewish background, he stood at at malnourished 5ft tall.

****   'Taking your peaceful share of Time, with joy to spare. / But the past is just the same--and War's a bloody game ... Have you forgotten yet?'

what he's best known for. A troubled man even before the war, he grew more so, but it gave his writing bite. Similarly, R.C. Sheriff could hardly be described as a one-hit wonder, having a long and distinguished career as a novelist, playwright and Oscar-nominated screenwriter, but *Journey's End* is easily his most famous work. A huge hit in 1928 when it ran for two years in the West End, it's frequently revived and has been made into a film four times.* Like Owen and Sassoon's poetry, it benefits from the writer's own war experiences (Vimy Ridge, Loos, Passchendaele), which he attempted to render as realistically as possible. The stage was the perfect medium for the claustrophobic atmosphere of a dug-out where the play is set – the book version does not work as well. However, not all ex-servicemen produced their best work about the war. Ford Madox Ford's quartet *Parade's End* (1924–28) is still highly rated. It's complex and experimental – more about the effect of war on the mind. But his literary reputation still rests on *The Good Soldier: A Tale of Passion* (1915), set before the war despite the title.

What all these writers have in common is a direct experience of the war. This made them a minority (less than 25 per cent of British war poets were in uniform)[4] yet it is their work we still read. The obvious conclusion is that non-combatants could not have adequately described what the First World War was actually like, but previously writers had imagined wars without actually fighting in them. Tolstoy never served in the Russian army during Napoleon's invasion but the battle scenes in *War and Peace* are brilliantly described. The newness of this industrialised warfare was beyond the imagination of those who had not been on the front line. Tolstoy, after all, had fought in the Crimean War, which was not so very different from Napoleonic encounters. Nothing like the battles of the Somme and Passchendaele had ever occurred so, not surprisingly, the best civilian novels written during the war were about the home front, like D.H. Lawrence's *Women in Love* and H.G. Wells' *Mr Britling Sees it Through*. Contemporary battlefront fiction rarely rose above the 'Boy's Own' variety, complete with glorious cavalry charges at the end. The best war novels had to wait for the demobilisation of writers who had actually been there.

They often remained obsessed by the trenches for years. Sassoon is the obvious example, but Edmund Blunden never got over his war. A year before his death he wrote, 'My experiences in the First World War have haunted me all my life and for many days I have, it seemed, lived in that world rather than this.'[5] This pastoral poet of the English countryside was prolific, but it is his distinguished soldier's memoir, *Undertones of War* (1928), that is his most popular work. Robert Graves' *Goodbye to All That* (1929), the memoir where the war featured so prominently,

---

*   In 1930, 2017, a German version in 1931 and as *Aces High* in 1976, which is set in the Royal Flying Corps rather than the infantry.

was meant to serve as an end to his life as a 'soldier poet'. But Graves never quite said goodbye; despite later being dismissive of his war writings, he could still remember trench songs in his dotage, if little else. Fussell described *Goodbye to All That*, along with Blunden's and Sassoon's trilogy, as 'one of the permanent works engendered by memories of the war'.[6]

Herbert Read must count as another writer whose career was formed by war. He had an unusual background for an officer, having grown up in a Halifax orphanage when his father died. Though he had written before, it was his collection of war poems *Naked Warriors* (1919) that marked his real literary debut. Like Blunden and Sassoon, he was haunted for the rest of his life, completing the last part of his autobiography in the 1960s, which prominently featured the war. He was almost manically active after being demobilised. Poet, novelist, art and literary critic, co-founder of the Institute of Contemporary Art and defender of modernism, he once explained:

I am always working under tremendous pressure, a fact you never seem to realize, and … devoting myself to other people, with no thought of my own genius or … fame … I found myself in a situation (in this country) where I was the only person with the … energy … to take on the defence of modern art. I would willingly have stood down … but I belong to a generation … decimated by the war, and people who might have done this necessary task – men like T.E. Hulme – were killed in that war, and I found myself a solitary survivor.[7]

Unlike Sassoon he had a more ambiguous view of the war, which might make him more typical of surviving soldiers. Read wrote that it was both a 'snake's head' and a 'ladder'.[8] He recognised the horrors and idiocies (he called it the 'quintessence of futility')[9] as well as the harmful effects on ex-servicemen ('Of the many who returned and yet were dead').[10] But the war also was the making of Read: a provincial orphan who now acquired the confidence to prosper in literary London. He described the war as giving 'self-understanding in battle'.[11]

The war was interwoven indirectly in writers' work as well. Tolkien's *Lord of the Rings* seems far removed from modern combat, but his trench experiences are there. He later wrote:

One has indeed personally to come under the shadow of war to feel fully its oppression; but as the years go by it seems now often forgotten that to be caught in youth by 1914 was no less hideous an experience than to be involved in 1939 and the following years.[12]

The war-ravaged landscapes of Mordor or the Dead Marshes that Tolkien wrote 'owe something to Northern France after the Battle of the Somme'.[13] The forms of long-dead soldiers disfigure the ground, 'grim faces and evil, noble faces and sad. Many faces proud and fair … But all foul, all rotting, all dead.'[14] Though he hated the war, he came away with a respect for the working-class troops he commanded. Like many front-line officers, he mixed with people from different social backgrounds for the first time. The character 'Sam Gamgee' was 'a reflection of the English soldier, of the privates and batmen I knew in the 1914 war, and recognised as so far superior to myself'.[15] This was also true of Sassoon and Graves, who moved to the left politically in the 1920s because of their experiences. Sassoon learnt that life, 'for the majority of the population, is an unlovely struggle against unfair odds, culminating in a cheap funeral'.

However, the war was a mixed blessing for some surviving writers. They had, after all, lost years of potential creativity, as Herbert Read noted about Wyndham Lewis: 'He is very bitter about the war: he feels that four years of the most vital period of his career have been torn from his life.'[16] Wyndham Lewis had been at the forefront of British art and literature in 1914 as the leader of the Vorticists, but never attained that position again. Much of the experimentation that had gone on during and immediately after the war was not by veterans. The vanguard was dominated by men and women who had not fought: D.H. Lawrence, Ezra Pound, T.S. Eliot, James Joyce, Virginia Woolf, Aldous Huxley. They had developed their styles in safety, dominating literary magazine and editorships of publishing houses. They were not especially welcoming to returning writers whose attempts at realistically depicting war were at odds with modernism – T.S. Elliot dismissed their work as mere 'reporting'.

Ex-servicemen also struggled, at least initially, if they were critical of the war. Memoirs of senior officers and positive accounts of Britain's glorious victory certainly sold in the aftermath but the mood of the nation wasn't ready for the war novels and poetry we now remember; they had to wait until the late 1920s to find an audience or even a publisher. A long time in a writer's career.

I am a messenger who will bring back word from the men who are fighting to those who want the war to go on forever. Feeble, inarticulate will be my message, but it will have a bitter truth and may it burn their lousy souls.[17]

Paul Nash, war artist

Britain's war artists have never received as much attention as its writers. It's a shame; talents like the Nash brothers, C.R.W. Nevinson, Henry Tonks, Stanley Spencer, Eric Kennington and Wyndham Lewis all produced fine work. Some had been soldiers, but most received honorary commissions as official war artists, which partly explains why they survived the war in greater numbers than war poets.

There was no official programme to produce art in 1914 but the head of the War Propaganda Bureau, Charles Masterman, was eventually persuaded of its value. However, the first officially commissioned war artist was an observer not a soldier. Muirhead Bone was 40 when he was given an honorary commission in 1916 to sketch the Western Front. He produced a series of competent, bloodless scenes. There is no sense of horror in 'On the Somme, Near Mametz 1916–17' but a calmness as the two soldiers talk, and another rides a horse. This could have been a drawing about a training exercise not the aftermath of one of the worst battles in British history. Wilfred Owen wrote to his mother that Bone's work was a laughing stock among the troops.[18]

Much better were the paintings by Paul Nash, Wyndham Lewis and C.R.W. Nevinson. All these artists had been at the Front before they became war artists: Nevinson was an orderly in an ambulance unit, Nash a second lieutenant, Lewis an artillery officer. This gave their work an edge that was missing in Bone's. These artists used Vorticist and Futurist techniques, as well realism, to render what the war was actually like. British painting had been more open to experiment than literature before the war and the Burlington House exhibition of war art in December 1919 reflected the degree to which war artists – with work by Nash, Wyndham Lewis, Nevinson, Spencer and William Roberts – had embraced the new. Vorticism tried to capture movement in images, Futurism celebrated the machine; both suited their subject matter. But it was not ultimately about whether a war artist was a modernist or a traditionalist, but whether he depicted the war in a truthful way. Like the poets, it was the combatants who came closest to achieving this. Bone's was realistic in the technical sense, but sanitised. Masterman, a learned, sensitive man, came to understand he needed to commission more soldiers and allowed his artists a good deal of freedom – 'Paint anything you please,'[19] he said to Nevinson. Some of the work was mediocre, like Charles Ernest Butler's dreadful *Blood and Iron* (1916), which depicts Christ comforting a figure representing Belgium as the cold-hearted Kaiser looks on unmoved. But much was good, and critical, of the war. Paul Nash did bring an honesty to his surrealist landscapes of the Western Front, as did Wyndham Lewis's Vorticist, *A Battery Shelled* (1919); his figures are angular, dehumanised automata.

After the war some artists continued to produce work of real quality. Stanley Spencer initially left the war alone after serving in Macedonia in the RAMC. He resumed a painting he'd started before joining up. He wrote, 'It is not proper or sensible to expect to paint after such experience.' Yet almost ten years later he started a series of murals for the Sandham Memorial Chapel at Burghclere based on his war service. They are among his finest work with their haunted, spiritual quality. William Orpen, never a combatant but who spent considerable time at the Front, agreed to paint three works about the Paris Peace Treaty of 1919. Yet he grew disgusted with the posturing of the politicians, who he called 'frocks', expressing views common to many ex-servicemen:

> I admit that all these little 'frocks' seemed to me very small personalities, in comparison with the fighting men I came into contact with during the war. They appeared to think so much – too much – of their own personal impor-tance, searching all the time for popularity, each little one for himself – strange little things. The fighting man alive, and those who fought and died – all the people who made the Peace Conference possible, were being forgotten, the 'frocks' reigned supreme.[20]

The last of the three paintings, *To the Unknown British Soldier*, is the most inter-esting. Instead of a group of politicians and generals (who were there in the beginning, but were eventually painted out) there is simply a coffin draped in a Union Jack. The Imperial War Museum refused to accept the picture.

The demand for war memorials offered a tremendous amount of work for sculptors (a number of them ex-servicemen) if they were prepared to work within the narrow guidelines of the commissioning committees. Most were simple affairs: a stone cross or obelisk. Some used chivalric, Christian or classical motifs that were starting to feel outmoded even by 1918, like Derwent Wood's Machine Gun Corps Memorial where an anachronistic David, having just slain Goliath, is flanked by two Vickers machine guns. A figure more at home in the Florentine Renaissance than the era of Picasso is juxtaposed against the ultimate symbol of the First World War's modernity. Few of the sculptures could be described as avant-garde, partly due to the resistance of local committees or regiments. One exception is Eric Kennington's 24th East Surrey Division War Memorial; with its cramped and (from a distance) trouserless figures, it has always divided opinion. Perhaps the only sculpture that measures up to Lutyens's Cenotaph is the Royal Artillery Memorial near Hyde Park. It's by the sculptor Charles Jagger, who saw active service in Gallipoli and the Western Front. It rejects both the formulaic and the abstract. It is realistic but unconventional. The central figure is howitzer ('no angels' wings there! No Georges and no dragons' as John Galsworthy noted), which Jagger chose for its awesome power. Below it is a cross-section of typical soldiers, including a dead man. Gavin Stamp, for the Twentieth Century Society, praised its 'truthful, brilliantly modelled realism about the brutal nature of conflict, though part of Jagger's genius was his ability to monumentalise the prosaic'.[21] Jagger's accomplishment was partly because he'd experienced the war first-hand and so rejected traditional forms of war memorials as completely inappropriate. Like so much of the best First World War art and writing, ex-servicemen were able to capture the 'bitter truth' better than any civilian could.

THE POLITICAL SCENE

'It was common ground to everyone that conditions before the War were often impossible and stupid ... no such opportunity had ever been given to any nation before – not even by the French Revolution.'

David Lloyd George[1]

Our masters – seeing us a little tired
Of war – for even wars begin to pall;
Seeing us growing restless; are inspired –
Lest we should once again begin to call
For liberty and justice, and to bawl
For things we've tended to forget of late –
To promise, lest some graves things befall,
They'll reconstruct our England while we wait.

'A Ballade of Reconstruction', W.N. Ewer[2]

For those who saw post-war reconstruction as an opportunity for reform, it began promisingly. The government instituted numerous committees and reports during the war. Ambitious and detailed plans were produced for industry, housing, health, education, agriculture and labour. The participants took their role as seriously as their counterparts in the Second World War and often came to similar conclusions about what needed to be done, like the expansion of social housing, education, welfare and the provision of public health on a national basis. It was an attempt at joined-up government where policy areas were interrelated. In particular, the issue of housing was pivotal. It was inseparable from health, as slum conditions increased diseases like tuberculosis. Without adequate housing, labour shortages would damage any economic recovery. A major house-building programme could create a million jobs and employ many of the demobilised soldiers. Poor housing was seen as a cause of industrial disputes by the Committee of Enquiry into Industrial Unrest.[3]

There were some long-time advocates of reform like Seebohm Rowntree, Beatrice Webb, Christopher Addison, Winston Churchill and William Beveridge. Lloyd George, the prime minister, had been a radical chancellor before the war and had helped steer through the welfare provisions of the last Liberal government.* Fabian socialists, 'new liberals' and progressive Tories** created a consensus for action. In part, they were a continuation of the previous reforms but the war had convinced some sceptics of the need for change. Wars shine a light on society's deficiencies – 'the spotlight effect', as it is sometimes called. Lloyd George said, 'the First World War has been like a gigantic star-shell, flashing all over the land, illuminating the country and showing up the deep, dark places. We have seen places that we have never noticed before, and we mean to put these things right.'[4] The poor health of many recruits was one example. In 1918 alone, over 1 million men were deemed unfit for front-line duty.[5] In the lowest physical category of fitness (Grade IV) the average height of a man examined in Lancashire and Cheshire was 4ft 9in.[6] This in the country with the largest empire in history.

Speed was of the essence. There was a belief that delay would be fatal to reform, and inertia and resistance would increase over time. The minutes of Lloyd George's opening address to his Reconstruction Committee captures this sense of urgency: 'The nation now was in a molten condition: it was malleable now and would continue to be so for a short time after the war, but not for long.'[7] Lloyd George was an inspired organiser and appointed men of 'push and go' like Christopher Addison, who was made Minister of Reconstruction in 1916 to coordinate the transition to peace. Addison thought reconstruction should not be a return to the pre-war world but should mould 'a better world out of the social and economic conditions which have come into being during the war'.[8]

One lasting outcome of the war was that most adults now received the vote. The complex system of property qualifications was largely swept away in the 1918 Representation of the People Act.*** Most men over 21 received the vote (women had to be 30, until 1928 when the voting age was finally equalised). It would have been politically unacceptable to deprive men who had fought for their country of the vote. The war finally realised the reformers' demand of universal manhood suffrage. In a further concession to the troops, those aged 19 and 20 were also enfranchised for the 1918 election. The electorate almost

---

* 1905–15.

** Bonar Law and Edward Carson were strong supporters of bold action, and even high Tories like Lord Salisbury were prominent advocates of government action over housing.

*** Residency requirement excluded almost 2 million men until 1928.

trebled. Ironically, many troops didn't vote as, still abroad, they didn't have time to register. Lloyd George was anxious to cash in on his wartime popularity and called the election for 14 December 1918. With only 57 per cent of the new electorate voting, it was a 'khaki election' without much khaki, but the die was cast: Britain's politicians would now have to be more sensitive to a wider range of public opinion.

So why was reconstruction so tepid compared to the reforms of the 1940s? Partly because the war ended too quickly. The conflict had been expected to go on into 1919 and politicians were caught off guard. There was still no housing legislation ready, despite its importance and the plethora of reports and recommendations the various committees had produced.* Time was lost switching prime ministers during the war. When Lloyd George replaced Asquith, he effectively started his own reconstruction plans and ignored his predecessor's. There was resistance from vested interests or opponents of reform. Poor Law Guardians, for instance, prevented any moves to abolish that most Victorian institution. They succeeded, but many destitute ex-veterans ended up in workhouses – something that reconstruction was designed to eradicate. The Local Government Board (LGB), with its powers over health, housing, local government and the Poor Law, became a beacon of obstruction under their Minister, William Hayes Fisher. Not only did they defend their political turf but they came up with little in the way of alternatives to Addison's proposals. Lloyd George prevaricated, anxious not to aggravate the spirit of wartime unity, but precious months were lost as a consequence.

The LGB's foot-dragging highlighted a major problem for the Ministry of Reconstruction. It had to work through existing ministries, unlike the Ministry of Munitions. This was another wartime department set up for a specific purpose, but it had huge, overarching powers due to the necessity of winning the war. Addison, spread thinly due to his wide remit, was increasingly isolated and dependent on the prime minister. Even when his plans might have saved money he was still met with resistance. Injured ex-servicemen who were treated during the war had to deal with a myriad of different bodies. Unemployment was dealt with by the Board of Trade, war pensions by the Ministry of Pensions and the National Insurance Commission was responsible for any previous National Insurance contributions, while the LGB still ran housing, the Poor Law and welfare. The health of a serviceman's wife and children came under the Board of Education.[9] The Reconstruction Committee recommended unifying these services under a Ministry of Health, which would have been more rational and

---

* The Salisbury Committee, the Carmichael Committee, the Tudor-Walters Committee and the Women's Housing Sub-Committee – the government was not short of information on what needed to be done.

ultimately less expensive, but as soon as this proposal became known there was resistance and a messy compromise – like so much of reconstruction.**

By 1921 reconstruction was effectively dead, as reforms had been abandoned or diluted. Post-war economic conditions became less favourable as the short boom ended. The decline in the balance of trade, inflation and persistently high unemployment meant the government focused on the economy rather than schemes now considered too costly. Conventional wisdom thought a return to the Gold Standard was essential for Britain's future prosperity and that meant eliminating the government deficit, not expanding its services. The British Government had borrowed extensively during the war, particularly from the Americans: in 1934 Britain still owed £866 million (over £40 billion in today's money). This meant the Treasury was even more hawkish than usual. The Department of Tax and Tears axed projects like Addison's expensive housing plans after only a quarter of the target had been met.[10] 'Homes for Heroes' would have to wait. Beatrice Webb, a member of the Reconstruction Committee during the war, presciently wrote, 'We are deciding on great expansions in housing, education, health. How is this expenditure, this huge war debt, to be met? If we leave it up to the Treasury no expenditure will be provided for except the interest on the War Debt.'[11]

The general election of 1918 was another setback, returning a House of Commons far less conducive to reform. The Liberal Party, the main agent of change before the war, was fatally split between supporters of Asquith and Lloyd George, who often ran against each other, ensuring the election of neither. It heralded the end of the once mighty Liberals as a party of government. Some eventually joined the Conservatives, like Winston Churchill; others felt more comfortable in Labour's ranks, like Addison. Lloyd George remained prime minister but was now dependent on Conservative support,*** as shown four years later when he was unceremoniously kicked out of office.

Labour did increase its vote by almost 2 million in 1918, however this yielded only fifteen more seats due to the unpredictability of the electoral system. Prominent anti-war Labour candidates like Philip Snowden and Ramsay MacDonald were defeated. This was galling, as most of its MPs had been broadly supportive of war and held ministerial office in the coalition. A belief that electoral reform would enfranchise Labour supporters was only partially true as 60 per cent of the working class did not vote Labour.[12] It was not yet the national party the Liberals had been. Rural areas and suburbia remained largely off-limits.

** The LGB's responsibilities were given to a new Ministry of Heath, along with the powers of the National Insurance Commission, but it was not the all-embracing ministry Addison had hoped for.

*** The make up was Conservative, 382; Coalition Liberal supporting Lloyd George, 127; Sinn Féin, 73; Labour, 57; Asquith Liberals, 36.

Though Labour would gain voters steadily throughout the 1920s, its support was still concentrated in the industrial heartlands. The split over whether to join the National Government during the Great Depression marginalised Labour in the 1930s. Their time would come after the next war.

This left the Conservative Party dominant. It provided the majority of MPs during Lloyd George's post-war coalition. After that it held power for fourteen out of the next seventeen years.* While it would be wrong to label the party as opponents of reform (with men like Winston Churchill, Harold Macmillan and Brunel Cohen as MPs), most Conservative politicians shied away from radical solutions that would have threatened the economic orthodoxy of laissez-faire economics and a balanced budget. They represented a powerful strand of opinion in Britain – those who desired to return to the world before the war. Labelled 'normalcy' in America, this was summed up by one Tory MP: 'The people of this country want the chance to live again after being buried beneath the mass of Regulations that have been imposed upon them since this War broke out.'[13] There was a nostalgic, and highly partial, longing for the Edwardian world, which limited the extent of change. Politicians didn't publicly dispute that something needed to be done for ex-servicemen, but what could be done was limited by the parameters of fiscal restraint and a minimum of government interference. One of the reasons why reform went deeper after the Second World War was there was not the same nostalgia for the 1930s; it was a decade scarred in popular memory by high unemployment, the Jarrow Marches and appeasement – the 'low, dishonest decade' in Auden's phrase. It was easier for reformers to argue for a new world after 1945.

It is doubtful things would have been much different if another party had been in control. Labour didn't form a government until 1924, after reconstruction had ended, and the settlement for veterans had largely been set in place. It lasted only ten months and was dependent on Liberal support. In 1929 it formed another minority government, which broke up in 1931 over the need for government cuts during the Great Depression. Even if it had gained a majority in parliament this wouldn't have made much of a difference. The Labour leadership was cautious and eager to prove its respectability. Bold measures would have to wait, or 'No monkeying' as Labour's first prime minister, Ramsay MacDonald, put it. Philip Snowden, Chancellor of the Exchequer in both governments, was more orthodox than any Conservative chancellor of the period and as eager as any treasury official to scotch high-spending schemes.

The Liberals were fading into permanent opposition but they still played a role in the first post-war Coalition (1918–22). Lloyd George's defenders have often

---

* Either solely or through the National Government after 1931 where it provided most MPs.

blamed his dependency on the Conservatives for the disappointments of recon-struction. Aside from the fact he was the one who engineered this situation,** Lloyd George showed himself more interested in foreign affairs than domestic reform. When he did stir himself, like recognising the need for housing legislation in 1919, it was due to domestic discontent and the 'Red Scare' gripping Europe. When those fears subsided, he was happy to throw one of his few reformers to the wolves. Christopher Addison, erstwhile Liberal ally, was removed from the Ministry of Health in 1921, to general Conservative rejoicing. Addison was seen as the chief 'squandamaniac' in the government. Lloyd George had come a long way in ten years from the radical scourge of the establishment.

Another problem was there was no critical mass of opinion to counter ortho-dox beliefs. Maynard Keynes was a lonely voice arguing against a return to the Gold Standard in the 1920s (and was ultimately vindicated). It wasn't until 1936 that he fully expounded his theories about the need for government to increase spending during recessions to counteract the effects of a slowdown in growth. When the Fabian Socialists, Beatrice and Sidney Webb, expounded similar (if less developed) theories a generation earlier they were seen as mavericks. It took the Great Depression and another world war for these beliefs to be widely accepted. It meant governments after the Second World War, whether Labour or Conservative, were prepared to treat their veterans more generously with greater educational opportunities, preferential treatment in employment and more gen-erous pensions and disability benefits. Both parties competed with each other to build the most social housing. Christopher Addison, now an elder statesman of the Labour Party, lived long enough to witness these changes. He was Leader of the House of Lords in the Attlee government and helped oversee a more gener-ous reconstruction programme second time around.

** By issuing Coupons for approved Coalition candidates before the 1918 election and withholding them from many Liberal candidates who were not thought sufficiently loyal, he maximised the number of Conservative MPs in the Coalition.

22

TO END ALL WARS: THE SEARCH FOR PEACE

'Those who had seen war — those who have experienced war — are the very people who will wish never to see it or experience it again; not only to avoid it for themselves, but to be able to hand on to those who come after a desire for peace.'
The Earl of Derby,[1] *former Secretary of State for War*

Perhaps the most depressing outcome of the war was the failure to secure a permanent peace. Ex-servicemen had fought the 'war to end all wars', yet twenty years on, Europe was squaring up for another terrible conflict. In the immediate aftermath, few could imagine this would happen. When one writer used the expression 'Second World War' in 1920 he was condemned as cynical. Private Walter Hare expressed the wish of most people when he recalled, 'I'd been one of the lucky ones. I'd survived and I hoped and felt that this was the end of war for all of us.'[2]

Between the wars, ex-servicemen reached different conclusions about how to prevent another one, but all were affected by their experiences of combat. Some veterans embraced pacifism, believing nothing could justify war again. There were chaplains who'd served in the army like Geoffrey Studdert Kennedy (better known as 'Woodbine Willie' for the cigarettes he gave troops) and Dick Sheppard (a famous 'radio parson' in the 1920s). 'War is awful,' wrote Sheppard. 'More awful than I supposed possible.' At the Front, he 'would identify himself with every dying man … sit there, just because he had promised the dying man that he would, just because he thought it might somehow comfort the poor fellow, who was long past any comfort really'.[3] Studdert Kennedy was awarded the Military Cross for helping the wounded at Messines. In 1914 he joined up out of patriotic reasons but became disillusioned. He later commented, 'War is only glorious when you buy it in the Daily Mail and enjoy it at the breakfast table. It goes

splendidly with bacon and eggs. Real war is the final limit of damnable brutality, and that's all there is in it.'[4] Neither could reconcile their religious faith with
what they had seen. Sheppard wrote in a letter to *The Manchester Guardian* 'war of
any kind or for any cause, is not only a denial of Christianity, but a crime against
humanity which is not to be permitted by civilised people'.[5]

In 1925 Sheppard protested against a victory ball being held on Armistice
Day. He commented, 'A fancy dress ball on a vast scale as a tribute to the Great
Deliverance which followed on the unspeakable agony of 1914–1918 seems to
me not so much irreligious as indecent.'[6] Instead he conducted a service that
became the annual Festival of Remembrance. Nine years later, he again wrote
to *The Manchester Guardian* asking men to pledge to never again support war
(women were thought to be already against). One hundred and thirty-five
thousand replied and this formed the basis of the Peace Pledge Union (PPU).
Sheppard's idealism led him to propose a peace army to stand between Japanese
and Chinese troops during the invasion of Manchuria. 'Most of those who read
it will laugh at us,' he admitted. Neither of these decent men lived to see the
Second World War and face the agonising decision of how pacifism could be
reconciled with opposing Nazi aggression.

Most prominent pacifists were not ex-servicemen. Two exceptions were
Siegfried Sassoon and Frank Crozier. Sassoon was hardly a typical ex-officer.
His public protest against the war in 1917 and his support for the Labour
Party in the 1920s, despite his privileged background, attest to an independent
spirit. Frank Crozier was also unusual. Born into a military family he fought in
the Boer War and supported the Curragh Mutiny. He then joined the Ulster
Volunteers and helped form the 36th (Ulster) Division. On the Western Front,
Crozier rose to the rank of brigadier. Afterwards, he put his military skills to
use and started advising the Lithuanian army. He then jumped at the chance
of seeing action by signing up with the Auxiliary Division during the Irish
War of Independence. It is only here that his career took an unusual turn. He
became disgusted over the treatment of the Irish by ex-British soldiers, dismiss-
ing twenty-one 'Auxies' for raids that left two men dead. He later resigned
when ordered to reinstate them. After this, Crozier stood unsuccessfully as a
Labour MP. Unlike Sassoon, it was the Irish uprising not the First World War
that led to his pacifism.

Appeasement in the 1930s had a wider appeal among ex-servicemen, as it did
with the population in general. The word appeasement is now associated with
the failure to oppose Hitler but, unlike pacifism, it was never about avoiding
conflict at any cost; rather, appeasers believed that every possible avenue should
be exhausted before war was declared. Neville Chamberlain, the prime minister
most associated with appeasement, increased Britain's rearmament programme
while negotiating with Hitler.

The leadership of the British Legion broadly adopted appeasement and attempted to foster better relations with Germany. The Prince of Wales, a former Grenadier Guard* and the Legion's patron, told the 1935 Annual Conference, 'There could be no more suitable body or organisation to stretch forth the hand of friendship to the Germans than the men who had fought them and had now forgotten all about it'.[7] A Legion delegation led by Major Francis Fetherston-Godley then went to Berlin and was cordially received by Hitler. They were fooled by his apparent sincerity but so were many experienced politicians who met him. Lloyd George came away from a meeting declaring Germany 'does not want war ... I have never seen a happier people than the Germans, and Hitler is one of the greatest of the many great men I have met'.[8] To criticise both the appeasers and pacifist ex-servicemen for their naivety is to forget that most British people shared the view in the 1930s that war solved nothing. This was the era when the Oxford Union voted for a motion 'that this House will in no circumstances fight for its King and Country'. The university had provided a disproportionate share of officers in the First World War and a disproportionate number of casualties. Now, many of the next generation were embracing a position little different from Dick Sheppard's.

The Legion certainly received the red-carpet treatment in Germany. After meeting the Führer, there was a drive past friendly, cheering crowds. They talked to the SS leader Heinrich Himmler, who Fetherston-Godley described as 'an unassuming man, anxious to do the best for his country'.[9] They got a chance to see some of Himmler's work in a visit to Dachau concentration camp, where inmates seemed well treated. They were duped of course: the inmates were SS men in disguise.[10] They would be fooled time and time again. On further trips to Germany they met former fighter pilot Hermann Goering and Hitler again. He chatted about his experiences at the Front and his respect for the British Army. German veterans came to Britain where they visited the Poppy Factory and the Royal Hospital, Chelsea. By 1938 the Nazis had already destroyed much of the Treaty of Versailles,** yet the Legion still offered to act as observers in a plebiscite in the Sudetenland.*** Three days before the war started, Sir Frederick Maurice, the Legion's president, appealed to German soldiers not to take part in

---

*   Though he saw little direct action as heir to the throne.

**   They had marched troops into the demilitarized zone in the Rhineland, broken naval limits (with the connivance of the British Government), introduced conscription for the German Army and invaded Austria.

*** The Sudetenland was a disputed area of Czechoslovakia that had a large German population and was claimed by the Nazi regime as part of Germany. The Czechs were reluctantly pushed by Britain and France to accept German demands and hold a plebiscite, which would obviously result in a transfer of the area to Germany. Hitler simply took the territory, halting the plebiscite.

the forthcoming Polish invasion. Any hope of avoiding conflict was long past, yet Maurice was still clutching at straws.

With hindsight, it is easy to see where the Legion went wrong. Its leaders assumed that senior Nazis were serious about avoiding war, and the old soldiers they met in Germany thought the same way as the Legion did – that the mutual respect soldiers had for each other during the war could be carried into peacetime. Lieutenant Colonel Graham Seton Hutchison, in *Legion*, approvingly quoted Germany's former army chief, General von Seeckt: 'The soldier, having experience of war, fears it far more than the doctrinaire who, being ignorant of war, talks only of peace.'[11] Brian Harding, author of a study on the Legion, describes this feeling among soldiers as a 'tremendous sense among them of being men apart'.[12]

We now know the Legion was being used. The German experience of the First World War gave ex-soldiers a different outlook. This was prevalent in, but not confined to, the Nazi Party. Many Germans thought they were robbed of victory in the First World War. Major General Frederick Maurice described their armies' return:

> The reception of the German troops by the German people, their march into the German towns through triumphal arches and beflagged streets with their helmets crowned with laurels, and the insistent statements in Germany that the German armies had not been defeat *that the Armistice had been accepted to save bloodshed, and to put an end to the sufferings of the women and children aroused amazement and disgust in the victors* [Author's italics].[13]

The 'stab in the back' myth was exactly as described – a myth. Germany asked for an Armistice because it was losing the war. It had not yet lost, but after the battles of Soissons and Amiens in the summer of 1918, the war had decisively turned in the Allies' favour. At Amiens, the British Fourth Army advanced over 7 miles on the first day. Inconceivable even a year before. General Ludendorff described it as 'the black day of the German army'. Certainly, disintegrating discipline, especially in the German Navy, and industrial unrest did not help, but these were a product not the cause of defeat. The belief that they had not lost partly explains German resentment at the peace imposed on them. It was a gift for the extreme right. 'The memory of the war became a weapon against those who had made the peace' and absolved Germans from taking responsibility for defeat. 'It was better to blame the un-German, the traitor.'[14] For the far right, the traitors were liberals, Jews, socialists and democrats who would all suffer under Hitler's regime; but even political moderates went along with the myth at the beginning. Chancellor Friedrich Ebert, the leader of the Social Democrats, told returning troops, 'I salute you who return unvanquished from the field of battle'.[15]

The Treaty of Versailles was a tough settlement but nowhere near as harsh as German reactions would suggest. It wasn't 'Carthaginian' nor as brutal as the treaty Germany had imposed on Russia the year before. But for many Germans, an inconclusive war should have resulted in a gentler settlement. The attraction of another war would be to right the wrongs of Versailles as well as remove the stain of the Armistice of 1918. This was exploited by Hitler to justify his initial conquests, but he went further than merely righting perceived wrongs: he established a racial empire in Eastern Europe. He was fooling many of his own people as well as the British Legion. It should be noted that the Royal British Legion (Scotland) refused to make any visit to Nazi Germany. They did not want to shake the hands of leading Nazis and contravene the Legion's democratic principles.[16] They showed considerably more political astuteness than their English counterparts.

Not all ex-servicemen were appeasers or pacifists. Many concluded that the totalitarian powers had to be resisted with force. The most obvious case is Churchill. He served briefly as a battalion commander and made numerous sorties in no-man's-land. He was never the warmonger some of his critics make out. He later reflected on the war's brutality: 'When all was over, Torture and Cannibalism were the only two expedients that the civilised, scientific, Christian States had been able to deny themselves: and they were of doubtful utility.'[17] His strategic interjections as prime minister in the Second World War were sometimes affected by his experiences in the last war. Delaying a second front in 1942 was partly due to his wish to avoid thousands of British troops dying in Flanders again. Churchill understood very early on that appeasement would not work with a man like Hitler. The Nazis were fully intent on a war of conquest and any concessions they made were merely tactical. He once said, 'An appeaser is one who feeds a crocodile, hoping it will eat him last.' In 1935 another ex-serviceman, Major Clement Attlee, was elected as leader of the Labour Party. His predecessor, George Lansbury, had been a committed pacifist. Attlee's election marked a significant turning point in Labour's road to supporting armed intervention against the Nazis. As Churchill's deputy during the war, he was part of a brilliant team. Churchill could rely on other First World War veterans like Anthony Eden (King's Royal Rifle Corps), a prominent anti-appeaser, who became his foreign secretary and Harold Macmillan, former grenadier guard, who was his minister in the Mediterranean. All shared a common conviction that war was unavoidable with a Nazi government like Nazi Germany.

This was perhaps the greatest let-down of all for First World War veterans. It still rankled with many ex-servicemen that twenty years after the Treaty of Versailles Britain was now once again heading for another war. Had their efforts been for nought? Billy Olsen looked back many years later and said, 'It accomplished nothing. It was continued in 1939. It wasn't worth it. We were mugs.'[18] Gordon

Page, who had flown with the Royal Flying Corps, was angry that his son had to leave Oxford and join the RAF in 1943.[19] Walter Hare, whose son was 16 in 1939, thought 'we'd wasted our time'. The war hadn't stopped German militarism but merely held it back for a while. Hare believed it wasn't fair 'that I did my bit and now my son was going to have to do what we failed to do'.[20]

23

'LEST WE FORGET': REFLECTIONS OF EX-SERVICEMEN

'We, who in manhood's dawn have been compelled to care not a damn for life or death, now care less still for the convention of glory and the intellectual apologies for what can never be to us other than a riot of ghastliness and horror, of inhumanity and negation.'

Herbert Read[1]

'It was terrible at times but I wouldn't have missed it.'
'Oh, yes, if I could have my time again, I'd go through it.'
'I can only say that I have never been so excited in my life.'

Ex-servicemen recalling the war[2]

For a long time, the First World War was overshadowed by the Second. The Second World War dominated public discourse with its sheer number of books, movies and documentaries. Yet the First World War was the start of so much of the modern age. Historian Fritz Stern called it 'the first calamity of the twentieth century, the calamity from which all other calamities sprang'.[3] The world's first industrialised war spawned the Russian Revolution and, ultimately, the Cold War, hastened American political and economic dominance, ended four empires and saw the birth of eight new European nations. Women obtained the right to vote in many countries. Its destabilising effects aided Mussolini and Hitler's rise to power. In British politics, Labour replaced the Liberals as the main party of the left. The Second World War sometimes felt like unfinished business. Charles de Gaulle and Winston Churchill both saw 1914–45 as a single conflict: the second Thirty Years' War.

Anniversaries started to stimulate interest: a slew of publications coincided with the 70th anniversary of the Armistice. A few years later, Sebastian Faulks was writing *Birdsong* and remembered being told how few people would read a

First World War novel; by the time it was published he was accused of jumping on the First World War bandwagon. There was also an awareness by the 1990s that First World War veterans were dying out. This was a generation who had not easily talked about their experiences. Faulks remembers being 'taught at school by people who could remember the First World War or who had lost brothers, fathers or friends … What intrigued me was how unwilling they seemed – even in the 1960s – to talk about it.'[4] Perhaps the most famous surviving veteran of recent years was Harry Patch, who fought in the war and was briefly the oldest man in Europe. He never publicly discussed the war until interviewed by the BBC in 1998. 'I've tried for 80 years to forget it. But I can't,' he commented. This opened a floodgate for Patch and he then spoke regularly about the war.

Like many survivors he was often critical, saying, 'Too many died. War isn't worth one life.' He later described it as the 'calculated and condoned slaughter of human beings.' Another famous veteran, Henry Allingham, who predeceased Patch by only a few days, was less bitter but also believed that war solved nothing. He felt that 'if any trigger-happy politician wants to start another war, it's my job to let people know what that means. Politicians today are pitiless humbugs. What do they know? Only those who were there can tell what really happened. Tell of the suffering and misery.'[5] The sense of wasted lives never left some ex-servicemen, even decades later. Bob Owen said, 'The age between 17 and 23, 24 is a lovely time of your life and you had to be fighting in the war and your friends, hundreds of them being killed … the cream age were killed unnecessarily, what for?'[6]

Some surviving veterans were more upset with the peace. This partly explains why letters, diaries and testaments at the end of the war tended to be more positive than ex-servicemen's later accounts. Men who lived through the disappointments of the interwar period later questioned why they had fought. Theirs was not the war to end all wars. Nor was Britain a land fit for heroes; its treatment of veterans was inferior to many other countries. J.B. Priestly wrote:

> They do not seem to see that it is not war that is right, for it is impossible to defend such stupid long-range butchery, but that it is peace that is wrong, the civilian life to which they returned, a condition of things in which they found their manhood stunted, their generous impulses baffled, their double instinct for leadership and loyalty completely checked.[7]

Lessons were learnt and the treatment of veterans after the Second World War was much better, but this was too late for the First World War generation. When Robert Graves wrote *Goodbye to All That* ten years after the war, he 'changed important details of his experience to fit his post-war disillusionment'.[8] John McCauley of the 2nd Border Regiment also felt let down by the peace:

'They died that England might live.' Every day I hear those words ringing in my ears, like the daily ringing of the shellfire of years ago. What if they who died could come back and survey this sorry world, and see what it fought for? I wonder what their thoughts would be? Perhaps they would say, 'We are better and happier in our world.' Who knows?

Cyril Jose of the King's Royal Rifle Corps was an enthusiastic volunteer in 1914 ('Stand back!! I've got my own rifle and bayonet new ones,' he wrote to his sister),[9] but at the end of the war he had become embittered against authority – an attitude that lasted, according to his granddaughter Pauline Wallace, until he died in the 1980s. 'He never really wanted to be part of that establishment.' She remembers him living in a caravan in Epping Forest, happy if he made enough money for his books.[10]

Some men found their religious faith tested by what they had experienced. Welshman O.M. Roberts had been a strong Christian, but was deeply affected when a friend lost a leg. He vowed 'never to go near a chapel again because the religious leaders had sent him to such a bloodbath'. Similarly, Percy Williams, who had a tough time as a POW, said, 'We were told it was a righteous war … and ever since then I've been a Doubting Thomas.'[11]

But not all survivors were so negative. Despite the hardships, the incompetency and the disappointing peace, despite all this, many thought the First World War was a just one. Germany had invaded neutral Belgium because that country just happened to be in the way of France.* This act certainly changed public opinion sharply during the crisis, sparked by the assassination of Franz Ferdinand on 28 June 1914. The nation and the Cabinet were by no means sold on the idea of a war with Germany during July. There was a huge peace demonstration in Trafalgar Square and the financial district of the City of London remained reluctant to support a war against Britain's biggest trading partner. But Belgium changed all that. A good example is Lloyd George; no flag-waving jingo, but a Welshman who felt an affinity for a small nation being bullied. This partly explains the large number of Irish Catholics who volunteered to fight for a country they had no loyalty to.

Certainly, the behaviour of politicians during the war and at the peace conference was often cynical. Lloyd George also saw the war as an opportunity to extend the British Empire. This so angered Siegfried Sassoon that he issued his famous soldier's declaration in 1917, saying, 'I believe that this war, upon which I entered as a war of defence and liberation, has now become a war of aggression and conquest.' But most soldiers were not prepared to stop fighting, as Sassoon

---

* The reasons for Germany invading Belgium were largely to fulfil the Schlieffen Plan. In order to avoid a two-front war, Belgium had to be quickly conquered before its ally Russia mobilised. In July 1914, Belgium had done nothing to justify a German invasion.

threatened to do (and he eventually went back to the Front), nor did this invalidate the rightness of the original reason for going to war. Someone like Private James Hewitt was closer to the views of most Tommies when he said, 'I have no regrets and I think that it was worthwhile overall. Whether the politicians think it was, I don't know, but I'd say on the basis of what we went for, yes, it was worthwhile.'[12] In a similar vein, the writer H.E.L. Mellersh later argued, 'I and my like entered the war expecting an heroic adventure and believing implicitly in the rightness of our cause ... we ended greatly disillusioned as to the nature of the adventure, but still believing that our cause was right and we had not fought in vain.' Brigadier General John Charteris believed 'many men went through the War and came back ennobled by the fact that they had taken part in it and had put into actual practice towards their fellow men some of the finest instincts in human nature'.[13]

We now know of German plans for Europe – known as the September Programme (1914) – if they had won. They would have given their enemies far harsher terms than the Peace of Versailles. The brutal Treaty of Brest-Litovsk imposed on Russia at the beginning of 1918 also gave the world a taste of German victory. The Kaiserreich was not as evil as Nazi Germany of course, but it was suffused by militaristic values and intent on Continental domination. Many decades later, Sid Coles still had no doubts about the need to fight:

> There's always got to be a point where you've got to make a stand and we had to make a stand with France against Germany who were, well, they would, the Germans in those days was out for expansion and they'd have been right down probably into France and that's the way they were going. See, they were led by a maniac and had to be checked and, course it was a good thing it was checked but – course they was ruthless people and they was well-equipped.[14]

Veterans were similarly conflicted over the Armistice commemorations. It was partly pressure from ex-servicemen that made 1919 a ceremony of remembrance rather than triumph. As dissatisfaction with their treatment grew, veterans started using the Armistice for protests. In 1921, former soldiers disturbed the Cenotaph commemorations. Other demonstrations followed, particularly over unemployment. The Ex-Officers' Association reminded the public they had a 'duty of remembrance' to ex-servicemen in need, renaming it 'Obligation Day'.[15] But most veterans scrupulously observed the Armistice throughout the 1920s, as did the majority of the public. A correspondent of *The Times* was on a bus with three others, all rather dismissive of the silence, until they observed:

> 10 or a dozen factory workers wearing their overalls but not their caps, standing rigidly at attention. Glancing along the road we saw at irregular intervals perhaps

twenty people, mostly women ... some with children in perambulators. Without exception they stood still ... it was then that we four cynics ... realized that we too were on our feet with our heads uncovered. At the end of the silence the factory workers gave three cheers for victory and the four 'scoffers' on the bus, *three of whom, significantly, were ex-soldiers, joined the cheering* [author's italics].[16]

As the likelihood of a new war grew, people became more critical. In 1937, one veteran interrupted the silence at the Cenotaph by shouting, 'All this hypocrisy!' A Mass Observation survey a year later found 43 per cent of people were against continuing the silence.[17] Yet many veterans still continued to support the Armistice commemorations throughout lives that sometimes stretched into the Millennium. Whatever their feeling about the conduct of the war, the two-minute silence and laying of wreaths marked a time to honour sacrifices. During the 1960s veterans defended local war memorials against demonstrations by the Campaign for Nuclear Disarmament – in one case, at St Ives, literally shoulder-to-shoulder.[18] Ninety years on, veteran Bill Stone, aged 108, still believed they should not be forgotten: 'If it wasn't for them [those who died] we wouldn't be here.'[19]

For some the war wasn't just a necessary evil but a worthwhile experience. There were dangers, but that was not their only experience of the war. The historian Charles Carrington MC published *A Subaltern's War* partly to counter the views that 'one was not always attacking or under fire. And one's friends were not always being killed.'[20] He felt the 'legend of disenchantment is false'.[21] Graham Greenwell, a captain in the Oxford and Buckinghamshire Light Infantry, wrote in his war memoirs:

> For my part I have to confess that I look back on the years 1914–1918 as among the happiest I have ever spent. That they contained moments of boredom and depression, or sorrow for the loss of friends and of alarm for my personal safety, is indeed true enough. But to be perfectly fit, to live among pleasant companions, to have responsibility and a clearly defined job – these are great compensations when one is very young.[22]

A study of the Leeds Rifles (territorials) 'drawn from a wide social spectrum' revealed a similar picture. 'When questioned late in their lives about their attitude towards it, the survivors ... emphasized how much they had found to enjoy in their war service. Nearly all of them ... described these as "the happiest days of my life." They recalled the sorrow of being discharged.'[23] Hal Kerridge acknowledged the hardships and the horrors but said 'nearly every old soldier will tell you the same; they hated it, they abhorred it, they loathed it, but they wouldn't have missed it'.[24] Others emphasised how formative an experience the war was for their later lives; as one ex-serviceman said, 'I don't think I should have ever been the man I am if it had been for having to serve. You learn to look after yourself ... if you can survive that you can survive anything.'[25] We do have to be cautious of old men recalling their youth, prone to remembering the past through the haze of nostalgia, but ex-servicemen's accounts from the immediate aftermath of the war often show a similar outlook.

Time and again the importance of comradeship comes up in men's reminiscences of the war. Those bonds were formed through shared experience and a reliance on one another. It helped soldiers keep going in the face of incredible dangers. Herbert Read believed a sense of comradeship was built on 'a mutual respect for each other's sufferings'.[26] The thought of 'letting down your mates' by not climbing out of a trench during an attack was a more important stimulant than patriotism or fear of punishment. Those friendships sometimes remained for life. Almost fifty years after the end of the war, Captain J. Glubb, MC recalled:

Many of the officers, NCOs and men of the 7th, Company wrote to me after I returned to England and some continued to do so for many years. Corporal Rennie, who was much older than I was, died many years ago. Sergeant Adams, who was with me in Sanctuary Wood in 1915, kept in touch until he died three years ago. The last of them was Driver Clemmitt, who became post-master at Appleton-le-Moors in Yorkshire. He kept bees on the moors and every year at Christmas he used to send me a present of honey in the comb, and continued to do so until he died in 1975, nearly sixty years since we had been together in France. Such were the comradeships of the Great War.[27]

Ex-servicemen's views on the war diverged, but there was general agreement on one thing: the sacrifices men had made should never be forgotten. Much as he criticised the generals and politicians, Sassoon also railed against the complacency of an interwar Britain that was only too eager to relegate the war to a distant memory. Sergeant William Peacock wrote:

England was saved. *Yes*, that is what our soldiers have done for you. How are we going to be rewarded for our services? ... Just think of the trials and hardships we had to endure to keep those foes from our shores. We are owed a debt of honour.[28]

Ninety years after the end of the war, Henry Allingham said, 'I hope people realise what my pals sacrificed on their behalf.'[29]

And the war hasn't faded. If anything, it's more part of the public consciousness than it has been for years. In 1956, someone noted, 'At 11 a.m. on last Remembrance Sunday I stood at a busy street corner in Westminster. People were strolling about unconcernedly, cars and taxis were on the move ...

a milkman clattered his rack of bottles.'[30] This wouldn't happen now. The 1914 Centenary showed a concerted effort by the media, schools and the government to commemorate the First World War. Armistice Day is once more a national event. Here is just one quiet example among the many acts of remembrance throughout the UK:

> A week-long programme of events to mark Armistice Day and Remembrance Sunday has begun in Inverness.
>
> On Friday, traffic will be stopped in the city centre – the first time since the Second World War that this has happened in Inverness to commemorate Armistice Day.
>
> Staff at council offices will also halt work for a two-minute silence.
>
> Events organised by Highland Council and Royal British Legion Scotland also include laying poppies at war graves in the Kilvean and Torvean cemeteries.
>
> Inverness Provost Jimmy Gray said the act of remembrance had grown in importance for the council and the city.
>
> He added: 'As a measure of its importance, this is the first time that traffic has been stopped in Inverness on Armistice Day since the Second World War.'[31]

The First World War finished over a hundred years ago but it's not been forgotten.

NOTES

Prologue

1   'The Speech: David Lloyd George, 23 November, 1918', *The Scotsman*, last modified 23 November 2007. Accessed 26 July 2018. www.scotsman.com/news-2-15012/the-speech-david-lloyd-george-23-november-1918-1-700345.
2   Thomas Zakharis, 'Book Review: All for the King's Shilling, The British Soldier Under Wellington, 1808–1814', *The History Website of the Fondation Napoleon*. Last accessed 22 November 2018. www.napoleon.org/en/history-of-the-two-empires/articles/book-review-all-for-the-kings-shilling-the-british-soldier-under-wellington-1808-1814.
3   Lord Angelsey, *A History of the British Cavalry 1816–1919: Volume 2 1851–1871* (Barnsley: Pen and Sword, 1993), p. 261.

Introduction

1   Pauline Thomas, 'The Mood of Edwardian Society', *FashionEra.com*. Accessed 19 July 2018. www.fashion-era.com/the_mood_of_edwardian_society.htm.
2   Philip Larkin, 'MCMXIV', *Poetry by Heart*, May 1960. Last accessed 15 December 2018. www.poetrybyheart.org.uk/poems/mcmxiv/.
3   'The Death of Queen Victoria', *The Economist*. Accessed 19 July 2018. www.economist.com/news/21663911-what-we-wrote-her-passing-1901-death-queen-victoria.
4   'Design, Politics and Commerce International Exhibitions 1851–1951', *University of Glasgow Special Collections*. Accessed 19 July 2018. special.lib.gla.ac.uk/teach/century/artnouveau.html.
5   Roy Hattersley, *The Edwardian* (London: Abacus, 2004), p. 15.
6   'The Death of Queen Victoria', *The Economist*.
7   'The History of Strikes in the UK', Office for National Statistics, last modified 21 September 2015. Accessed 2 August 2019. www.ons.gov.uk/employmentand-

labourmarket/peopleinwork/employmentandemployeetypes/articles/thehistoryof-strikesintheuk/2015-09-21

7   Andrew Thorpe, *The Longman Companion to Britain in the Era of the Two World Wars 1914–1945* (Harlow, Essex: Longman, 1994), p. 83.

8   Paul A.B. Clarke and Andrew Linzey, *Dictionary of Ethics, Theology and Society* (Abingdon: Routledge, 2013), p. 671.

9   E.M. Forster, *Howard's End* (London: Penguin Classics, 2012), Chapter 6.

10 W.H. Greenleaf, *Rise in Collectivism* (Abingdon: Taylor and Francis, 2003), p. 167.

11 J.M. Winter, *The Great War and the British People* (Basingstoke: Macmillan Education, 1987), p. 9.

12 *Ibid.*, p. 150.

13 *Ibid.*, p. 151.

14 'CIA World Factbook', *Central Intelligence Agency*. Accessed 23 July 2017. www.cia.gov/library/publications/resources/the-world-factbook/geos/af.html.

15 Richard Toye (ed.), *Winston Churchill: Politics, Strategy and Statecraft* (London: Bloomsbury, 2017), p. 14.

16 George Donaldson and Mara Kalnins (eds.), *D. H. Lawrence in Italy and England* (New York: Springer, 1999), p. 15.

17 Forster, *Howard's End*, Chapter 6.

18 John P. Mckay, *History of Western Society Since 1300*, 11th ed. (New York: Bedford/St Martin's, 2014), p. 902.

19 Neil Oliver, *Not Forgotten* (London: Hodder & Stoughton, 2005), p. 176.

20 'Women's Clothing', *Landscape Change Program*, last modified June 2012. Accessed 23 July 2018. www.uvm.edu/landscape/dating/clothing_and_hair/1910s_clothing_women.php.

Chapter 1

1   Richard Holmes, *Tommy: The British Soldier on the Western Front, 1914–1918* (London: HarperCollins, 2004), p. 614.

2   Winter, *The Great War and the British People*, p. 72.

3   Sean Howard, 'Dominions of the Dead', *Cape Breton Post*, last modified 7 November 2018. Accessed 16 December 2018. www.capebretonpost.com/opinion/columnists/guest-shot-dominions-of-the-dead-257298/.

4   Stanley Weintraub, *A Stillness Heard Round the World: The End of the Great War, November 1918* (New York: E.P. Dutton, 1985), p. 216.

5   Peter Liddle, *The Soldier's War, 1914–18* (London: Blandford, 1988), p. 232.

6   Martin Marix Evans, *1918: The Year of Victories* (London, Chartwell, 2004), p. 235.

7   Lyn Macdonald, *1914–1918: Voices & Images of the Great War* (London: Penguin, 1991), p. 316.

8   Richard van Emden, *The Soldier's War: The Great War Seen Through Veterans' Eyes* (London: A&C Black, 2010), p. 368.

9   John Hayes-Fisher, 'The Last Soldiers to Die in World War I', *BBC News*, last modified 29 October 2008. news.bbc.co.uk/1/hi/magazine/7696021.stm.

10 Laurence V. Keegan, *Victory Must be Ours: Germany in the Great War 1914–1918* (Barnsley: Pen and Sword, 1995), p. 298.

11 Weintraub, *A Stillness Heard Round the World*, p. 175.

12 Joe Cotrill, 'AP European History Practice Exam', *College Board Advanced Placement Program*. Accessed 12 June 2018. files5.pdesas.org/012254089243214063165145109 053021226205079172004/Download.ashx?hash=2.2.

13 Richard Garrett, *The Final Betrayal: The Armistice 1918 … and Afterwards* (Southampton: Buchan & Enright, 1989), p. 48.

14 Brown, *The Imperial War Museum Book of the Western Front* (London: Pan, 2001), pp. 342–3.

15 Holmes, *Tommy*, p. 614.

16 Macdonald, *1914–1918: Voices & Images of the Great War*, p. 308.

17 Rudyard Kipling, *The Irish Guards in the Great War: The First Battalion* (Staplehurst: Spellmount, 1997), pp. 286–7.

18 Adams, 'Herbert Read and the Fluid Memory of the First World War: Poetry, Prose and Polemic', *Historical Research*, vol. 88, no. 240 (2015), pp. 333–54.

19 *Ibid.*

20 Peter Parker, *The Last Veteran: Harry Patch and the Legacy of War* (London: HarperCollins, 2010), p. 8.

21 Cecil Lewis, *Sagittarius Rising* (London: Greenhill, 1993), p. 255.

22 *They Shall Not Grow Old*, Peter Jackson (dir.), Fathom Events, 2018.

23 Liddle, *The Soldier's War*, p. 232.

24 C.P. Blacker, *Have You Forgotten Yet? The First World War Memoirs of C.P. Blacker, MC* (Barnsley: Sword and Pen, 2000), p. 284.

25 Cross, *In Memoriam: Remembering the Great War* (London: Ebury Press, 2008), p. 240.

26 Van Emden and Steve Humphries, *Veterans: The Last Survivors of the Great War* (Barnsley: Pen and Sword, 2005), p. 221.

27 Kipling, *The Irish Guards in the Great War*, pp. 286–7.

28 Van Emden, *Britain's Last Tommies: Final Memories from Soldiers of the 1914–18 War – In their Own Words* (Barnsley: Sword and Pen, 2006), p. 317.

29 Lewis, *Sagittarius Rising*, p. 255.

30 Van Emden and Humphries, *Veterans*, p. 220.

31 Van Emden, *Britain's Last Tommies*, p. 315.

32 Gregor Dallas, *1918: War and Peace* (London: Pimlico, 2002), accessed via Google Books.

33 Garrett, *The Final Betrayal*, p. 8.

Chapter 2

1 Alan G.V. Simmonds, *Britain and World War One* (Abingdon: Routledge, 2013), p. 283.

2 'Daily Mirror Headlines: Armistice, Published 12 November 1918', *BBC*. Accessed 17 July 2018. www.bbc.co.uk/history/worldwars/wwone/mirror07_01.shtml.

3 Evangeline Holland, 'A Glimpse of Armistice Day in London, 1918', *Edwardian Promenade*, last modified 10 November 2011. Accessed 17 July 2018. www.edwardianpromenade.com/war/a-glimpse-of-armistice-day-in-london-1918/.

4 Katie Allen, 'Armistice Day in London, 1918', *The Bookseller*, last modified 10 February 2015. Accessed 17 July 2018. www.thebookseller.com/feature/armistice-day-london-1918-339105.

5 Andrew Gumbel, 'RIP Alex, the Parrot that Learnt to Count and Communicate', *The Independent*, last modified 18 September 2011. Accessed 17 July 2018. www.

independent.co.uk/news/world/americas/rip-alex-the-parrot-that-learnt-to-count-and-communicate-402076.html.

6   'Daily Mirror Headlines: Armistice, Published 12 November 1918'.

7   Weintraub, *A Stillness Heard Round the World*, 262.

8   Garrett, *The Final Betrayal*, p. 55.

9   'Lord Robert Baden-Powell by Winston S. Churchill, Great Contemporaries, London, 1938', *tripod.com*, last modified 1997. Accessed 17 July 2018. troop485. tripod.com/documents/bp-churchhill.htm.

10 Holmes, *Tommy*, pp. 616-7.

11 Samuel Hynes. *A War Imagined: The First World War and English Culture* (London: Pimlico, 1990), p. 255.

12 Weintraub, *A Stillness Heard Round the World*, p. 273.

13 Gregory, *The Last Great War: British Society and the First World War* (Cambridge: Cambridge University Press, 2009), p. 251.

14 'Jubilation on the Day the Guns Fell Silent', *Walesonline*, last modified 28 March 2013. Accessed 17 July 2018. www.walesonline.co.uk/news/local-news/jubilation-day-guns-fell-silent-2139014.

15 *Ibid.*

16 Kitchen, 'Part 5: Now This Bloody War Is Over', *Days of Pride: The Story of Wolverton & New Bradwell 1913–1918*, last modified November 2004. Accessed 17 July 2018. www.mkheritage.co.uk/la/DaysofPride/docs/partfive.html.

17 Marty Johnston, 'Your Place and Mine: Antrim – WWII Nell Martin', *BBC*. Accessed 17 July 2018. www.bbc.co.uk/northernireland/yourplaceandmine/antrim/nell_martin.shtml.

18 Kitchen, 'Now This Bloody War Is Over'.

19 Robert Graves, *Goodbye to All That* (London: Penguin Classics, 2000), p. 228.

20 Van Emden, *The Soldier's War*, p. 365.

Chapter 3

1   Gerard J. DeGroot, *Blighty: British Society in the Era of the Great War* (Harlow, Essex, Longman, 1996), p. 255.

2   'Extract from a speech by the war secretary Lord Milner on demobilisation, December 1918', *The National Archives*, last modified 1 January 1970. Accessed 17 July 2018. www.nationalarchives.gov.uk/pathways/firstworldwar/spotlights/demobilisation.htm.

3   *Ibid.*

4   Johnson, *Land Fit for Heroes* (Chicago: University of Chicago, 1968), p. 207.

5   'Voices of the First World War: Homecoming', *Imperial War Museums*, accessed 21 February 2019. www.iwm.org.uk/history/voices-of-the-first-world-war-homecoming.

6   Garrett, *The Final Betrayal*, p. 148.

7   Weintraub, *A Stillness Heard Round the World*, p. 365.

8   Andrew Rothstein, *The Soldiers' Strikes of 1919* (New York: Springer, 1980), p. 68.

9   Lamb, 'Mutinies 1917–1920', *Libcom.org*, 31 December 2005. Accessed 17 July 2018. libcom.org/library/mutinies-dave-lamb-solidarity.

10 Anthony Read, *The World on Fire* (London: Random House, 2009), p. 59.

11   Simon Webb, *1919: Britain's Year of Revolution* (Barnsley: Pen & Sword History, 2016), accessed via Google Books.
12   Lamb, 'Mutinies 1917–1920'.
13   *Ibid.*
14   Webb, *1919: Britain's Year of Revolution.*
15   'Demobilisation in Britain, 1918–20', *National Archives.* .
16   Jeroen Sprenger, 'The Objectives of the Triple Alliance', *The Triple Alliance: A Threat of Revolution That Never Was.* Accessed 17 July 2018. www.jeroensprenger.nl/Triple Alliance/chapter-ii---the-objectives-of-the-triple-alliance.html.
17   Winston Churchill, *The World Crisis: The Aftermath* (London: Thornton Butterworth, 1929), p. 60.

Chapter 4

1   G. R. Searle, *A New England? Peace and War 1886–1918* (Oxford: Oxford University Press, 2005), p. 803.
2   E.R.M. Fryer, *Reminiscences of a Grenadier 1914–1919* (London: Digby, Long & Co., 1921), p. 241.
3   Van Emden, *Britain's Last Tommies*, p. 322.
4   'Episode 2', *Welsh Memories of World War 1* (2014: Cardiff, BBC Wales), television broadcast.
5   'Episode 4: Lost Peace (1919)', *The People's Century* (1995: London, BBC), television broadcast.
6   Pat Cryer, 'Celebrating Peace After World War One: The Street Party', *Join Me in the 1900s.* Accessed 17 July 2018. www.1900s.org.uk/1919-peaceparty-edmonton.htm.
7   Van Emden (ed.), *Sapper Martin: The Secret Great War Diary of Jack Martin* (London: Bloomsbury, 2009), p. 272.
8   'This Month in History: Peace Day, July 1919', *The Gazette Official Public Record.* Accessed 17 July 2018. www.thegazette.co.uk/awards-and-accreditation/content/100215.
9   'Peace Day', *Peace Pledge Union.* Accessed 26 December 2018. archive.ppu.org.uk/remembrance/rem03.html.
10   Jeremy Laurance, 'Flu: How Britain Coped in the 1918 Epidemic', *The Independent*, last modified 22 October 2005. Accessed 17 July 2018. www.independent.co.uk/life-style/health-and-families/health-news/flu-how-britain-coped-in-the-1918-epidemic-5348535.html.
11   Everett Sharp, 'The Etaples Flu Pandemic?', *World War I Centenary.* Accessed 17 July 2018. ww1centenary.oucs.ox.ac.uk/body-and-mind/the-etaples-flu-pandemic/.
12   Garrett, *The Final Betrayal*, p. 74.
13   Stedman, *Salford Pals: A History of the Salford Brigade* (Barnsley: Leo Cooper, 2007), p. 222.
14   *Ibid.*
15   Max Arthur, *The Road Home: The Aftermath of the Great War Told by the Men and Women Who Survived It* (London: Phoenix, 2010), pp. 29–30.

16 Mark Honigsbaum, 'The 1918 Flu Pandemic Remembered', *The Guardian*, last modified 5 November 2005. Accessed 17 July 2018. www.theguardian.com/society/2005/nov/05/health.birdflu.

17 Juliet Nicolson, 'The War Was Over – but Spanish Flu Would Kill Millions More', *The Telegraph*, last modified 11 November 2009. Accessed 17 July 2018. www.telegraph.co.uk/news/health/6542203/The-war-was-over-but-Spanish-Flu-would-kill-millions-more.html.

18 'Wilson, Ernest J. (Oral History)', *Imperial War Museums*. Accessed 17 July 2018. www.iwm.org.uk/collections/item/object/80004393.

19 'Hunt, W. (Oral History)', *Imperial War Museums*. Accessed 17 July 2018. www.iwm.org.uk/collections/item/object/80023206.

20 Van Emden, *Britain's Last Tommies*, p. 314.

21 'British Prisoners of War in German Captivity, 1914–1918', *Imperial War Museums*. Accessed 17 July 2018. www.iwm.org.uk/collections/item/object/205222132.

22 Chris Baker, 'Records of British Prisoners of War 1914–1918', *The Long, Long Trail*. Accessed 22 November 2018. www.longlongtrail.co.uk/soldiers/how-to-research-a-soldier/records-of-british-prisoners-of-war-1914-1918/.

23 Anita Singh, 'First World War PoWs: Why Has History Forgotten Them?', *The Telegraph*, last modified 28 May 2014. Accessed 17 July 2018. www.telegraph.co.uk/culture/hay-festival/10861012/First-World-War-PoWs-why-has-history-forgotten-them.html.

24 Yucel Yanikdag, 'Prisoners of War (Ottoman Empire/Middle East)', *Encyclopedia 1914–1918*. Accessed 17 July 2018. encyclopedia.1914-1918-online.net/article/prisoners_of_war_ottoman_empiremiddle_east.

25 'Episode 2', *Welsh Memories of World War 1*.

26 Max Arthur, *The Road Home*, 37.

27 *Ibid.*, p. 45.

28 Kitchen, 'Now This Bloody War Is Over'.

29 Brian Wilson, 'New Year's Day 1919 / A Private Tragedy at Lewis', *The Independent*, last modified 18 September 2011. Accessed 17 July 2018. www.independent.co.uk/voices/new-years-day-1919-a-private-tragedy-at-lewis-1397469.html.

30 'The *Iolaire* Disaster, where 200 Men Died Yards from Shore', *The Scotsman*, last modified 12 June 2006. Accessed 17 July 2018. www.scotsman.com/heritage/people-places/the-iolaire-disaster-where-200-men-died-yards-from-shore-1-465122.

31 *Ibid.*

32 *Ibid.*

33 Wilson, 'A Private Tragedy at Lewis.'.

Chapter 5

1 Sinéad Joy, *The IRA in Kerry 1916–1921* (Cork: The Collins Press, 2005), accessed via Google Books.

2 Gerry Doherty and James MacGregor, *Hidden History: The Secret Origins of the First World War* (New York: Random House, 2013), accessed via Google Books.

3 Keith Jeffrey, *Ireland and the Great War* (Cambridge: Cambridge University Press, 2000), accessed via Google Books.

4   *Ibid.*
5   *Ibid.*
6   Tom Barry, 'Guerilla Days in Ireland', *Mercier Press*. Accessed 17 July 2018. www.mercierpress.ie/irish-books/guerilla_days_in_ireland/.
7   'Irish Soldiers of the Great War', *1916 Commemorations – Battle of the Somme*, Department of the Taoiseach. Accessed 17 July 2018. www.taoiseach.gov.ie/attached_files/Pdf%20files/1916Commemorations-BattleOfTheSomme.pdf.
8   'Ireland and the Great War/Post-war Ireland', *Royal Dublin Fusiliers Association*. Accessed 17 July 2018. greatwar.ie/ireland-and-the-great-war-2/post-war-ireland/.
9   'What Tommy Did Next: Veterans' Activities and Organisations of the First World War, in the UK and Beyond', *Men, Women and Care*. Accessed 11 November 2018. menwomenandcare.leeds.ac.uk/what-tommy-did-next-veterans-activities-and-organisations-of-the-first-world-war-in-the-uk-and-beyond/.
10   Keith Jeffery, 'Ireland and the First World War', *Irish History Live*. Accessed 27 December 2018. www.qub.ac.uk/sites/irishhistorylive/IrishHistoryResources/.
11   Robert Lynch, *The Northern IRA and the Early Years of Partition* (New Bridge: Irish Academic Press, 2006), p. 127.
12   Brendan O Cathaoir, 'An Irishman's Diary', *The Irish Times*, last modified 2 October 2012. Accessed 17 July 2018. www.irishtimes.com/opinion/an-irishman-s-diary-1.546549.
13   Joy, *The IRA in Kerry*.
14   McKittrick, 'Ireland's War of Independence', *The Independent*, last modified 17 September 2011. Accessed 17 July 2018. www.independent.co.uk/news/world/europe/irelands-war-of-independence-the-chilling-story-of-the-black-and-tans-5336022.html.
15   R.F. Foster, *Modern Ireland, 1600–1972* (New York: Penguin, 1989), p. 498.
16   John Ainsworth, 'The Black & Tans and Auxiliaries in Ireland', presented to the Annual Conference of the Queensland History Teachers' Association in Brisbane, 12 May 2001. Accessed: 17 July 2018. eprints.qut.edu.au/9/1/Ainsworth_Black_conf.PDF.
17   McKittrick, 'Ireland's War of Independence'.
18   Max Arthur, *The Last Post* (London: Weidenfeld & Nicholson, 2005), p. 250.
19   J.J. Lee (ed.), *Kerry's Fighting Story 1916–21: Told by the Men Who Made It* (Cork: Mercier Press, 2009), p. 199.
20   Foster, *Modern Ireland*, p. 498.
21   Roy Jenkins, *Churchill: A Biography* (New York: Farrar, Straus and Giroux, 2001), pp. 362–3.
22   Ronan McGreevy, *The Mad Guns: Reflections on the Battle of the Somme* (Dublin: Irish Times Books, 2016), p. 46.
23   Jeffery, 'Ireland and the First World War'.
24   Geoff Dyer, *The Missing of the Somme* (New York: Vintage, 2011), pp. 106–7.
25   Bridget Haggerty, 'The Irish Soldiers in WWI – World Cultures European', *Irish Culture and Customs*. Accessed 17 July 2018. www.irishcultureandcustoms.com/ACalend/VetsWW1.html.
26   Donal Fallon, 'Poppy-snatching in Dublin', *Come Here to Me!: Dublin Life & Culture*, last modified 4 November 2015. Accessed 9 December 2018. comeheretome.com/2015/11/04/poppy-snatching-in-dublin/.

27   Gerry White, 'An Open Letter to Cork's Unknown Soldier', *Evening Echo*, accessed
     27 December 2018. www.eveningecho.ie/opinion/An-open-letter-to-Corks-
     unknown-soldier-c43d563d-42da-44d1-819a-d0bb91fece7f-ds.
28   Haggerty, 'The Irish Soldiers in WWI'.
29   'The Fallen . When Both Sides Fought and Died Together', *The Belfast Telegraph*,
     last modified 8 December 2012. Accessed 17 July 2018. www.belfasttelegraph.
     co.uk/life/the-fallen-when-both-sides-fought-and-died-together-28068143.html.

Chapter 6

1   'Bolshevism: "Foul Baboonery … Strangle at Birth"', *The Churchill Project*, Hillsdale
     College, last modified 29 March 2016. Accessed 22 November 2018. winston-
     churchill.hillsdale.edu/bolshevism/.
2   'Brig Roy Smith-Hill (Obituary, *The Times*)', *The Sunday Times*, last modified
     21 August 1996. Accessed 17 July 2018. www.curioussymbols.com/john/brig/
     times.html.
3   *Ibid.*
4   'Earnshaw, R.H. (Oral History)', *Imperial War Museums*. Accessed 27 July 2018.
     www.iwm.org.uk/collections/item/object/80000959.
5   Martin Gilbert, *Churchill: A Life* (New York: Random House, 2000), p. 410.
6   Lamb, 'Mutinies 1917–1920'.
7   'Allied Intervention in Russia, 1918–19', The National Archives. Accessed
     11 August 2018. www.nationalarchives.gov.uk/pathways/firstworldwar/
     spotlights/allies.htm.
8   Kevin Myers, 'The Bitter Sting in the Tail of World War', *The Telegraph*, last
     modified 11 November 2001. Accessed 17 July 2018. www.telegraph.co.uk/
     comment/4266725/The-bitter-sting-in-the-tail-of-world-war.html.
9   'Stories of Britain's Forgotten Role in Russia's Civil War on Display', *University of
     Exeter*, last modified 18 October 2017. Accessed 22 November 2018. www.exeter.
     ac.uk/news/featurednews/title_616668_en.html.
10   'Archangel Cemetery', *CWGC Archive*. Accessed 18 August 2018. www.cwgc.org/
     find-a-cemetery/cemetery/54102/ARCHANGEL MEMORIAL.
11   Chuck DeVore, 'America's Foreign Policy Must Be Sustainable in Public
     Opinion, Too', *The Federalist*, last modified 8 August 2014. Accessed 17 July 2018.
     thefederalist.com/2014/08/04/americas-foreign-policy-must-be-sustainable-in-
     public-opinion-too/.
12   Chris Wrigley, *Winston Churchill: A Biographical Companion* (Santa Barbara:
     ABS-CLIO, 2002), p. 317.

Chapter 7

1   David Olusoga, *The World's Wars* (London: Head of Zeus, 2014), p. 267.
2   *Ibid.*, p. 233.
3   Cross, *In Memoriam*, p. 251.
4   Jonathan Glancey, 'Comment: Gas, Chemicals, Bombs: Britain Has Used Them All
     before in Iraq', *The Guardian*, last modified 19 April 2003. Accessed 17 July 2018.
     www.theguardian.com/world/2003/apr/19/iraq.arts.

5   Barker, 'Policing Palestine', *Questia*, accessed 28 November 2018. www.questiaschool.
    com/reader/printPaginator/3360.

6   David Cronin, 'Winston Churchill Sent the Black and Tans to Palestine', *The Irish
    Times*, last modified 19 May 2017. Accessed 17 July 2018. www.irishtimes.com/
    culture/books/winston-churchill-sent-the-black-and-tans-to-palestine-1.3089140.

7   *Ibid*.

8   Barker, 'Policing Palestine'.

9   'The Story of Africa', *BBC World Service*. Accessed 17 July 2018. www.bbc.co.uk/
    worldservice/specials/1624_story_of_africa/page13.shtml.

10 Peter Fryer and Paul Gilroy, *Staying Power: The History of Black People in Britain*
    (London: Pluto, 2010), p. 319.

11 Shashi Tharoor, 'Why the Indian Soldiers of WW1 Were Forgotten', *BBC
    Magazine*, last modified 2 July 2015. Accessed 9 December 2018. www.bbc.co.uk/
    news/magazine-33317368.

12 Simon Rogers, 'First World War: Volunteers from the Colonies – the Forgotten
    Soldiers', *The Guardian*, last modified 10 November 2008. Accessed 17 July 2018.
    www.theguardian.com/world/2008/nov/10/first-world-war-colonial-soldiers-racism.

13 Budheswar Pati, *India and the First World War* (New Delhi: Atlantic Publishers,
    1996), p. 9.

14 Karl J. Schmidt, *An Atlas and Survey of South Asian History* (London: Routledge:
    2015), p. 34.

15 Harriet Sherwood, 'Indians in the Trenches: Voices of Forgotten Army Are Finally
    to Be Heard', *The Guardian*, last modified 27 October 2018. Accessed 28 October
    2018. www.theguardian.com/world/2018/oct/27/armistice-centenary-indian-
    troops-testimony-sacrifice-british-library.

16 *Ibid*.

17 Steven Johns, 'The British West Indies Regiment Mutiny, 1918', *Libcom.org*, last
    modified 7 August 2013. Accessed 17 July 2018. libcom.org/history/british-west-
    indies-regiment-mutiny-1918.

18 The Times, *The Times History of the War* (London: The Times, 1918), p. 89.

19 Caroline Coxon, 'The Sinking of the SS Mendi', *History Today*, vol. 57, no. 2, last
    modified February 2007. Accessed 9 December 2018. www.historytoday.com/
    archive/sinking-ss-mendi.

20 Rogers, 'Volunteers from the Colonies'.

21 *Ibid*.

22 Stephen Bourne, 'How Black Soldiers Helped Britain in First World War', *Black
    History Month*, last modified 11 November 2018. Accessed 22 July 2018. www.
    blackhistorymonth.org.uk/article/section/bhm-heroes/how-black-soldiers-helped-
    britain-in-first-world-war/.

23 Gabriel Christian, 'The Interwar Years & the Caribbean Soldier in Social
    Transformation', *GenTwenty*. Accessed 17 July 2018. www.da-academy.org/
    uploads/9/2/0/3/92034718/thecaribbeansoldierinsocialtransformation.pdf.

24 Glenford D. Howe, 'A White Man's War? World War One and the West Indies',
    BBC, last modified 10 March 2011. Accessed 17 July 2018. www.bbc.co.uk/
    history/worldwars/wwone/west_indies_01.shtml.

25 Johns, 'The British West Indies Regiment Mutiny'.

26 *Ibid*.

27 Howe, 'A White Man's War? World War One and the West Indies'.

28   Christian, 'The Interwar Years'.
29   David Van Leeuwen, 'Marcus Garvey and the Universal Negro Improvement Association', *TeacherServe*, National Humanities Center. Accessed 17 July 2018. nationalhumanitiescenter.org/tserve/twenty/tkeyinfo/garvey.htm.
30   Christian, 'The Interwar Years'.
31   Christian, 'The History of Honourable Cecil Edgar Allen Rawle', *HAS Newsletter*, no. 115. Accessed 18 July 2018. www.antiguanice.com/v2/documents/HASNewsletter2011-4.pdf.
32   Rogers, 'First World War'.
33   Olusoga, *The World's Wars*, p. 279.
34   *Ibid.*, p. 101.
35   'The Story of Africa', BBC World Service.
36   *Ibid.*
37   Olusoga, *The World's Wars*, p. 143.
38   *Ibid.*, pp. 271–2.
39   'The Story of Africa', BBC World Service.

Chapter 8

1   Montague, *Disenchantment* (London: MacGibbon & Kee, 1968), p. 130.
2   Margaret MacMillan, *Peacemakers: Six Months That Changed the World* (London: John Murray, 2002), pp. 180–1.
3   Brown, *The Imperial War Museum Book of the Western Front*, p. 346.
4   Fryer, *Reminiscences of a Grenadier*, p. 236.
5   Michael Duffy, 'Philip Gibbs on the Allied Occupation of the Rhineland, December 1918', *First World War.com*, last modified 22 August 2009. Accessed 17 July 2018. www.firstworldwar.com/source/rhineoccupation_gibbs.htm.
6   Fryer, *Reminiscences of a Grenadier*.
7   *Ibid.*
8   Van Emden, *Britain's Last Tommies*, p. 326.
9   'Occupation of Rhineland', British Pathé Historical Collection. Accessed 17 July 2018. www.britishpathe.com/video/occupation-of-rhineland.
10   Arthur, *Last Post*, p. 49.
11   Montague, *Disenchantment*, p. 133.
12   *Ibid.*, p. 132.
13   *Ibid.*, pp. 131–2.
14   Violet Markham, *Watching on the Rhine* (New York: George H. Doran, 1921), p. 28.
15   *Ibid.*
16   'The Occupation of the Rhineland', *The Spectator*, published 27 August 1927. Accessed 22 July 2018. archive.spectator.co.uk/article/27th-august-1927/4/the-occupation-of-the-rhineland.

Chapter 9

1   Hynes. *A War Imagined*, p. 384.
2   *They Shall Not Grow Old*.
3   Hynes. *A War Imagined*, p. 29.

4   Graves, *Goodbye to All That*, p. 205.

5   DeGroot, *Blighty*, p. 245.

6   Holmes, *Tommy*, p. 530.

7   Graves, *Goodbye to All That*, p. 120.

8   Marina MacKay, *Modernism, War, and Violence* (London: Bloomsbury, 2017), accessed via Google Books.

9   Vera Brittain, *Testament of Youth: An Autobiographical Study of the Years 1900–1925* (London: Fontan, 1980), p. 618.

10   Arthur, *The Road Home*, p. 239.

11   James Mellow, *Charmed Circle: Gertrude Stein and Company* (New York: Houghton Mifflin, 1991), p. 273.

12   Van Emden, *Britain's Last Tommies*, p. 331.

13   Alf Ludtke and Bernd Weisbrod (eds), *No Man's Land of Violence: Extreme Wars in the 20th Century* (Gottingen: Wallstein Verlag, 2006), p. 125.

14   'Charles Stewart Alexander - Letters to Cousin Amy Reid', *Auckland War Memorial Museum*. Accessed 27 December 2018. www.aucklandmuseum.com/collection/object/am_library-manuscriptsandarchives-9155.

15   Scott Anderson, 'The True Story of Lawrence of Arabia', *Smithsonian.com*, last modified 1 July 2014. Accessed 22 November 2018. www.smithsonianmag.com/history/true-story-lawrence-arabia.

16   Graves, *Goodbye to All That*, p. 244.

17   A.R. Basov and T.A. Basova, 'Emir Dynamite: A Biography of T. E. Lawrence', *Elite Spirit*. Accessed 4 October 2018. www.elitespirit.org/read_chapters/t_e_lawrence_blog.html.

18   Francis Beckett, 'State Spying Helps to Create Extremists. My Father Was One of Them', *The Guardian*, last modified 31 August 2016. Accessed 4 October 2018. www.theguardian.com/commentisfree/2016/aug/31/state-spying-extremists-father-john-beckett.

19   Dennis Healey, *The Time of My Life* (London: Penguin, 1990), p. 53.

20   Holmes, *Tommy*, p. 613.

21   Macdonald, *1914–1918*, pp. 333–4.

22   Richard Aldington, *Life for Life's Sake* (California: Cassell, 1968), quoted in Robert Wohl, *The Generation of 1914* (Cambridge MA: Harvard University Press, 2009), p. 293.

23   Michael Reeve, 'Smoking and Cigarette Consumption', *International Encyclopedia of the First World War*, last modified 23 May 2018. Accessed 6 December 2018. encyclopedia.1914-1918-online.net/article/smoking_and_cigarette_consumption.

24   Tony Allen, 'Cigarettes & Tobacco and WW1 Soldiers', *Picture Postcards from the Great War*. Accessed 7 December 2018. www.worldwar1postcards.com/smokes-for-the-troops.php.

25   *Ibid.*

26   Reid, *Broken Men*, p. 167.

27   Van Emden and Humphries, *Veterans*, p. 218.

28   Van Emden, *Britain's Last Tommies*, p. 303.

29   Caroline Davies, '"It Was Very Hard for Him": Relatives Remember First World War Survivors', *The Guardian*, last modified 9 November 2018. Accessed 10 November 2018. www.theguardian.com/world/2018/nov/09/relatives-remember-first-world-war-survivors.

30   Van Emden and Humphries, *Veterans*, p. 218.
31   Howard Jacobson, 'To Truly Remember the Holocaust, We Must Stay Alert to Prejudice', *New Statesman*, last modified 1 February 2008. Accessed 17 July 2018. www.newstatesman.com/2018/02/truly remember-holocaust-we-must-stay-alert-prejudice.
32   Magnus Linklater, 'We Must Not Avert Our Eyes to Horrors of War', *The Times*, 22 December 2016. Accessed 22 July 2018. www.thetimes.co.uk/article/we-must-not-avert-our-eyes-to-horrors-of-war-lw92cjr9f.
33   Magnus Linklater, 'Remembering Our Fathers: A Generation That Fought and Died Without Complaint', *The Times*, 4 August 2004. www.thetimes.co.uk/article/remember-our-fathers-a-generation-that-fought-and-died-without-complaint-rl367lvvqv5.
34   Graves, *Goodbye to All That*, p. 260.
35   Richards, *Old Soldiers Never Die* (Uckfield: The Naval & Military Press, 2006), p. 323.
36   Graves, *Goodbye to All That*, pp. 239–40.
37   Fussell, *The Great War and Modern Memory* (New York: Oxford University Press, 1975), p. 325.
38   Anne Roze and John Foley, *Fields of Memory: A Testimony to the Great War* (London: Cassell, 1999), p. 228.
39   Kowalsky, 'Enabling the Great War: Ex-Servicemen, the Mixed Economy of Welfare and the Social Construction of Disability, 1830–1930', Ph.D Diss., University of Leeds, 2007. etheses.whiterose.ac.uk/680/.
40   Robin Truda, 'Nightmares: The Navel of Freud's Dreaming', *Australasian Journal of Psychotherapy*, vol. 26, no. 2 (2007), pp. 1-14. Accessed 18 July 2018. www.ajppsy-chotherapy.com/pdf/26_2/RobinTruda_Nightmaresthe.pdf.
41   Macdonald, *1914–1918*, p. 335.
42   Weintraub, *A Stillness Heard Round the World*, p. 368.
43   Graves, *Goodbye to All That*, p. 235.
44   Bourke, 'Shell Shock during World War One', *BBC*, last modified 10 March 2011. Accessed 18 July 2018. www.bbc.co.uk/history/worldwars/wwone/shellshock_01.shtml.
45   Van Emden, *Britain's Last Tommies*, pp. 318–9.
46   *Ibid.*, p. 303.
47   *Teenage Tommies* (London: BBC Two, 31 October 2018), television broadcast.
48   Clive Emsley, 'Violent Crime in England in 1919: Post-War Anxieties and Press Narratives', *Continuity and Change*, vol. 23, no. 1 (2008), p. 176.
49   *Ibid.*, p. 183.
50   Fiona Guy, 'The Green Bicycle Case: The Murder of Bella Wright in 1919', *Crime Traveller*, last modified 30 June 2018. Accessed 15 August 2018. www.crimetraveller.org/2015/09/green-bicycle-case-bella-wright-murder/.
51   Emsley, 'Violent crime in England in 1919', p. 175.
52   J. Lawrence, 'Forging a Peaceable Kingdom: War, Violence, and Fear of Brutalization in Post–First World War Britain', *The Journal of Modern History*, vol. 75, no. 3 (2003), pp. 557–89.
53   Grayling, *A Land Fit for Heroes: British Life after the Great War* (London: Buchan & Enright, 1987), p. 39.
54   *Ibid.*, p. 32.

55 Roz Laws, 'Forgotten Bravery of Tragic Hero Who Took His Own Life',
    Birmingham Mail, last modified 26 July 2014. Accessed 23 December 2018. www.
    birminghammail.co.uk/news/midlands-news/ww1-captain-branded-coward-
    after-7512658.
56 Emsley, 'Violent crime in England in 1919', p. 181.
57 J. Holmes, N.T. Fear and S. Wessely, 'Suicide among Falkland War Veterans', *BMJ*,
    vol. 346 (May 2013).
58 Emsley, 'Violent crime in England in 1919', p. 181.

Chapter 10

1   Reese, *Homecoming Heroes: An Account of the Reassimilation of British Military
    Personnel into Civilian Life* (London: L. Cooper, 1992), p. 10.
2   'Peace Day', Peace Pledge Union.
3   Holmes, *Tommy*, p. 619.
4   Ed Butchart, 'Unemployment and Non-Employment in Interwar Britain',
    Discussion Papers in Economic and Social History University of Oxford, Number 16
    (May 1997), p. 15.
5   'Oral History Audio Recording of Frank Gillard (b.1891) and His Experiences
    in the Army in World War One', *Living Archive*. Accessed 18 July 2018. www.
    livingarchive.org.uk/content/catalogue_item/days-of-pride-collection-2/
    oral-history-recordings-of-memories-of-world-war-one-by-people-from-
    wolverton-and-new-bradwell/oral-history-audio-recording-of-frank-gillard-b-
    1891-and-his-experiences-in-the-army-in-world-war-one-2.
6   Van Emden, *Britain's Last Tommies*, p. 328.
7   *Ibid.*, p. 332.
8   Arthur, *The Road Home*, p. 203.
9   Reese, *Homecoming Heroes*, p. 72.
10 *Ibid.*, p. 55.
11 Carlos E. Negron, 'Nomination of The Great Ocean Road for recognition under
    the Heritage Recognition Program', *Australia Engineers*. Accessed 18 July 2018.
    portal.engineersaustralia.org.au/system/files/engineering-heritage-australia/
    nomination-title/Great%20Ocean%20Road%20-%20Nomination.pdf.
12 Reese, *Homecoming Heroes*, pp. 70–1.
13 *Ibid.*, p. 59.
14 *Ibid.*, p. 71.
15 Niall Barr, *The Lion and the Poppy: British Veterans, Politics, and Society, 1921–1939*
    (Westport CT: Greenwood, 2005), p. 10.
16 Reese, *Homecoming Heroes*, p. 70.
17 Stevenson, *British Society 1914–45* (London: Penguin, 1990), p. 252.
18 Arthur, *The Road Home*, p. 200.
19 Graves, *Goodbye to All That*, p. 230.
20 Stevenson, *British Society*, p. 248.
21 *Ibid.*, p. 253.
22 Arthur, *The Last Post*, p. 207.
23 House of Lords, 'Instruction in The Army', *Hansard*, 18 March 1919. Accessed
    6 August 2018. hansard.parliament.uk/Lords/1919-03-19/debates/987212d7-b6ea-
    4a80-bf65-2fa85b111300/InstructionInTheArmy.

24   Roderick Floud and Johnson (eds), *The Cambridge Economic History of Modern Britain* (Cambridge: Cambridge University Press, 2003), p. 63.

25   'Spotlights on History', *The National Archives*, last modified 1 January 1970. Accessed 18 July 2018. www.nationalarchives.gov.uk/pathways/firstworldwar/spotlights/demobilisation.htm.

26   Ascherson, 'Armistice Day: Victory and Beyond', *The Guardian*, last modified 11 November 2018. Accessed 11 November 2018. www.theguardian.com/world/2018/nov/11/armistice-day-victory-and-beyond-first-world-war-neal-ascherson-essay.

27   Keith Laybourn, *Britain on the Breadline: A Social and Political History of Britain 1918–1939* (Stroud: Sutton Publishing, 1998), p. 9.

28   *They Shall Not Grow Old.*

29   Brian Harding, *Keeping Faith: The Royal British Legion (1921–2001)* (Barnsley: Pen and Sword, 2001), p. 69.

30   Garrett, *The Final Betrayal*, p. 227.

31   Jim Hooley, *A Hillgate Childhood* (Stockport: Age Concern Stockport, 1981).

32   'Settlement of Returned Soldiers and Sailors 1914–18', *Australian Bureau of Statistics*, Australian Government. Accessed 18 July 2018. www.abs.gov.au/AUSSTATS/abs@.nsf/featurearticlesbyCatalogue/72BB159FA215052FCA2569DE0020331D?OpenDocument.

33   Reese, *Homecoming Heroes*, p. 138.

34   Ann Evans, 'Clement Attlee – MP for Limehouse 1922', *The Port of London Study Group*, last modified 13 October 2017. Accessed 18 July 2018. portoflondonstudy.wordpress.com/2017/10/13/clement-attlee-mp-for-limehouse-1922-by-ann-evans/.

35   '2014 – War and Impairment', *Unite the Union*. Accessed 20 July 2018. worldofinclusion.com/v3/wp-content/uploads/2014/09/UK-Disability-history-month-2014.pdf.

36   Gary Mead, *The Good Soldier: A Biography of Douglas Haig* (London: Atlantic, 2007), accessed via Google Books.

37   'A Land Fit for Heroes', *Aftermath*. Accessed 26 December 2018. www.aftermathww1.com/landfit.asp.

38   Stephen Ward (ed.), *The War Generation*, p. 30, quoted in Fedorowich '"Foredoomed to failure" The Resettlement of British Ex-Servicemen in the Dominions 1914–1930', Ph.D Diss., University of London, 1991, www.researchgate.net/publication/297279233_Foredoomed_to_failure'_The_resettlement_of_British_ex-servicemen_in_the_Dominions_1914-1930.

39   Rex Pope, *War and Society in Britain, 1899–1948* (London: Longman, 1991), p. 103.

40   'World War 1: The Final Hours' (London: BBC, 12 November 2018), television broadcast.

41   Marjorie Levine-Clark. '"The Whole World Had Gone against Them": Ex-Servicemen and the Politics of Relief', *Unemployment, Welfare, and Masculine Citizenship. Genders and Sexualities in History* (London: Palgrave Macmillan, 2015), p. 138

42   Nicholas Horsewood, Somnath Sen and Anca Voicu, 'Beggar Thy Neighbour: British Imports during the Inter-War Years and the Effect of the 1932 Tariff', *University of Birmingham Department of Economics Discussion Paper* (2009). www.researchgate.net/publication/228645685_Beggar_Thy_Neighbour_British_Imports_during_the_Inter-War_Years_and_the_effect_of_the_1932_tariff.

43 Stevenson, *British Society 1914–45*, p. 271.

44 *Ibid.*, p. 280.

45 James Brady, 'Survivor: Private James Brady', *Curriculum Bites: World War One*, BBC. Accessed 18 July 2018. www.bbc.co.uk/schools/worldwarone/survivor/memoir12.shtml.

46 Garrett, *The Final Betrayal*, p. 176.

47 Macdonald, *1914–1918*, p. 334.

48 Niall Barr, 'Service not Self: The British Legion, 1921-1939', PhD Diss. University of St Andrews, 1994. research-repository.st-andrews.ac.uk/handle/10023/7101.

49 Jeremy Paxman, *Great Britain's Great War* (London: Penguin, 2013), p. 283.

50 George Coppard, *With a Machine Gun to Cambrai: The Tale of a Young Tommy in Kitchener's Army 1914–1918* (London: Imperial War Museum, 1969), p. 133.

51 Harding, *Keeping Faith*, p. 197.

52 DeGroot, *Blighty*, p. 298.

53 Harding, *Keeping Faith*, p. 196.

54 Macdonald, *1914–1918*, p. 333.

55 Graham Wooton, quoted in Garrett, *The Final Betrayal*, p. 227.

56 E. Hills, 'J.B. Priestley's Wars by Neil and Jack Hanson: The Last Time I Gave a Talk about Priestley', *World War One Art*. Accessed 18 July 2018. ww1art.files.wordpress.com/2014/12/j-b-priestleys-wars.pdf.

57 Grayling, *A Land Fit for Heroes*, p. 75.

58 *Ibid.*, p. 102.

59 Barr, 'Service not Self'.

60 Graves, *Goodbye to All That*, p. 234.

61 Arthur, *The Road Home*, p. 247.

62 Paxman, *Great Britain's Great War*, p. 284.

63 The information was supplied with kind permission from his grandson, Graham Page.

64 Arthur, *The Last Post*, pp. 86–7.

65 Stevenson, *British Society 1914–45*, p. 273.

66 Thorpe, *The Longman Companion to Britain*, p. 57.

67 Barr, 'Service not Self'.

68 Richards, *Old Soldiers Never Die*, p. 322.

69 Martin Middlebrook, *The First Day of the Somme* (Barnsley: Pen and Sword, 2006), p. 319.

70 Harding, *Keeping Faith*, p. 71.

71 W.R. Garside, *British Unemployment 1919–1939: A Study in Public Policy* (Cambridge: Cambridge University Press, 2002), p. 37.

72 Peter Hart, *The IRA and Its Enemies: Violence and Community in Cork, 1916–1923* (Oxford: Oxford University Press, 1999), p. 312.

73 Stevenson, *British Society 1914–45*, p. 297.

74 *Ibid.*, p. 298.

75 Butchart, 'Unemployment and Non-Employment in Interwar Britain', p. 4.

76 Middlebrook, *The First Day of the Somme*, p. 319.

Chapter 11

1   Coppard, *With a Machine Gun to Cambrai*, p. 56.
2   Winter, *The Great War*, pp. 250-3.
3   *Ibid.*, p. 256.
4   Simon Heffer, 'Dark Shadow of the Great War as We Are Still Living with Its Legacy in Ukraine and Gaza', *Daily Mail Online*, last modified 3 August 2014. Accessed 18 July 2018. www.dailymail.co.uk/debate/article-2714390/Dark-shadow-Great-War-Tomorrow-marks-100-years-Europe-plunged-war-end-wars-But-brilliant-analysis-argues-living-appalling-legacy-Ukraine-Gaza.html#ixzz4pFE6Ook8.
5   Per 1,000 males aged 15–49. Britain 63, Germany 125 and France 133 Winter, *The Great War*, p. 75.
6   *Ibid.*, p. 251.
7   Amanda Cable, 'Condemned to Be Virgins: The Two Million Women Robbed by the War', *Daily Mail Online*, last modified 15 September 2007. Accessed 18 July 2018. www.dailymail.co.uk/femail/article-481882/Condemned-virgins-The-million-women-robbed-war.html.
8   *Ibid.*
9   Clive James, *Falling Towards England* (Omnibus Edition) (London: Quality Paperback Direct, 1990), p. 207.
10   'UK Marriage and Divorce Figures', *Kaggle*, last modified 20 March 2018. Accessed 11 December 2018. www.kaggle.com/osbornep/uk-marriage-and-divorce-figures.
11   Arthur, *The Last Post*, p. 239.
12   'Episode 2', *Welsh Memories of World War 1*.
13   Arthur, *The Road Home*, p. 241.
14   Winter, *The Great War*, p. 251.
15   Searle, *A New England?*, p. 742.
16   Jessica Chamberlain and Baljit Gill, 'Fertility and mortality' in Roma Chapel (ed.), *Focus on People and Migration* (London: Palgrave Macmillan, 2005), pp. 71–89. Accessed 18 July 2018. link.springer.com/chapter/10.1007/978-1-349-75096-2_5.
17   Winter, *The Great War*, p. 271.
18   Joe Hicks and Grahame Allen, *A Century of Change: Trends in UK Statistics Since 1900*, vol. 99, no. 11 (London: House of Commons Library, 1999). Accessed 30 July 2018. www.researchgate.net/profile/Grahame_Allen/publication/235361286_A_Century_of_Change_Trends_in_UK_Statistics_since_1900/links/56f1390d08ae5c367d4a9aa5/A-Century-of-Change-Trends-in-UK-Statistics-since-1900.pdf.
19   Mark Harrison, 'The British Army and the Problem of Venereal Disease in France and Egypt during the First World War', *Advances in Pediatrics*, last modified April 1995. Accessed 18 July 2018. www.ncbi.nlm.nih.gov/pmc/articles/PMC1036972/?page=1.
20   Graves, *Goodbye to All That*, p. 195.
21   John Lichfield, 'Inside the Brothels that Served the Western Front', *The Independent*, last modified 3 August 2014. Accessed 3 September 2018. www.independent.co.uk/news/world/world-history/inside-the-brothels-that-served-the-western-front-how-one-first-world-war-soldier-found-love-in-the-9643738.html.

22 David Smith, 'A Book Lifts the Lid on the Carnal Comforts Sought by First World War Troops', *The Guardian*, last modified 23 August 2008. Accessed 18 July 2018. www.guardian.co.uk/world/2008/aug/24/firstworldwar.military.

23 Graves, *Goodbye to All That*, p. 151.

24 C.N. Trueman, 'Brothels and the Western Front', *History Learning Site*, last modified 31 March 2015. Accessed 18 July 2018. www.historylearningsite.co.uk/brothels_western_front.htm.

25 Clare Makepeace, 'Sex and the Somme: The Officially Sanctioned WWI Brothels on the Front Line Laid Bare for the First Time', *Daily Mail Online*, last modified 29 October 2011. Accessed 18 July 2018. www.dailymail.co.uk/news/article-2054914/Sex-Somme-Officially-sanctioned-WWI-brothels-line.html.

26 Richard Marshall, 'The British Army's Fight against Venereal Disease in the "Heroic Age of Prostitution"', *World War I Centenary*. Accessed 18 July 2018. ww1centenary.oucs.ox.ac.uk/body-and-mind/the-british-army's-fight-against-venereal-disease-in-the-'heroic-age-of-prostitution'/.

27 Sir George Arthur, *Life of Lord Kitchener, Volume 3* (New York: Cosimo Inc., 2007), accessed via Google Books.

28 Marshall, 'The British Army's Fight against Venereal Disease'.

29 Frances Osborne, 'Sex in The Downton Abbey Era', *The Huffington Post*, last modified 14 August 2012. Accessed 18 July 2018. www.huffingtonpost.com/frances-osborne/sex_b_1597879.html.

30 *Ibid.*

31 *Ibid.*

32 DeGroot, *Blighty*, p. 234.

33 Marshall, 'The British Army's Fight against Venereal Disease'.

34 I. Palmer, 'Sexuality and Soldiery Combat & Condoms, Continence & Cornflakes', *Journal of the Royal Army Medical Corps* (2003), pp. 38-46. jramc.bmj.com/content/jramc/149/1/38.full.pdf.

35 Harrison, 'The British Army and the Problem of Venereal Disease'.

36 Holmes, *Tommy*, p. 483.

37 *Ibid.*

38 Makepeace, 'Sex and the Somme'.

39 John Frith, 'Syphilis – Its early history and Treatment until Penicillin and the Debate on its Origins', *Journal of Military and Veterans' Health*, vol. 20, no. 4 (2012), pp. 49–56.

40 Marshall, 'The British Army's Fight against Venereal Disease'.

41 Simon Szreter, 'The Prevalence of Syphilis in England and Wales on the Eve of the Great War: Re-Visiting the Estimates of the Royal Commission on Venereal Diseases 1913–1916', *Social History of Medicine* (2014), pp. 508–29. Accessed 18 July 2018. www.ncbi.nlm.nih.gov/pmc/articles/PMC4109696/.

42 '1912–1949: The Early Years at the BBFC', *bbfc.co.uk*. Accessed 18 July 2018. www.bbfc.co.uk/education-resources/student-guide/bbfc-history/1912-1949.

43 DeGroot, *Blighty*, p. 236.

44 Osborne, 'Sex in The Downton Abbey Era'.

45 Winter, *The Great War*, p. 253.

46 *Ibid.*, p. 271.

47 Grayling, *A Land Fit for Heroes*, p.18.

48 Alfred Noyes, 'A Victory Dance', *The Saturday Evening Post*. Accessed 17 December 2018. www.blueridgejournal.com/poems/an-victory.htm.
49 Brittain, *Testament of Youth*, p. 469.
50 James J. Nott, *Classes, Cultures, and Politics: Essays on British History for Ross McKibbin*, Clare V. J. Griffiths, James J. Nott, William Whyte (eds) (Oxford: Oxford University Press, 2003), p. 231.

Chapter 12

1   Kitchen, 'Now This Bloody War Is Over'.
2   Jenny Du Feu, 'Factors Influencing Rehabilitation of British Soldiers After World War 1', *Historia Medicinae*, vol. 2, no. 1 (2009), p. 1.
3   Seth Koven, 'Remembering and Dismemberment: Crippled Children, Wounded Soldiers, and the Great War in Great Britain', *The American Historical Review*, vol. 99, no. 4 (1 October 1994), pp. 1167–1202.
4   Mike Mantin, 'Coalmining and the National Scheme for Disabled Ex-Servicemen after the First World War', *Social History*, vol. 41, no. 2 (2016), p. 156.
5   Dr Saleyha Ahsan, 'How Did WW1 Change the Way We Treat War Injuries Today?', *World War One BBC*, BBC iWonder. Accessed 18 July 2018. www.bbc.co.uk/guides/zs3wpv4.
6   Dan Snow, 'How Did So Many Soldiers Survive the Trenches?', *World War One BBC*, BBC iWonder. Accessed 18 July 2018. www.bbc.co.uk/guides/z3kgjxs.
7   Cohen, *The War Come Home: Disabled Veterans in Britain and Germany, 1914–1939* (Berkeley: University of California, 2001), p. 46.
8   Mantin, 'Coalmining', p. 157.
9   Bourke, quoted in Jenny De Feu, 'Factors Influencing Rehabilitation of British Soldiers After World War 1', *Dismembering the Male: Men's Bodies, Britain and the Great War* (London: Reaktion Books, 1996), p. 3.
10 Reese, *Homecoming Heroes*, p. 95.
11 Cohen, *The War Come Home*, p. 111.
12 Gerber (ed.), *Disabled Veterans in History: Enlarged and Revised Edition* (Ann Arbor: The University of Michigan Press, 2015), p. 300.
13 *Ibid.*, p. 296.
14 Cohen, *The War Come Home*, p. 110.
15 'War and Impairment', *Unite the Union*.
16 Cohen, *The War Come Home*, p. 111.
17 Reese, *Homecoming Heroes*, p. 55.
18 Harding, *Keeping Faith*, p. 197.
19 Arthur, *The Road Home*, pp. 208–9.
20 Mantin, 'Coalmining', p. 166.
21 *Ibid.*, p. 162.
22 *Ibid.*, p. 164.
23 Gerber (ed.), *Disabled Veterans in History*, p. 296.
24 *Secret History: WWI's Forgotten Heroes* (London: Channel 4, 2 November 2004), television broadcast.

25 Rachel Hasted and Paul Stamper, *Domestic Housing for Disabled Veterans, 1900-2014* (England: Heritage England, 2016). Accessed 18 July 2018. retail.historicengland-services.org.uk/domestic-housing-for-disabled-veterans-1900-2014.html.

26 Reese, *Homecoming Heroes*, p. 96.

27 Cohen, *The War Come Home*, pp. 35–6.

28 Matthew Lloyd, 'Sir Oswald Stoll', *ArthurLloyd.co.uk*. Accessed 18 July 2018. www.arthurlloyd.co.uk/OswaldStoll.htm.

29 'War and Impairment', *Unite the Union*.

30 Anderson, *War, Disability and Rehabilitation in Britain: 'Soul of a Nation'* (Manchester: Manchester University Press, 2011), p. 49.

31 'History & Timeline', *The Poppy Factory*. Accessed 18 July 2018. www.poppyfactory.org/history-timeline.

32 Reese, *Homecoming Heroes*, p. 95.

33 Alexander Dean, 'An Analytical Study into the Rehabilitation of the Wounded from the Great War', *Academia.edu*. Accessed 13 December 2018. www.academia.edu/27091561/An_analytical_study_into_the_rehabilitation_of_the_wounded_from_the_Great_War.

34 Anderson, *War, Disability and Rehabilitation in Britain*, p. 46.

35 Cohen, *The War Come Home*, p. 45.

36 *Ibid.*

37 Gerber (ed.), *Disabled Veterans in History*, pp. 296-7.

38 Cohen, *The War Come Home*, p. 120.

39 Anderson, *War, Disability and Rehabilitation in Britain*, 54.

40 *Ibid.*, pp. 124–5.

41 *Secret History: WWI's Forgotten Heroes* (London: Channel 4, 28 October 2014), television broadcast.

42 Caroline Alexander, 'Faces of War', *Smithsonian Magazine*, last modified 1 February 2007. Accessed 18 July 2018. www.smithsonianmag.com/history/faces-of-war-145799854/?no-ist=&fb_locale=ja_JP&page=3.

43 Anderson, *War, Disability and Rehabilitation in Britain*, p. 53.

44 Trevor Wilson, *The Myriad Faces of War: Britain and the Great War, 1914–1918* (Cambridge: Polity, 1988), p. 755.

45 Battersby, 'Heroic Pal Joined Up at 14, Lost Leg at 17', *Accrington Observer*, last modified 6 February 2013. Accessed 6 November 2018. www.accringtonobserver.co.uk/news/local-news/heroic-pal-joined-up-at-14-1268132.

46 Ronald Blythe, *The View in Winter: Reflections on Old Age* (Norwich: Hymns Ancient and Modern Ltd, 2005), p.164.

47 Suzannah Biernoff, 'The Rhetoric of Disfigurement in First World War Britain', *Oxford University Press Academic*, last modified 27 February 2011. Accessed 21 February 2019. academic.oup.com/shm/article/24/3/666/1630765.

48 Battersby, 'Heroic Pal Joined Up at 14, Lost Leg at 17'.

49 Biernoff, 'The Rhetoric of Disfigurement in First World War Britain'.

50 Michael Mosley, 'How Do You Fix a Face That's Been Blown off by Shrapnel?', *World War One BBC*, BBC iWonder. Accessed 22 November 2018. www.bbc.co.uk/guides/zxw42hv.

51 Biernoff, 'The Rhetoric of Disfigurement in First World War Britain'.

52 Alexander, 'Faces of War'.

53 *Ibid.*

54   *Secret History: WWI's Forgotten Heroes.*
55   David Silbey, *The British Working Class and Enthusiasm for War, 1914–1916* (Abingdon: Routledge, 2015), p. 43.
56   John Welshman, 'Eugenics and Public Health in Britain, 1900–40: Scenes from Provincial Life', *Urban History*, vol. 24, no. 1 (1997) 57.
57   *The Nineteenth Century and After,*vol. 95 (London: Leonard Scott Publishing Company, 1924), p. 177.
58   Cohen, *The War Come Home*, p. 123.
59   Anderson, *War, Disability and Rehabilitation in Britain*, p. 62.
60   *Ibid.*, pp. 55-64.
61   Bourke, 'Masculinity, Men's Bodies and the Great War', *History Today*, vol. 46, no. 2 (2 February 1996).
62   'Four Decades since Disability Act', *BBC News Liverpool*, last modified 20 May 2010. Accessed 26 July 2018. news.bbc.co.uk/local/liverpool/low/people_and_places/newsid_8691000/8691968.stm.
63   Andrew Roth, 'Lord Morris of Manchester Obituary', *The Guardian*, last modified 14 August 2012. Accessed 26 July 2018. www.theguardian.com/politics/2012/aug/14/lord-morris-of-manchester.

Chapter 13

1   Shephard, *A War of Nerves: Soldiers and Psychiatrists, 1914–1994* (London: Pimlico, 2002), p. 144.
2   Alex Horton, 'Battle in Their Hearts', *VAntage Point*, last modified 30 January 2017. Accessed 18 July 2018. www.blogs.va.gov/VAntage/459/battle-in-their-hearts/.
3   Anthony Babington, *Shell Shock* (Barnsley: Pen and Sword, 1990), p. 7.
4   William Shakespeare, *Henry IV, Part 1*, Act 2, Scene 3.
5   Henry G. Cole, 'Reflections on Courage', *Strategic Studies Institute* (Winter 1997-98), pp. 147–57. Accessed 20 July 2018. ssi.armywarcollege.edu/pubs/parameters/articles/97winter/win-essa.htm.
6   David Payne, 'Furthering Interest in the Great War 1914–18 Shell Shock: Genesis and Outcomes in The Great War' (Presentation, The Western Front Association, Thursday, 22 May 2008).
7   'Frederick W Mott', *King's Collections: Online Exhibitions: The Treaty of Utrecht.* Accessed 26 July 2018. www.kingscollections.org/exhibitions/specialcollections/mind-matters/war-psychiatry/frederick-w-mott.
8   Reid, *Broken Men*, p. 57.
9   John Simkin, 'Shellshock', *Spartacus Educational.* Accessed 18 July 2018. spartacus-educational.com/FWWshellshock.htm.
10   Payne, 'Furthering Interest in the Great War.
11   Bourke, 'Shell Shock during World War One'.
12   Barham, *Forgotten Lunatics of the Great War* (New Haven: Yale University Press, 2004), pp. 14–21.
13   Leese, *Shell Shock: Traumatic Neurosis and the British Soldiers of the First World War* (London: Palgrave Macmillan, 2002), p. 34.
14   Fionnuala Barrett, 'Perspectives on "Shell Shock"', *World War I Centenary*, University of Oxford. Accessed 18 July 2018. ww1centenary.oucs.ox.ac.uk/body-and-mind/shell-shock-on-film/.

15 David Reynolds. 'Long Shadows of Old Wars', *New Statesman*, last modified 17 August 2016. Accessed 2 August 2019. www.newstatesman.com/politics/uk/2016/08/long-shadows-old-wars.

16 Peter Mulvany, 'Shot at Dawn; Justice Does Not Have an Expiry Date', *History Ireland*, last modified 10 April 2013. Accessed 18 July 2018. www.historyireland.com/20th-century-contemporary-history/shot-at-dawn-justice-does-not-have-an-expiry-date/.

17 Payne, 'Furthering Interest in the Great War'.

18 'Shell Shock', *BBC Inside Out*, last modified 3 March 2004. Accessed 2 August 2019. www.bbc.co.uk/insideout/extra/series-1/shell_shocked.shtml.

19 Graves, *Goodbye to All That*, p. 144.

20 *Ibid.*

21 Shephard, *A War of Nerves*, p. 29.

22 Reid, *Broken Men*, pp. 60–1.

23 *Ibid.*, p. 31.

24 Stefanie C. Linden, Edgar Jones and Andrew J. Lees, 'Shell Shock at Queen Square: Lewis Yealland 100 Years On', *Brain*, vol. 136, no. 6 (2013), pp. 1,976–88.

25 *Ibid.*

26 Virginia Woolf, quoted in Tonya Krouse, *The Opposite of Desire* (Lanham, MD: Lexington Books, 2009), p. 80.

27 Matthew Levay. *Violent Minds: Modernism and the Criminal* (Cambridge: Cambridge University Press, 2019), p. 70..

28 Shephard, *A War of Nerves*, p. 167.

29 Linden, Jones and Lees, 'Shell Shock at Queen Square', pp. 976–88.

30 *Ibid.*

31 Barham, *Forgotten Lunatics of the Great War*, p. 29.

32 Leese, *Shell Shock*, p. 89.

33 Shephard, *A War of Nerves*, p. 110.

34 Peter W. Howarth, 'The treatment of shell-shock: Cognitive therapy before its time', *Psychiatric Bulletin*, vol. 24, no. 6 (2000), pp. 225–7. www.cambridge.org/core/journals/psychiatric-bulletin/article/treatment-of-shellshock/738DC9BBF9DFEB6304C411D4E9DA700B

35 Vicki Caren, 'Treatment of Shell Shock', *Merseyside at War 1914–1918*. Accessed 18 July 2018. www.merseyside-at-war.org/story/treatment-of-shell-shock/#_ftn4.

36 Reid, *Broken Men*, p. 133.

37 War Office Committee, *Report of the War Office Committee of Enquiry into 'Shell-Shock'*, (1922). Accessed 18 July 2018. wellcomelibrary.org/item/b18295496#?c=0&m=0&s=0&cv=0

38 Ted Bogacz, 'War Neurosis and Cultural Change in England, 1914–22: The Work of the War Office Committee of Enquiry into "Shell-Shock"', *Journal of Contemporary History*, vol. 24, no. 2 (1989), pp. 227–56. www.jstor.org/stable/260822.

39 *Ibid.*

40 Leese, *Shell Shock*, p. 38.

41 Reid, *Broken Men*, p. 133.

42 'Broadcast Appeal by an Unknown Soldier', *Trades Union Congress*, Warwick Digital Collections. Accessed 26 October 2018. cdm21047.contentdm.oclc.org/digital/collection/tav/id/4022.

43 House of Lords, 'Neurasthenia and Shell-Shock', *Hansard*, 15 April 1919. api.parliament.uk/historic-hansard/lords/1919/apr/15/neurasthenia-and-shell-shock.

44 Jones and Wessely, *Shell Shock to PTSD*, p. 133.

45   Leese, *Shell Shock*, p. 141.

46   Bourke, 'Shell Shock during World War One'.

47   *World War 1's Secret Shame: Shell Shock* (London: BBC Two, 12 November 2018), television broadcast.

48   Paul Chapman and Ted Smith, *A Haven in Hell* (Oxford: ISIS, 2001), p. 116.

49   Winter, 'Britain's "Lost Generation" of the First World War', *Population Studies*, vol. 31, no. 3 (Nov., 1977), pp. 461.

50   Bourke, 'Shell Shock during World War One'.

51   Leese, *Shell Shock*, p. 148.

52   Cohen, *The War Come Home*, p. 58.

53   Edgar Jones and Simon Wessely, *Shell Shock to PTSD: Military Psychiatry from 1900 to the Gulf War* (Hove: Psychology Press, 2005), p. 143.

Chapter 14

1   Barr, *Service not self*.

2   Kowalsky, 'Enabling the Great War'.

3   *Ibid*.

4   Kipling, 'The Absent-Minded Beggar', *The Kipling Society*. Accessed 18 July 2018. www.kiplingsociety.co.uk/poems_beggar.htm.

5   DeGroot, *Blighty*, p. 258.

6   Arthur, *The Road Home*, pp. 131–2.

7   Kowalsky, 'Enabling the Great War'.

8   Richards, *Old Soldiers Never Die*, p. 319.

9   Kowalsky, 'Enabling the Great War'.

10   Arthur, *The Road Home*, pp. 169–70.

11   Pension Appeal Tribunal (Assessment), Vernon House, Surrey. Ref. no. O.A. 87410. With permission from his grandson, Graham Page.

12   Barr, *The Lion and the Poppy*, p. 123.

13   Kowalsky, 'Enabling the Great War'.

14   *Ibid*.

15   Arthur, *The Road Home*, p. 161.

16   Kowalsky, 'Enabling the Great War'.

17   *Ibid*.

18   Cohen, *The War Come Home*, p. 53.

19   *Ibid*., p. 48.

20   *Ibid*., p. 194.

21   Kowalsky, 'Enabling the Great War'.

22   Barr, *Service not self*.

23   Cohen, *The War Come Home*, p. 25.

24   *Ibid*., p. 58.

25   *Ibid*., p. 19.

Chapter 15

1 Robert F. Drake, *Understanding Disability Policies* (Basingstoke: Palgrave Macmillan, 1999), p. 50.
2 Winter, *The Great War*, p. 139.
3 Christopher Harvie, *A Floating Commonwealth: Politics, Culture, and Technology on Britain's Atlantic Coast, 1860–1930* (Oxford: Oxford University Press, 2008), p. 148.
4 Marie Luise Schroeter Gothein, *A History of Garden Art* (Cambridge: Cambridge University Press, 2014), p. 416.
5 Crabtree and Evans, 'The Sociality of Domestic Environments' (ESPRC Project, University of Nottingham, 2001), vol. 36. www.cs.nott.ac.uk/~pszaxc/work/Equator-01-003.pdf.
6 Benson, *The Working Class in Britain: 1850–1939* (London: I.B.Tauris, 2003), p. 80.
7 *Ibid.*
8 'Council Housing', *Living Heritage*, UK Parliament. Accessed 27 September 2018. www.parliament.uk/about/living-heritage/transformingsociety/towncountry/towns/overview/councilhousing/.
9 Crabtree and Evans, 'The Sociality of Domestic Environments'.
10 Alan Crisp, 'The Working-Class Owner-Occupied House of the 1930s', PhD diss., University of Oxford, 1998.
11 *Ibid.*
12 Benson, *The Working Class in Britain*, pp. 74-5.
13 Thorpe, *The Longman Companion to Britain*, p. 61.
14 Crabtree and Evans, 'The Sociality of Domestic Environments'.
15 'A Brief History of Social (Council) Housing', *Historic England*. Accessed 14 December 2018. http://www.heritage-explorer.co.uk/file/he/content/upload/9527.doc.
16 Finn Jensen, *The English Semi-Detached House: How and Why the Semi Became Britain's Most Popular House-Type* (Huntingdon: Ovolo, 2007), p. 162.
17 George Orwell, *Road to Wigan Pier* (London: Penguin Modern Classics, 2001), Chapter 4.

Chapter 16

1 Fussell, *The Great War and Modern Memory*, p. 231.
2 *Ibid.*, pp. 231–44.
3 Mark Bostridge, 'The Shepherd in a Soldier's Coat', *The Independent*, last modified 22 October 2011. Accessed 22 November 2018. www.independent.co.uk/arts-entertainment/the-shepherd-in-a-soldiers-coat-1313625.html.
4 Graves, *Goodbye to All That*, p. 241.
5 '90th Anniversary of the End of the First World War', *The War Poetry Website*. Accessed 27 September 2018. www.warpoetry.co.uk/end_of_First_World_War_90th_anniversary.html.
6 *Teenage Tommies*, BBC Two.
7 Barr, *Service not self.*
8 Leah Leneman, 'Land Settlement in Scotland after World War I', *The Agricultural History Review*, vol. 37, no. 1 (1989), pp. 52–64.

9   *Ibid.*
10   *Ibid.*
11   Chris Coates, 'Utopian Scotland', *Utopia Britannica*. Accessed 19 July 2018. www.utopia-britannica.org.uk/pages/SCOTLAND.htm.
12   Leneman, 'Land Settlement in Scotland after World War I'.
13   *Ibid.*
14   Barr, *Service not Self.*
15   Field, 'Exporting "People of British Stock": Training and Emigration Policy in Inter-War Britain', in *40th Annual SCUTREA Conference*, University of Leeds, 2010. www.leeds.ac.uk/educol/documents/191542.pdf.
16   Barr, *Service not Self.*
17   Fedorowich, 'Foredoomed to Failure'.
18   *Ibid.*
19   Field, 'Exporting "People of British Stock"'.
20   *Ibid.*
21   Barr, *Service not Self.*
22   Fedorowich, 'Foredoomed to Failure'.
23   *Ibid.*
24   *Ibid.*
25   Alec Tritton, 'Empire Settlement Schemes after WWI', *Exodus: Movement of the People*, last modified 2 July 2013. Accessed 19 July 2018. www.exodus2013.co.uk/empire-settlement-schemes-after-wwi/.
26   Fedorowich, 'Foredoomed to Failure'.
27   *Ibid.*

Chapter 17

1   Fussell, *The Great War and Modern Memory*, p. 327.
2   Michael Hughes, 'After the War', *Graham: World Traveller*. Accessed 19 July 2018. www.stephengrahamworldtraveller.com/after-the-war.html.
3   Volker Rolf Berghahn and Martin Kitchen, *Germany in the Age of Total War* (London, Croom Helm, 1981), p. 108.
4   Jay Winter, *Sites of Memory, Sites of Mourning: The Great War in European Cultural History* (Cambridge: Cambridge University Press, 2014), p. 52.
5   Graham, *The Challenge of the Dead: A Vision of the War and the Life of the Common Soldier in France, Seen Two Years Afterwards Between August and November, 1920* (Cassell and Company Limited, 1921). Digitised by Project Gutenberg.
6   Neil Tweedie, '"Sacred" Battlefield Still Gives up Its Dead', *The Telegraph*, last modified 11 November 2000. Accessed 19 July 2018. www.telegraph.co.uk/news/uknews/1373997/Sacred-battlefield-still-gives-up-its-dead.html.
7   Winter, *Sites of Memory, Sites of Mourning*, p. 52.
8   'Pilgrimage', *Aftermath*, accessed 19 July 2018. www.aftermathww1.com/pilgrim.asp.
9   Joanna Legg, Graham Parker and David Legg, 'The Menin Gate Inauguration Ceremony – Sunday 24th July, 1927', *The Great War 1914–1918*. Accessed 19 July 2018. www.greatwar.co.uk/ypres-salient/memorial-menin-gate-inauguration.htm.

10   Siegfried Sassoon, 'On Passing the New Menin Gate', *Peace Pledge Union*. Accessed 19 July 2018. www.ppu.org.uk/learn/poetry/poetry_ww1_4.html.

11   Grayling, *A Land Fit for Heroes*, p. 83.

12   Barr, *Service not Self*.

13   Stedman, *Salford Pals*, p. 226.

14   Holmes, *Tommy*, p. 24.

15   C.N. Trueman, 'Commonwealth War Graves Commission', *The History Learning Site*, last modified 17 April 2015. Accessed 19 July 2018. www.historylearningsite. co.uk/world-war-one/world-war-one-and-casualties/commonwealth-war-graves-commission/.

16   Norman Bonney, 'The Cenotaph: A Consensual and Contested Monument of Remembrance', *London: National Secular Society*, October 2014. Accessed 26 July 2018. www.secularism.org.uk/uploads/cenotaph-a-consensual-and-contested-monument-of-remembrance.pdf.

17   Gavin Stamp, *The Memorial to the Missing of the Somme* (London: Profile Books, 2010), p. 77.

18   John Masefield, *The Old Front-line* (Barnsley: Pen and Sword, 2006), p. 75.

19   Brown, *The Imperial War Museum Book of The Western Front*, p. 347.

20   'The Blog', *History Today*. Accessed 19 July 2018. www.historytoday.com/ blog/2011/11/remains-german-soldiers-ww1-found-france.

21   Rob Ruggenberg, 'Burials of the Great War: Near Ypres Newly Found Corpses and Mortal Remains Are Reburied in Flemish Earth -/- Begrafenissen Van De Groote Oorlog: Pas Opgedolven Soldatenlijken En Menselijke Resten Worden Begraven in Vlaamse Aarde', *The Heritage of the Great War*. Accessed 19 July 2018. www.denblanken.com/ieper/burial.html.

22   Bird, *Thirteen Years After: The Story of the Old Front Revisited* (Toronto: Maclean, 1932), p. 31.

23   Holmes, *Tommy*, p. 23.

24   'The Iron Harvest', *Flanders Today*, last modified 1 December 2010. Accessed 19 July 2018. www.flanderstoday.eu/living/iron-harvest.

25   'Behind the Scenes with Belgium's Bomb Disposal Unit – BBC News', *BBC*, last modified 21 March 2014. Accessed 19 July 2018. www.bbc.co.uk/news/ world-europe-26663643?ocid.

26   Constant Brand, 'On WWI Killing Field, an Iron Harvest', *USA Today*, last modified 7 July 2010. Accessed 28 July 2018. www.usatoday.com/news/ world/2007-07-10-384369162_x.htm.

27   Graham, 'The Challenge of the Dead'.

28   Bird, *Thirteen Years After*, p. 225.

29   Stedman, *Salford Pals*, p. 221.

30   Bird, *Thirteen Years After*, p. 51.

31   *Ibid.*, p. 28.

32   'Pilgrimage', *Aftermath*.

33   Graham, 'The Challenge of the Dead'.

34   Jay Winter and Blaine Baggett, *1914–18: The Great War and the Shaping of the 20th Century* (London: BBC, 1996), p. 382.

35   Dennis Winter, *Death's Men Soldiers of the Great War* (London: Penguin, 1979), p. 262.

Chapter 18

1   DeGroot, *Blighty*, p. 269.
2   Deanna Spingola, *The Ruling Elite: Death, Destruction, and Domination* (Bloomington: Trafford Publishing, 2014), p. 673.
3   Winter, *The Great War*, p. 229.
4   E.J. Hobsbawm, *Age of Extremes: 1914–1991* (New York: Vintage, 1995), p. 125.
5   Oswald Mosley, *My Life* (New York: Arlington House, 1972), p. 50.
6   Bret Rubin, 'The Rise and Fall of British Fascism: Sir Oswald Mosley and the British Union of Fascists', *Intersections*, vol. 11, no. 2 (2010), p. 327.
7   *Ibid.*, p. 337.
8   G. Lebzelter, *Political Anti-Semitism in England 1918–1939* (New York: Springer, 1978), p. 103.
9   Constance Kell, *A Secret Well Kept: The Untold Story of Sir Vernon Kell, Founder of MI5* (London: Bloomsbury Publishing, 2017), p. 11.
10 Andrew Richards, 'Mobilizing the Powerless. Collective Protest Action of the Unemployed in the Interwar Period', Estudio/Working paper 2002/175, Juan March Institut, Madrid 2002, last modified 2002. Accessed 26 August 2018. citeseerx.ist.psu.edu/viewdoc/download?doi=10.1.1.586.228&rep=rep1&type=pdf.
11 Graves, *Goodbye to All That*, p. 238.
12 Lamb, 'Mutinies 1917–1920'.
13 Claire McKim, 'Red Clydeside Remembered: The Battle of George Square', *The Scotsman*, last modified 1 February 2016. www.scotsman.com/lifestyle/red-clydeside-remembered-the-battle-of-george-square-1-4017559.
14 Rob Sewell, '1919: Britain on the Brink of Revolution', *In Defence of Marxism*, last modified 16 May 2013. Accessed 19 July 2018. www.marxist.com/1919-britain-on-the-brink-of-revolution.htm.
15 Lamb, 'Mutinies 1917–1920'.
16 Webb, *1919: Britain's Year of Revolution*, p. 107.
17 '1919 Race Riots', *Making Britain: Discover How South Asians Shaped the Nation, 1870-1950*, (The Open University). Accessed 19 July 2018. www.open.ac.uk/researchprojects/makingbritain/content/1919-race-riots.
18 Roy Jenkins, *Churchill* (London: Pan, 2001), p. 339.
19 Thorpe, 'The Membership of the Communist Party of Great Britain, 1920–1945', *The Historical Journal 43*, no. 3 (2000), p. 781.
20 *Ibid.*, p. 781.
21 James Vernon, *Hunger: A Modern History* (Cambridge MA: Harvard University Press, 2009), accessed via Google Books.

Chapter 19

1   Mark Garnett and Richard Weight, *The A–Z Guide to Modern British History* (London: Jonathan Cape, 2003), p. 76.
2   Reese, *Homecoming Heroes*, p. 111.
3   Barr, *The Lion and the Poppy*, p. 18.
4   Reese, *Homecoming Heroes*, p. 112.
5   Harding, *Keeping Faith*, p. 5.

6   Alwyn Turner, 'The Most Degrading and Bestial Business in the World', *Lion &*
      Unicorn, last modified 25 November 2017. Accessed 19 July 2018. thelionand-
      unicorn.wordpress.com/2015/11/08/the-most-degrading-and-bestial-business-in-
      the-world/.
7   Harding, *Keeping Faith*, p. 45.
8   Barr, *Service not self*.
9   Barr, *The Lion and the Poppy*, p. 19.
10   Barr, *Service not self*.
11   Stuart Bell and Ian Holliday, *Mass Conservatism: The Conservatives and the Public since*
      the 1880s (Abingdon: Routledge, 2013), p. 49.
12   Barr, *Service not self*.
13   Harding, *Keeping Faith*, p. 15.
14   *Ibid.*, p. 434.
15   *Ibid.*
16   Cohen, *The War Come Home*, p. 53.
17   Harding, *Keeping Faith*, p. 12.
18   *Ibid.*, p. 21.
19   Cohen, *The War Come Home*, p. 54.
20   *Ibid.*, p. 50.
21   Reese, *Homecoming Heroes*, p. 137.
22   *Ibid.*, p. 138.
23   Barr, *Service not self*.
24   'War and Impairment', *Unite the Union*.
25   Cohen, *The War Come Home*, p. 46.
26   Hasted and Stamper, *Domestic Housing for Disabled Veterans*.
27   Harding, *Keeping Faith*, p. 38.
28   Barr, *Service not Self*.
29   Arthur, *The Road Home*, p. 221.
30   Robin Bowman, 'Tubby Clayton and the Story of Toc-H', *Trenches on the Web*.
      Accessed 29 December 2018. www.worldwar1.com/sftoch.htm.
31   'History of TocH', TocH International Charity. Accessed 29 December 2018.
      toch-uk.org.uk/history-of-toch/.
32   David Englander, 'The National Union of Ex-Servicemen and the Labour
      Movement, 1918–1920', *History*, vol. 76, no. 246 (1991), pp. 24–42. Accessed
      7 August 2018.
33   Turner, 'The Most Degrading and Bestial Business in the World'.
34   *Ibid.*
35   Ian F.W. Becket, *The Great War 1914–1918* (Abingdon: Rouledge, 2014), p. 572.
36   Reid, *Broken Men*, p. 105.
37   'Ex-Services Welfare Society: public appeal for funds on behalf of mentally broken
      ex-servicemen 1922–1924', *The National Archives*. Accessed 21 July 2018. national-
      archives.gov.uk/documents/filesonfilm/ex-services-welfare-society-public-appeal-
      for-funds-pin-15-2499.pdf.
38   Reid, *Broken Men*, p. 116.
39   *Ibid.*, p. 115.
40   *Ibid.*, p. 122.
41   *Ibid.*, p. 125.

Chapter 20

1   Fussell, *The Great War and Modern Memory*, p. 157.
2   Alan R. Ruff, *Arcadian Visions: Pastoral Influences on Poetry, Painting and the Design of Landscape* (Barnsley: Windgather Press, 2015), p. 198.
3   Janet S.K. Watson, *Fighting Different Wars: Experience, Memory, and the First World War in Britain* (Cambridge: Cambridge University Press, 2004), p. 239.
4   Hynes, *A War Imagined*, p. 29.
5   'Edmund Blunden', *Poetry Foundation*. Accessed 19 July 2018. www.poetry-foundation.org/poets/edmund-blunden.
6   Fussell, *The Great War and Modern Memory*, p. 255.
7   Adams, 'Herbert Read and the Fluid Memory of the First World War', pp. 333–54.
8   *Ibid.*
9   *Ibid.*
10   *Ibid.*
11   *Ibid.*
12   Nancy Marie Ott, 'JRR Tolkien and World War I', *GreenBooks*. Accessed 19 July 2018. greenbooks.theonering.net/guest/files/040102_02.html.
13   *Ibid.*
14   *Ibid.*
15   *Ibid.*
16   Hynes, *A War Imagined*, p. 237.
17   'We Are Making a New World', *Tate Britain*. Accessed 18 December 2018. www.tate.org.uk/whats-on/tate-britain/exhibition/paul-nash/room-guide/we-are-making-new-world.
18   Hynes, *A War Imagined*, p. 161.
19   *Ibid.*, p. 195.
20   Winter and Baggett, *1914–18*, p. 350.
21   Gavin Stamp, 'London: Royal Artillery Memorial', *The Twentieth Century Society*. Accessed 4 November 2018. c20society.org.uk/war-memorials/london-royal-artillery-memorial/.

Chapter 21

1   Johnson, *Land Fit for Heroes*, p. 38.
2   Hynes, *A War Imagined*, p. 263.
3   Thane, *The Foundations of the Welfare State* (London: Longman, 1996), p. 129.
4   Ascherson, 'Armistice Day: Victory and beyond'.
5   Winter, *The Great War*, p. 59.
6   *Ibid.*, p. 62.
7   Johnson, *Land Fit for Heroes*, p. 38.
8   Thane, *The Foundations of the Welfare State*, p. 129.
9   *Ibid.*
10   L.C.B. Seaman, *Post-Victorian Britain: 1902–1951* (Abingdon: Routledge, 1993), p. 90.
11   Johnson, *Land Fit for Heroes*, p. 55.
12   DeGroot, *Blighty*, p. 318.
13   Johnson, *Land Fit for Heroes*, p. 68.

Chapter 22

1   Stedman, *Salford Pals*, p. 226.
2   'Episode 4: Lost Peace (1919)', *The People's Century*.
3   'Dick Sheppard', *Peace Pledge Union*. Accessed 19 July 2018. www.ppu.org.uk/
    people/N_sheppard_dick.html.
4   'Woodbine Willie: A Different Kind of War Hero', *Birminghampost*, last modified
    30 May 2013. Accessed 19 July 2018. www.birminghampost.co.uk/lifestyle/
    woodbine-willie-different-kind-war-3948562.
5   Charles Messenger, *Broken Sword: The Tumultuous Life of General Frank Crozier
    1897–1937* (Barnsley: Pen and Sword, 2013), p. 191.
6   'Dick Sheppard', *Peace Pledge Union*.
7   Neil Tweedie, 'How British Legion Flirted with Hitler', *The Telegraph*, last modified
    17 August 2001. Accessed 14 December 2018. www.telegraph.co.uk/news/
    uknews/1337705/How-British-Legion-flirted-with-Hitler.html.
8   Spingola, *The Ruling Elite*, p. 58.
9   'Scots Refused to Shake the Hand of Nazis Legion Members Were Appalled at
    English "Naivety" over Dachau Visit', *HeraldScotland*, last modified 18 August 2001.
    Accessed 19 July 2018. www.heraldscotland.com/news/12172177.Scots_refused_
    to_shake_the_hand_of_Nazis_Legion_members_were_appalled_at_English__apos_
    naivety_apos__over_Dachau_visit/.
10 Reese, *Homecoming Heroes*, p. 181.
11 *Ibid*.
12 'Scots Refused to Shake the Hand of Nazis', *HeraldScotland*.
13 Michael Duffy, 'Sir Frederick Maurice, ed. Charles F. Horne, Source Records of the
    Great War', *FirstWorldWar.com*, last modified 22 August 2009. Accessed 19 July 2018.
    www.firstworldwar.com/source/armistice_maurice.htm.
14 Gregory, *The Silence of Memory: Armistice Day, 1919–1946* (London: A & C
    Black, 2014), p. 6.
15 Cross, *In Memoriam*, p. 246.
16 'Scots Refused to Shake the Hand of Nazis', *HeraldScotland*.
17 Jeffrey C. Alexander, *Fin de Siecle Social Theory: Relativism, Reduction, and the Problem
    of Reason* (London: Verso, 1995), p. 76.
18 '"The War to End all War" Was Just the Start of Many More', *South Wales Echo*,
    11 November 2009.
19 The information was supplied with kind permission from his grandson, Graham Page.
20 'Episode 4: Lost Peace (1919)', *The People's Century*.

Chapter 23

1   Adams, 'Herbert Read'.
2   *They Shall Not Grow Old*.
3   Christopher Clark, 'The First Calamity: July, 1914', *London Review of Books*, last
    modified 28 August 2013. Accessed 21 November 2018. www.lrb.co.uk/v35/n16/
    christopher-clark/the-first-calamity.
4   Sebastian Faulks, 'I'll Never Forget How My Personal Birdsong Saga Began',
    The Independent, last modified 21 January 2012. Accessed 19 July 2018. www.

independent.co.uk/voices/commentators/sebastian-faulks-ill-never-forget-how-my-personal-birdsong-saga-began-6292553.html.

5   Arthur, *The Road Home*, p. 264.
6   'Episode 2', *Welsh Memories of World War 1.*
7   Ascherson, 'Armistice Day'.
8   Adam, 'Herbert Read'.
9   'Private William Cyril Jose', *Lives of the First World War* (IWM). Accessed 6 November 2018. livesofthefirstworldwar.org/lifestory/2187435.
10 *Teenage Tommies*, BBC Two.
11 'Episode 2', *Welsh Memories of World War 1.*
12 Arthur, *The Road Home*, p. 257.
13 Hynes, *A War Imagined*, p. 450.
14 'Oral History Recording of Sid Coles (b.1893) Memories of the Wolverton Park and Recreation Ground', *Living Archive*. Accessed 23 January 2019. www.livingarchive.org.uk/content/catalogue_item/days-of-pride-collection-2/oral-history-recordings-of-memories-of-world-war-one-by-people-from-wolverton-and-new-bradwell/oral-history-recording-of-sid-coles-b-1893-memories-of-the-wolverton-park-and-recreation-ground-2.
15 Reid, 'In Focus: Remembrance Day Traditions', *BBC History Magazine*, last modified 25 June 2018. Accessed 27 October 2018. www.historyextra.com/period/first-world-war/in-focus-remembrance-day-traditions/.
16 Gregory, *The Silence of Memory*.
17 Joe Moran, 'The Two-Minute Silence Keeps a Delicate Balance between Public Coercion and Private Reflection', *The Guardian*, last modified 11 November 2006. Accessed 27 October. 2018. www.theguardian.com/commentisfree/2006/nov/11/comment.mainsection.
18 Harding, *Keeping Faith*, p. 219.
19 'WWI Veterans Mark Armistice Day', *BBC News*, last modified 11 November 2008. Accessed 27 October 2018. news.bbc.co.uk/1/hi/uk/7720601.stm.
20 Wohl, *The Generation of 1914*, p. 109.
21 Hynes, *A War Imagined*, p. 450.
22 Holmes, *Tommy*, p. 623.
23 Wilson, *The Myriad Faces of War*, p. 755.
24 Van Emden and Humphries, *Veterans*, p. 223.
25 *They Shall Not Grow Old.*
26 Hynes, *A War Imagined*, p. 440.
27 Sir John Bagot Glubb, *The Changing Scenes of Life: An Autobiography* (London: Quartet Books, 1983), accessed via Google Books.
28 Van Emden, *The Soldiers' War*, p. 376.
29 'WWI Veterans Mark Armistice Day', *BBC News*.
30 Harding, *Keeping Faith*, p. 218.
31 'Traffic to Stop in Inverness for Armistice Day', *BBC News*, last modified 7 November 2011. Accessed 19 July 2018. www.bbc.co.uk/news/uk-scotland-highlands-islands-15618855.

BIBLIOGRAPHY

'1912-1949', *The Early Years at the BBFC*. Accessed 18 July 2018. www.bbfc.co.uk/education-resources/student-guide/bbfc-history/1912-1949.

'2014 – War and Impairment: The Social Consequences of Disablement', *Unite the Union*. Accessed 20 July 2018. worldofinclusion.com/v3/wp-content/uploads/2014/09/UK-Disability-history-month-2014.pdf.

'The Absent Minded Beggar', *Poems – The Glory of the Garden*. Accessed 18 July 2018. www.kiplingsociety.co.uk/poems_beggar.htm.

Ackerley, J.R. *My Father and Myself.* New York: New York Review Books, 1999.

Adams, M.S. 'Herbert Read and the Fluid Memory of the First World War: Poetry, Prose and Polemic', *Historical Research*, vol. 88, no. 240 (2015), pp. 333–54. .

Ahsan, Dr Saleyha. 'How Did WW1 Change the Way We Treat War Injuries Today?' *BBC*. Accessed 18 July 2018. www.bbc.co.uk/guides/zs3wpv4.

Ainsworth, John. 'The Black & Tans and Auxiliaries in Ireland', a paper presented to the Annual Conference of the Queensland History Teachers' Association in Brisbane, 12 May 2001. eprints.qut.edu.au/9/1/Ainsworth_Black_conf.PDF.

Alexander, Caroline. 'Faces of War', *Smithsonian.com*, 1 February 2007. Accessed 18 July 2018. www.smithsonianmag.com/history/faces-of-war-145799854/?no-ist=&fb_locale=ja_JP&page=3.

'Alexander, Charles Stewart: Letters to Cousin Amy Reid', *Auckland War Memorial Museum*. Accessed 27 December 2018. www.aucklandmuseum.com/collection/object/am_library-manuscriptsandarchives-9155.

Alexander, Jeffrey C. *Fin de Siecle Social Theory: Relativism, Reduction, and the Problem of Reason.* London: Verso, 1995.

Allen, Katie. 'Armistice Day in London, 1918'. *The Bookseller*, last modified 11 November 2011. Accessed 17 July 2018 www.thebookseller.com/feature/armistice-day-london-1918-339105

Allen, Tony. 'Cigarettes & Tobacco and WW1 Soldiers', *WorldWar1Postcards.com*. Accessed 7 December 2018. www.worldwar1postcards.com/smokes-for-the-troops.php.

'Allied Intervention in Russia, 1918-19', *National Archives*. Accessed 11 August 2018. www.nationalarchives.gov.uk/pathways/firstworldwar/spotlights/allies.htm.

Anderson, Julie. *Men After War*. Stephen McVeigh and Nicola Cooper (eds). Abingdon: Routledge, 2013.

Anderson, Julie. *War, Disability and Rehabilitation in Britain*. Manchester: Manchester University Press, 2016.

Anderson, Scott, 'The True Story of Lawrence of Arabia', *Smithsonian.com*, last modified 1 July 2014. Accessed 22 November 2018. www.smithsonianmag.com/history/ true-story-lawrence-arabia.

Angelsey, Lord. *A History of the British Cavalry 1816–1919: Volume 2 1851–1871*. Barnsley: Pen and Sword, 1993.

'Archangel Cemetery', *CWGC Archive*. Accessed 18 August 2018. www.cwgc.org/ find-a-cemetery/cemetery/54102/ARCHANGEL MEMORIAL.

'Armistice Day 1918 and Peace Day 1919', *Exploring Twentieth-Century London*, last modified 6 August 2014. Accessed 19 July 2018. www.20thcenturylondon.org.uk/ server.php?show=conInformationRecord.63.

Arthur, George. *Life of Lord Kitchener George Arthur, Volume 3*. New York: Cosimo Inc., 2007.

Arthur, Max. *The Faces of World War 1: The Great War in Words and Pictures*. London: Cassell, 2007.

Arthur, Max. *Forgotten Voices of the Great War*. London: Ebury, 2002.

Arthur, Max. *The Last Post*. London: Weidenfeld & Nicholson, 2005.

Arthur, Max. *The Road Home: The Aftermath of the Great War Told by the Men and Women Who Survived It*. London: Phoenix, 2010.

Ascherson, Neal. 'Armistice Day: Victory and beyond', *The Guardian*, 11 November 2018. Accessed 11 November 2018. www.theguardian.com/world/2018/nov/11/armistice- day-victory-and-beyond-first-world-war-neal-ascherson-essay.

Babington, Anthony. *Shell Shock*. Barnsley: Pen and Sword, 1990.

Baker, Chris. 'Records of British Prisoners of War 1914-1918', *The Long Long Trail*. Accessed 22 November 2018. www.longlongtrail.co.uk/soldiers/how-to-research-a- soldier/records-of-british-prisoners-of-war-1914-1918/.

Barham, Peter. *Forgotten Lunatics of the Great War*. New Haven: Yale University Press, 2007.

Barrett, Fionnuala. 'Perspectives on 'Shell Shock', *World War I Centenary*. Accessed 18 July 2018. ww1centenary.oucs.ox.ac.uk/body-and-mind/shell-shock-on-film/.

Barr, Niall. *The Lion and the Poppy: British Veterans: Politics, and Society, 1921–1939*. Westport, CT: Greenwood, 2005.

Barr, Niall. 'Service Not Self: The British Legion 1921–1939', PhD thesis, University of St Andrews, 1994. research-repository.st-andrews.ac.uk/handle/10023/7101.

Barry, Tom. 'Guerilla Days In Ireland', *Mercier Press*. Accessed 17 July 2018. www. mercierpress.ie/irish-books/guerilla_days_in_ireland/.

'The Story of Africa', *BBC World Service*. Accessed 17 July 2018. www.bbc.co.uk/ worldservice/specials/1624_story_of_africa/page13.shtml.

Beckett, Ian F.W. *The Great War 1914–1918*. Abingdon: Rouledge, 2014.

Beckett, Ian F W. *A Nation in Arms*. Barnsley: Pen and Sword, 2004.

'Behind the Scenes with Belgium's Bomb Disposal Unit', *BBC*, last modified 21 March 2014. Accessed 20 July 2018. www.bbc.co.uk/news/av/world-europe- 26663643/behind-the-scenes-with-belgium-s-bomb-disposal-unit.

Bell, Stuart and Ian Holliday. *Mass Conservatism: The Conservatives and the Public since the 1880s*. Abingdon: Routledge, 2013.

Benson, John. *The Working Class in Britain: 1850–1939*. London: I.B. Tauris, 2003.

Berghahn, Volker R., Kitchen, Martin and Carsten, F.L. *Germany in the Age of Total War*. London: Croom Helm, 1981.

Best, Geoffrey. *Churchill, A Study in Greatness*. London: A & C Black, 2001.

Bird, Will R. *Thirteen Years After: The Story of the Old Front Revisited*. Ontario: CEF Books, 2001.

Blacker, C. P. *Have You Forgotten Yet?: The First World War Memoirs of C.P.Blacker, M.C.*, Barnsley: Pen and Sword, 2000.

Blakeway, Denys. *The Last Dance: 1936: The Year Our Lives Changed*. London: Hachette, 2010.

'The Blog', *History Today*. Accessed 19 July 2018. www.historytoday.com/ blog/2011/11/remains-german-soldiers-ww1-found-france.

Blunden, Edmund. *Undertones of War*. London: Penguin, 2000.

Blythe, Ronald. *The View in Winter*, Norwich: Canterybury Press, 2005.

Bogacz, Ted. 'War Neurosis and Cultural Change in England, 1914–22: The Work of the War Office Committee of Enquiry into "Shell-Shock"', *Journal of Contemporary History* ,vol. 24, no. 2 (1989), pp. 227–56. www.jstor.org/stable/260822.

'Bolshevism: 'Foul Baboonery ... Strangle at Birth', *The Churchill Project – Hillsdale College*, last modified 29 March 2016. Accessed 22 November 2018. winston-churchill.hillsdale.edu/bolshevism/.

Bonney, Professor Norman. 'The Cenotaph: A Consensual and Contested Monument of Remembrance Norman Bonney Emeritus Professor at Edinburgh Napier University', *Secularism.org.uk*. Accessed 26 July 2018. www.secularism.org.uk/ uploads/cenotaph-a-consensual-and-contested-monument-of-remembrance.pdf.

Bostridge, Mark. 'The Shepherd in a Soldier's Coat', *The Independent*, last modified 22 October 2011. Accessed 22 November 2018. www.independent.co.uk/ arts-entertainment/the-shepherd-in-a-soldiers-coat-1313625.html.

Bourke, Joanna. 'Shell Shock during World War One', *BBC History*, last modified 10 March 2011. Accessed 20 July 2018. www.bbc.co.uk/history/worldwars/wwone/ shellshock_01.shtml.

Bourke, Joanna. 'Masculinity, Men's Bodies and the Great War', *History Today*, vol. 46, no. 2 (1996).

Bourne, Stephen. 'How Black Soldiers Helped Britain in First World War', *Black History Month*, last modified 11 November 2018. Accessed 22 July 2018. www.blackhisto-rymonth.org.uk/article/section/bhm-heroes/how-black-soldiers-helpedbritain-in-first-world-war/.

Bowman, Robin. 'Tubby Clayton and the Story of Toc-H', *WorldWar1.com*. Accessed 29 December 2018. www.worldwar1.com/sftoch.htm.

Brand, Constant. 'On WWI Killing Field, an Iron Harvest', *USA Today*. Accessed 28 July 2018. www.usatoday.com/news/world/2007-07-10-384369162_x.htm.

'A Brief History of Social (Council) Housing', *English Heritage*. Accessed 21 July 2018. www.heritage-explorer.co.uk/file/he/content/upload/9527.doc.

'Brig Roy Smith-Hill', *The Sunday Times*, last modified 21 August 1996. Accessed 17 July 2018. www.curioussymbols.com/john/brig/times.html.

'British Prisoners of War in German Captivity, 1914–1918,' *Imperial War Museums*. Accessed 17 July 2018. www.iwm.org.uk/collections/item/object/205222132.

'British Utopian Experiments 1325–1945', *Utopia Britannica*. Accessed 19 July 2018. www.utopia-britannica.org.uk/pages/SCOTLAND.htm.

Brittain, Vera. *Testament of Youth: An Autobiographical Study of the Years 1900–1925*. London: Fontana, 1980.

'Broadcast Appeal by an Unknown Soldier', *Trades Union Congress*. Accessed 26 October 2018. cdm21047.contentdm.oclc.org/digital/collection/tav/id/4022.

Brown, Malcolm. *The Imperial War Museum Book of the Western Front*. London: Pan, 2001.

Butchart, Ed. 'Unemployment and Non-Employment in Interwar Britain.' *Discussion Papers in Economic and Social History University of Oxford*, no. 16 (May 1997).

Cable, Amanda. 'Condemned to Be Virgins: The Two Million Women Robbed by the War.' *Daily Mail Online*, last modified 15 September 2007. Accessed 18 July 2018. www.dailymail.co.uk/femail/article-481882/Condemned-virgins-The-million-women-robbed-war.html.

Caren, Vicki. 'Treatment of Shell Shock', *Merseyside at War*. Accessed 18 July 2018. www.merseyside-at-war.org/story/treatment-of-shell-shock/#_ftn4.

Cathaoir, Brendan O. 'An Irishman's Diary', *The Irish Times*, last modified 2 October 2012. Accessed 17 July 2018. www.irishtimes.com/opinion/an-irishman-s-diary-1.546549.

'Celebrating Peace After World War One: The Street Party', *Wounded Soldiers and Military Hospitals in WW1*. Accessed 17 July 2018. www.1900s.org.uk/1919-peaceparty-edmonton.htm.

Chamberlain, J. and Gill, B. 'Fertility and mortality', *Springer Link*. Accessed 18 July 2018. link.springer.com/chapter/10.1007/978-1-349-75096-2_5.

Chapman, Paul, and Smith, Ted. *A Haven in Hell*. Oxford: ISIS, 2001.

Christian, Gabriel. 'The Interwar Years & the Caribbean Soldier in Social Transformation', *Dominica Academy of Arts and Sciences*. Accessed 17 July 2018. www.da-academy.org/uploads/9/2/0/3/92034718/thecaribbeansoldierinsocial-transformation.pdf .

Churchill, Winston. 'Lord Robert Baden-Powell by Winston S. Churchill, Great Contemporaries, London, 1938', *Troop485*, last modified 1997. Accessed 17 July 2018. troop485.tripod.com/documents/bp-churchhill.htm.

Churchill, Winston. *The World Crisis, Vol. IV: 1918–28*. London: Bloomsbury, 2015.

'CIA World Factbook', *CIA.gov*. Accessed 23 July 2017. www.cia.gov/library/publications/the-world-factbook/geos/uk.html.

Clark, Christopher. 'The First Calamity: July, 1914', *London Review of Books*, last modified 28 August 2013. Accessed 21 November 2018. www.lrb.co.uk/v35/n16/christopher-clark/the-first-calamity.

Clarke, Paul A.B. and Linzey, Andrew. *Dictionary of Ethics, Theology and Society*. Abingdon: Routledge, 2013.

Cohen, Deborah. *The War Come Home: Disabled Veterans in Britain and Germany, 1914–1939*. Berkeley: University of California, 2001. .

Cole, Henry G. 'Reflections on Courage', *Strategic Studies Institute*. Accessed 20 July 2018. strategicstudiesinstitute.army.mil/pubs/parameters/articles/97winter/win-essa.htm#gole.

Cole, Sarah. *Modernism, Male Friendship, and the First World War*. Cambridge: Cambridge University Press, 2003.

Coleman, Marie. *The Republican Revolution, 1916–1923*. Abingdon: Routledge, 2013.

Cook, Chris and Stevenson, John. *The Longman Handbook of Modern British History 1714–1980*. Harlow: Longman, 1983.

Coombs, Rose E.B. *Before Endeavours Fade*. London: After the Battle, 1994.

Coppard, George. *With a Machine Gun to Cambrai: The Tale of a Young Tommy in Kitchener's Army 1914–1918*. London: Cassell, 1969.

Cotrill, Joe. 'AP European History Practice Exam', College Board Advanced Placement Program. Accessed 21 June 2018. files5.pdesas.org/012254089243214063165145109 053021226205079172004/Download.ashx?hash=2.2.

Crabtree, Andy and Evans, Terry. 'The Sociality of Domestic Environments', *ESPRC Project*, University of Nottingham. Accessed 25 July 2018. www.cs.nott. ac.uk/~pszaxc/work/Equator-01-003.pdf.

Crisp, Alan. 'The Working-class Owner-Occupied House of the 1930s', M.Litt, Oxford University Press, 1998.

Cronin, David. 'Winston Churchill Sent the Black and Tans to Palestine', *The Irish Times*, last modified 19 May 2017. Accessed 17 July 2018. www.irishtimes.com/ culture/books/winston-churchill-sent-the-black-and-tans-to-palestine-1.3089140.

Cross, Robin. *In Memoriam: Remembering the Great War*. London: Ebury Press, 2008.

'Daily Mirror Headlines: Armistice, Published 12 November 1918', *BBC*. Accessed 20 July 2018. www.bbc.co.uk/history/worldwars/wwone/mirror07_01.shtml.

Dallas, Gregor. *1918: War and Peace*, London: Pimlico, 2002.

Dean, Alexander. 'An Analytical Study into the Rehabilitation of the Wounded from the Great War', *Academia.edu*. Accessed 13 December 2018. www.academia. edu/27091561/An_analytical_study_into_the_rehabilitation_of_the_wounded_ from_the_Great_War.

'The Death of Queen Victoria', *The Economist*. Accessed 19 July 2018. www.economist. com/news/21663911-what-we-wrote-her-passing-1901-death-queen-victoria.

DeGroot, Gerard J. *Blighty: British Society in the Era of the Great War*. Harlow: Longman, 1996.

'Demobilisation in Britain, 1918–20', *The National Archives*. Accessed 18 July 2018. www.nationalarchives.gov.uk/pathways/firstworldwar/spotlights/demobilisation.htm.

'Design, Politics and Commerce International Exhibitions 1851–1951', *University of Glasgow Special Collections*. Accessed 19 July 2018. special.lib.gla.ac.uk/teach/century/ artnouveau.html.

DeVore, Chuck. 'America's Foreign Policy Must Be Sustainable In Public Opinion, Too', *The Federalist*, last modified 8 August 2014. Accessed 17 July 2018. thefederalist.com/2014/08/04/americas-foreign-policy-must-be-sustainable-in- public-opinion-too/.

Dewey, P. E. *War and Progress: Britain, 1914–1945*. Harlow: Longman, 1997.

'Dick Sheppard', *Peace Pledge Union*. Accessed 19 July 2018. www.ppu.org.uk/ people/N_sheppard_dick.html.

Dillon, Martin. *The Shankill Butchers: A Case Study of Mass Murder*. London: Hutchinson, 1989.

Doherty, Gerry and MacGregor, James. *Hidden History: The Secret Origins of the First World War*. London: Random House, 2013.

'Domestic Housing for Disabled Veterans 1900–2014,' *Historic England*, accessed 18 July 2018. historicengland.org.uk/images-books/publications/iha-domestic- housing-for-disabled-veterans-1900-2014/.

Donaldson, George and Kalnins, Mara (eds). *D. H. Lawrence in Italy and England*. New York: Springer, 1999.

Drake, Robert F. *Understanding Disability Policies*. Basingstoke: Palgrave Macmillan, 1999.

Du Feu, Jenny. 'Factors Influencing Rehabilitation of British Soldiers After World War 1', *Historia Medicinae*, vol. 2, no. 1 (2009).

Duffy, Michael. 'Life in the Trenches', *First World War.com*. Accessed 20 July 2018. www. firstworldwar.com/source/armisticeterms.htm.

Duffy, Michael. 'Philip Gibbs on the Allied Occupation of the Rhineland, December 1918', *First World War.com*, last modified 22 August 2009. Accessed 17 July 2018. www.firstworldwar.com/source/rhineoccupation_gibbs.htm.

Dyer, Geoff. *The Missing of the Somme*. London: Phoenix, 2004.

'Earnshaw, R H (Oral History)', *Imperial War Museums*. Accessed 27 July 2018. www.iwm. org.uk/collections/item/object/80000959.

'Edmund Blunden', *Poetry Foundation*. Accessed 19 July 2018. www.poetryfoundation. org/poets/edmund-blunden.

Ekstein, Modris. *Rites of Spring: The Great War and the Birth of the Modern Age*. London: Papermac, 2000.

Emden, Richard van. *Britain's Last Tommies: Final Memories from Soldiers of the 1914–18 War in Their Own Words*. Barnsley: Sword and Pen, 2006. .

Emden, Richard van. *Sapper Martin: The Secret Great War Diary of Jack Martin*. London: Bloomsbury, 2009.

Emden, Richard van. *The Soldiers' War: The Great War through Veterans' Eyes*. London: Bloomsbury, 2009.

Emden, Richard van, and Steve Humphries. *Veterans: The Last Survivors of the Great War*. Barnsley: Pen and Sword, 2005.

Emsley, Clive. 'Violent Crime in England in 1919: Post-War Anxieties and Press Narratives', *Continuity and Change*, vol. 23, no. 1 (2008).

Englander, David. 'The National Union of Ex-Servicemen and the Labour Movement, 1918–1920', *History*, vol. 76, no. 246 (1991), pp. 24–42. Accessed 7 August 2018.

Evans, Ann. 'Clement Attlee – MP for Limehouse 1922', *The Port of London Study Group*, last modified 13 October 2017. Accessed 18 July 2018. portoflondonstudy. wordpress.com/2017/10/13/clement-attlee-mp-for-limehouse-1922-by-ann-evans/.

Evans, Martin Marix. *1918: The Year of Victories*. London: Chartwell, 2004. .

Evans, Richard J. *The Coming of the Third Reich*. New York: Penguin, 2004. .

'Experiences of Colonial Troops', *The British Library*, 9 December 2013. Accessed 20 July 2018. www.bl.uk/world-war-one/articles/colonial-troops.

'Extract from a speech by the war secretary Lord Milner on demobilisation, December 1918', The National Archives, last modified 1 January 1970. Accessed 17 July 2018. www.nationalarchives.gov.uk/pathways/firstworldwar/spotlights/ demobilisation.htm.

'Ex-Services Welfare Society: public appeal for funds on behalf of mentally broken ex-servicemen 1922–1924', *The National Archives*. Accessed 21 July 2018. national-archives.gov.uk/documents/filesonfilm/ex-services-welfare-society-public-appeal-for-funds-pin-15-2499.pdf.

'The Fallen. When Both Sides Fought and Died Together', *The Belfast Telegraph*, last modified 8 December 2012. Accessed 17 July 2018. www.belfasttelegraph.co.uk/ life/the-fallen-when-both-sides-fought-and-died-together-28068143.html.

Fallon, Donal. 'Poppy-snatching in Dublin', *Come Here to Me!: Dublin Life & Culture*, last modified 4 November 2015. Accessed 9 December 2018. comeheretome. com/2015/11/04/poppy-snatching-in-dublin/.

Faulks, Sebastian. 'I'll Never Forget How My Personal Birdsong Saga', *The Independent*, last modified 21 January 2012. Accessed 19 July 2018. www.independent.co.uk/ voices/commentators/sebastian-faulks-ill-never-forget-how-my-personal-birdsong-saga-began-6292553.html.

'Feature Article – Settlement of Returned Soldiers and Sailors 1914–18', *Australian Bureau of Statistics, Australian Government*. Accessed 18 July 2018. www.abs.gov.au/ AUSSTATS/abs@.nsf/featurearticlesbyCatalogue/72BB159FA215052FCA2569DE0 020331D?OpenDocument.

Fedorowich, E.K. '"Foredoomed to Failure": The Resettlement of British Ex-Servicemen in the Dominions 1914–1930', Ph.D Diss., University of London, 1991. www.researchgate.net/publication/297279233_Foredoomed_to_failure'_The_resettlement_of_British_ex-servicemen_in_the_Dominions_1914-1930.

Field, John. 'Exporting "People of British Stock": Training and Emigration Policy in Inter-War Britain', paper presented at the 40th Annual SCUTREA Conference, 6–8 July 2010, University of Warwick, Coventry). www.leeds.ac.uk/educol/documents/191542.pdf.

'First World War', *CWGC Archive*. Accessed July 20, 2018. www.cwgc.org/history-and-archives/cwgc-archive.

'Flu: How Britain Coped in the 1918 Epidemic', *The Independent*, last modified 22 October 2005. Accessed 17 July 2018. www.independent.co.uk/life-style/health-and-families/health-news/flu-how-britain-coped-in-the-1918-epidemic-5348535.html.

Floud, Roderick and Johnson, Paul (eds). *The Cambridge Economic History of Modern Britain*. Cambridge: Cambridge University Press, 2003.

'Four Decades since Disability Act', *BBC News Liverpool*, last modified 20 May 2010. Accessed 26 July 2018. news.bbc.co.uk/local/liverpool/low/people_and_places/newsid_8691000/8691968.stm.

Forster, E. M. *Howard's End*. London: Penguin Classics, 2012.

Foster, R. F. *Modern Ireland, 1600–1972*. London: Penguin, 1989.

'Frederick W Mott', *King's Collections Online*. Accessed 26 July 2018. www.kingscollections.org/exhibitions/specialcollections/mind-matters/war-psychiatry/frederick-w-mott.

Frith, John. 'Syphilis – Its Early History and Treatment until Penicillin and the Debate on its Origins', *Journal of Military and Veterans' Health*, vol. 20, no. 4 (2012). pp. 49–56.

Fryer, E. R. M. *Reminiscences of a Grenadier, 1914–1919*. London: Digby, Long & Company, 1921.

Fryer, Peter, and Gilroy, Paul. *Staying Power: The History of Black People in Britain*. London: Pluto, 2010. .

Fussell, Paul. *The Great War and Modern Memory*. Oxford: Oxford University Press, 1977.

Garnett, Mark and Weight, Richard. *The A-Z Guide to Modern British History*. London: Jonathan Cape, 2003.

Garrett, Richard. *The Final Betrayal: The Armistice 1918 and Afterwards*. Shedfield, Southampton: Buchan & Enright, 1989.

Garside, W. R. *British Unemployment, 1919-1939: A Study in Public Policy*. Cambridge: Cambridge University Press, 1990.

Gerber, David A., Ed., *Disabled Veterans in History: Enlarged and Revised Edition*. Ann Arbor: University of Michigan Press, 2015.

Gilbert, Martin. *Churchill: A Life*. New York: Random House, 2000.

Glancey, Jonathan. 'Comment: Gas, Chemicals, Bombs: Britain Has Used Them All before in Iraq', *The Guardian*, last modified 19 April 2003. Accessed 17 July 2018. www.theguardian.com/world/2003/apr/19/iraq.arts.

Gothein, Marie Luise Schroeter. *A History of Garden Art*. Cambridge: Cambridge University Press, 2014.

Graham, Stephen. *The Challenge of the Dead: An Impression of France and the Battlefields Just after the War*. London: Ernest Benn, 1930.

Grayling, Christopher. *A Land Fit for Heroes: British Life after the Great War*. London: Buchan & Enright, 1987.

Graves, Robert. *Goodbye to All That*. London: Penguin Classics, 2000.

Greenleaf, W. H. *Rise in Collectivism*. Abingdon: Taylor and Francis, 2003.

Gregory, Adrian, *The Last Great War: British Society and the First World War*. Cambridge: Cambridge University Press, 2009.

Gregory, Adrian. *The Silence of Memory: Armistice Day, 1919–1946*. London: A&C Black, 2014.

Gregory, Phil; Crichton, Sean; Sherwood, Marika; and Morgan, Marjorie. 'Black Soldiers', *The Black Presence in Britain*. Accessed 20 July 2018. www.blackpresence. co.uk/category/black-history/black-soldiers-black-history.

Gumbel, Andrew. 'RIP Alex, the Parrot That Learnt to Count and Communicate', *The Independent*, last modified 18 September 2011. Accessed 17 July 2018. www. independent.co.uk/news/world/americas/rip-alex-the-parrot-that-learnt-to-count-and-communicate-402076.html.

Guy, Fiona. 'The Green Bicycle Case: The Murder of Bella Wright in 1919', *Crime Traveller*. Accessed 30 June 2018. www.crimetraveller.org/2015/09/green-bicycle-case-bella-wright-murder/.

Hadley, Kathryn. 'Remains of German Soldiers from WW1 Found in France', *History Today*. Accessed 30 July 2018. www.historytoday.com/blog/2012/04/may-issue-history-today?page=23.

Haggerty, Bridget. 'The Irish Soldiers in WWI – World Cultures European', *Irish Culture and Customs*. Accessed 17 July 2018. www.irishcultureandcustoms.com/ACalend/VetsWW1.html.

Harding, Brian. *Keeping Faith: The Royal British Legion (1921–2001)*. Barnsley: Pen & Sword, 2001.

Harrison, Mark. 'The British Army and the Problem of Venereal Disease in France and Egypt during the First World War', *Advances in Pediatrics*, last modified April 1995. Accessed 18 July 2018. www.ncbi.nlm.nih.gov/pmc/articles/PMC1036972/?page=1.

Harvey, A.D. *A Muse of Fire: Literature, Art and War*. London: Hambledon, 1998. .

Harvie, Christopher. *A Floating Commonwealth: Politics, Culture, and Technology on Britain's Atlantic Coast, 1860–1930*. Oxford: Oxford University Press, 2008.

Hattersley, Roy. *The Edwardian*. London: Abacus, 2004.

Hayes-Fisher, John. 'The Last Soldiers to Die in World War I', *BBC News*, last modified 29 October 2008. news.bbc.co.uk/1/hi/magazine/7696021.stm.

Healey, Dennis. *The Time of My Life*. London: Penguin, 1990.

Heffer, Simon. 'Dark Shadow of the Great War as We Are Still Living with Its Legacy in Ukraine and Gaza', *Daily Mail Online*, last modified 3 August 2014. Accessed 18 July 2018. www.dailymail.co.uk/debate/article-2714390/Dark-shadow-Great-War-Tomorrow-marks-100-years-Europe-plunged-war-end-wars-But-brilliant-analysis-argues-living-appalling-legacy-Ukraine-Gaza.html#ixzz4pFE6Ook8.

Hicks, Joe and Allen, Grahame. *A Century of Change: Trends in UK Statistics Since 1900*, vol. 99, no. 11 (London: House of Commons Library, 1999). Accessed 30 July 2018. www.researchgate.net/profile/Grahame_Allen/publication/235361286_A_Century_of_Change_Trends_in_UK_Statistics_since_1900/links/56f1390d08ae5c367d4a9aa5/A-Century-of-Change-Trends-in-UK-Statistics-since-1900.pdf.

'History: The B Specials', *Royal Ulster Constabulary*. Accessed 20 July 2018. royalulster-constabulary.org/history3.htm.

'History & Timeline', *The Poppy Factory*. Accessed 18 July 2018. www.poppyfactory. org/history-timeline.

'History of TocH', TocH International Charity. Accessed 29 December 2018. toch-uk. org.uk/history-of-toch/.

Hobsbawm, E.J. *Age of Extremes: 1914–1991*. New York: Vintage, 1996.

Holmes, Richard. *Tommy: The British Soldier on the Western Front, 1914–1918*. London: HarperCollins, 2004.

Holland, Evangeline. 'A Glimpse of Armistice Day in London, 1918', *Edwardian Promenade* last modified 10 November 2011. Accessed 17 July 2018. www.edwardi-anpromenade.com/war/a-glimpse-of-armistice-day-in-london-1918/.

Honigsbaum, Mark. 'The 1918 Flu Pandemic Remembered,' *The Guardian*, last modified 5 November 2005. Accessed 17 July 2018. www.theguardian.com/ society/2005/nov/05/health.birdflu.

Hooley, Jim. *A Hillgate Childhood*. Stockport: Age Concern Stockport, 1981.

Horton, Alex. 'Battle in Their Hearts', *VAntage Point*, last modified 30 January 2017. Accessed 18 July 2018. www.blogs.va.gov/VAntage/459/battle-in-their-hearts/.

House of Lords. 'Instruction in The Army', *Hansard*, 18 March 1919. Accessed 6 August 2018. hansard.parliament.uk/Lords/1919-03-19/debates/987212d7-b6ea-4a80-bf65-2fa85b111300/InstructionInTheArmy.

House of Lords. 'Neurasthenia and Shell-Shock', *Hansard*, 15 April 1919. api.parliament. uk/historic-hansard/lords/1919/apr/15/neurasthenia-and-shell-shock.

Howard, Sean. 'Dominions of the Dead', *Cape Breton Post*, last modified 7 November 2018. Accessed 16 December 2018. www.capebretonpost.com/ opinion/columnists/guest-shot-dominions-of-the-dead-257298/.

Howe, Glenford D. 'A White Man's War? World War One and the West Indies', *BBC*, last modified 10 March 2011. Accessed 17 July 2018. www.bbc.co.uk/history/ worldwars/wwone/west_indies_01.shtml.

Howorth, Peter W. 'The Treatment of shell-shock: Cognitive therapy before its time', The Psychiatric Bulletin, 2000. www.merseyside-at-war.org/story/treatment-of-shell-shock/#_ftn2.

Hughes, Michael. 'After the War', *Graham: World Traveller*. Accessed 20 July 2018. www. stephengrahamworldtraveller.com/after-the-war.

'Hunt, W. (Oral History)', Imperial War Museums. Accessed 17 July 2018. www.iwm. org.uk/collections/item/object/80023206.

Hynes, Samuel. *A War Imagined: The First World War and English Culture*. London: Pimlico, 1990.

'In Their Own Words: The Unpublished Photos and Letters from the Frontline on the 90th Anniversary of the Armistice', *Daily Mail Online*, last modified 10 November 2008. Accessed 20 July 2018. www.dailymail.co.uk/news/article-1084298/In-words-The-unpublished-photos-letters-frontline-90th-anniversary-Armistice.html.

'The *Iolaire* Disaster, Where 200 Men Died Yards from Shore', *The Scotsman*, last modified 12 June 2006. Accessed 17 July 2018. www.scotsman.com/ heritage/people-places/the-iolaire-disaster-where-200-men-died-yards-from-shore-1-465122.

'Ireland and the Great War/Post-war Ireland', *Royal Dublin Fusiliers Association*. Accessed 17 July 2018. greatwar.ie/ireland-and-the-great-war-2/post-war-ireland/.

'Irish Soldiers of the Great War', *1916 Commemorations – Battle of the Somme*, Department of the Taoiseach. Accessed 17 July 2018. www.taoiseach.gov.ie/attached_files/Pdf%20files/1916Commemorations-BattleOfTheSomme.pdf.

'The Iron Harvest', *Flanders Today*, last modified 1 December 2010. Accessed 19 July 2018. www.flanderstoday.eu/living/iron-harvest.

Jacobson, Howard. 'To Truly Remember the Holocaust, We Must Stay Alert to Prejudice', *New Statesman*, last modified 1 February 2008. Accessed 17 July 2018. www.newstatesman.com/2018/02/truly remember-holocaust-we-must-stayalert-prejudice.

James, Clive. *Falling Towards England* (Omnibus Edition). London: Quality Paperback Direct, 1990.

Jeffery, Keith. *Ireland and the Great War*. Cambridge: Cambridge University Press, 2000.

Jeffery, Keith. 'Ireland and the First World War', *Irish History Live*. Accessed 27 December 2018. www.qub.ac.uk/sites/irishhistorylive/IrishHistoryResources/.

Jenkins, Roy. *Churchill: A Biography*. London: Pan, 2002.

Jensen, Finn. *The English Semi-Detached House: How and Why the Semi Became Britain's Most Popular House-Type*. Huntingdon: Ovolo, 2007.

Johns, Steven. 'The British West Indies Regiment Mutiny, 1918', *Libcom.org*, last modified 7 August 2013. Accessed 17 July 2018. libcom.org/history/british-west-indies-regiment-mutiny-1918.

Johnson, Paul Barton. *Land Fit for Heroes; the Planning of British Reconstruction, 1916–1919*. Chicago: University of Chicago, 1968.

Johnstone, Philip. 'First World War: High Wood, a Poem by Philip Johnstone', *The Guardian*, last modified 14 November 2008. Accessed 17 January 2019. www.theguardian.com/world/2008/nov/14/high-wood-philip-johnstone.

Jones, Edgar and Wessely, Simon. *Shell Shock to PTSD: Military Psychiatry from 1900 to the Gulf War*. Hove: Psychology Press, 2005.

Joy, Sinéad. *The IRA in Kerry 1916–1921*. Dublin: Gill & Macmillan Ltd, 2005.

'Jubilation on the Day the Guns Fell Silent', *Walesonline*, last modified 28 March 2013. Accessed 20 July 2018. www.walesonline.co.uk/news/local-news/jubilation-day-guns-fell-silent-2139014.

Keegan, Laurence V. *Victory Must be Ours: Germany in the Great War 1914–1918*. Barnsley: Pen and Sword, 1995.

Kell, Constance. *A Secret Well Kept: The Untold Story of Sir Vernon Kell, Founder of MI5*. London: Bloomsbury Publishing, 2017.

King, Alex. *Memorials of the Great War in Britain: The Symbolism and Politics of Remembrance*. Oxford: Berg, 1998.

Kipling, Rudyard. *The Irish Guards in the Great War*. Staplehurst: Spellmount, 1997. .

Kitchen, Roger. 'Part 5: Now This Bloody War Is Over', *Days of Pride: The Story of Wolverton & New Bradwell 1913–1918*, last modified November 2004. Accessed 17 July 2018. www.mkheritage.co.uk/la/DaysofPride/docs/partfive.html.

Koven, Seth. 'Remembering and Dismemberment: Crippled Children, Wounded Soldiers, and the Great War in Great Britain', *The American Historical Review*, vol. 99, no. 4 (1 October 1994), pp. 1167–202.

Kowalsky, Meaghan and Marie, Melssia. 'Enabling the Great War: Ex-Servicemen. The Mixed Economy of Welfare and the Social Construction of Disability, 1830-1930', PhD Diss., University of Leeds, 2007. etheses.whiterose.ac.uk/680/.

'A Land Fit for Heroes', *Aftermath*. Accessed 26 December 2018. www.aftermathww1.com/landfit.asp.

Lamb, Dave. 'Mutinies 1917-1920,' *Libcom.org*. Accessed 17 July 2018. libcom.org/library/mutinies-dave-lamb-solidarity.

Larkin, Philip. 'MCMXIV', *Poetry By Heart*. Last accessed 15 December 2018. www.poetrybyheart.org.uk/poems/mcmxiv/.

Laybourn, Keith. *Britain on the Breadline: A Social and Political History of Britain 1918–1939*. Stroud: Sutton Publishing, 1998.

Lawrence. J. 'Forging a Peaceable Kingdom: War, Violence, and Fear of Brutalization in Post–First World War Britain', *The Journal of Modern History*, vol. 75, no. 3 (2003), pp. 557-89.

Laws, Roz. 'Forgotten Bravery of Tragic Hero Who Took His Own Life', *Birmingham Mail*, last modified 26 July 2014. Accessed 23 December 2018. www.birminghammail.co.uk/news/midlands-news/ww1-captain-branded-cowardafter-7512658.

Lebzelter, G. *Political Anti-Semitism in England 1918–1939*. New York: Springer, 1978.

Lee, J.J. (Editor). *Kerry's Fighting Story 1916-21: Told by the Men Who Made It*. Cork: Mercier Press, 2009.

Leese, Peter. *Shell Shock: Traumatic Neurosis and the British Soldiers of the First World War*. London: Palgrave Macmillan, 2014.

Leeuwen, David Van. 'Marcus Garvey and the Universal Negro Improvement Association', *TeacherServe*, National Humanities Center. Accessed 17 July 2018. nationalhumanitiescenter.org/tserve/twenty/tkeyinfo/garvey.htm.

Legg, Joanna; Legg, David; and Park, Graham. 'The Menin Gate Inauguration Ceremony – Sunday 24th July, 1927', *The Great War 1914–1918*. Accessed 19 July 2018. www.greatwar.co.uk/ypres-salient/memorial-menin-gateinauguration.htm.

Leneman, Leah. 'Land Settlement in Scotland after World War I.' *The Agricultural History Review*, vol. 37, no. 1 (1989), pp. 52–64.

Levine-Clark, Marjorie. *Unemployment, Welfare, and Masculine Citizenship: 'So Much Honest Poverty' in Britain, 1870–1930*. Basingstoke: Palgrave Macmillan, 2015.

Lewis, Cecil. *Sagittarius Rising*. London: Greenhill, 1993.

Liddle, Peter. *The Soldier's War, 1914–18*. London: Blandford, 1988.

Linden, Stefanie C.; Jones, Edgar; and Lees, Andrew J. 'Shell Shock at Queen Square: Lewis Yealland 100 Years on', *Brain*, vol. 136, no. 6 (2013), pp. 1976–88.

Linklater, Magnus. 'We Must Not Avert Our Eyes to Horrors of War', *The Times*, 22 December 2016. Accessed 22 July 2018. www.thetimes.co.uk/article/we-mustnot-avert-our-eyes-to-horrors-of-war-lw92cjr9f.

Linklater, Magnus. 'Remembering Our Fathers: A Generation That Fought and Died Without Complaint', *The Times*, 4 August 2004. www.thetimes.co.uk/article/remember-our-fathers-a-generation-that-fought-and-died-without-complain-trl367lvvqv5.

Ludtke, Alf and Weisbrod, Bernd (eds) *No Man's Land of Violence: Extreme Wars in the 20th Century*. Gottingen: Wallstein Verlag, 2006.

Lynch, Robert. *The Northern IRA and the Early Years of Partition*. New Bridge: Irish Academic Press, 2006.

Macdonald, Lyn. *1914–1918: Voices & Images of the Great War*. London: Penguin, 1991.

MacKay, Marina. *Modernism, War, and Violence*. London: Bloomsbury, 2017.

McGreevy, Ronan. *The Mad Guns: Reflections on the Battle of the Somme*. Dublin: Irish Times Books, 2016.

Mckay, John P. *History of Western Society Since 1300*. Bedford: St. Martin's, 2014 (11th ed.)

McKibbin, Ross. *Parties and People: England 1914–1951*. Oxford: Oxford University Press, 2010.

McKim, Claire. 'Red Clydeside Remembered: The Battle of George Square', *The Scotsman*, last modified 1 February 2016. Accessed 20 July 2018. www.scotsman.com/lifestyle/red-clydeside-remembered-the-battle-of-george-square-1-4017559.

McKittrick, David. 'Ireland's War of Independence', *The Independent*, last modified 17 September 2011. Accessed 20 July 2018. www.independent.co.uk/news/world/europe/irelands-war-of-independence-the-chilling-story-of-the-black-and-tans-5336022.html.

MacMillan, Margaret. *Peacemakers: Six Months that Changed the World*. London: John Murray, 2012.

'The Mad Guns Reflections on the Battle of the Somme', *The Irish Times: Books*. Accessed July 19, 2018. docplayer.net/45603383-Published-by-the-irish-times-limited-irish-times-books-the-irish-times-2016.html.

Makepeace, Clare. 'Sex and the Somme: Officially Sanctioned WWI Brothels on the Front Line', *Daily Mail Online*. Last modified 29 October 2011. Accessed 18 July 2018. www.dailymail.co.uk/news/article-2054914/Sex-Somme-Officially-sanctioned-WWI-brothels-line.html.

'Making Britain', *The Open University*. Accessed 19 July 2018. www.open.ac.uk/researchprojects/makingbritain/content/1919-race-riots.

Manning, Frederick. *Her Privates We*. London: Serpent's Tail, 1999.

Mantin, Mike. 'Coalmining and the National Scheme for Disabled Ex-Servicemen after the First World War', *Social History*, vol. 41, no. 2 (2016).

Markham, Violet R. *Watching on the Rhine*. New York: George H. Doran, 1921.

Marshall, Richard. 'The British Army's Fight against Venereal Disease in the "Heroic Age of Prostitution"', *World War I Centenary*. Accessed 18 July 2018. ww1centenary.oucs.ox.ac.uk/body-and-mind/the-british-army's-fight-against-venereal-disease-in-the-'heroic-age-of-prostitution'/.

Marwick, Arthur. 'British Life and Leisure and the First World War', *History Today*, vol. 15, no. 6 (1965). pp. 409–19.

Masefield, John. *The Old Front Line*. Barnsley: Pen and Sword, 2006.

Mellow, James. *Charmed Circle: Gertru de Stein and Company*. New York: Houghton Mifflin, 1991.

Messenger, Charles. *Broken Sword: The Tumultuous Life of General Frank Crozier 1897–1937*. Barnsley: Pen and Sword, 2013.

Middlebrook, Matthew. *The First Day of the Somme*. Barnsley: Pen and Sword, 2006.

Miley, Frances, and Read, Andrew. 'The Purgatorial Shadows of War: Accounting, Blame and Shell Shock Pensions, 1914–1923', *Accounting History*, vol. 22, no. 1 (2016). pp. 5-28.

Montague, C. E. *Disenchantment*. London: MacGibbon & Kee, 1968.

Moore, Christopher. *Trench Fever*. London: Little, Brown, 1998.

Moore, Lucinda. 'The Human Repair Factory at Roehampton – Rehabilitation of Amputees', *Picturing the Great War*. Accessed 13 January 2019. blog.maryevans.com/2013/09/the-human-repair-factory-at-roehampton-rehabilitation-of-amputees.html.

Mosley, Michael. 'How Do You Fix a Face That's Been Blown off by Shrapnel?', *World War One BBC*, BBC iWonder. Accessed 22 November 2018. www.bbc.co.uk/guides/zxw42hv.

Mosley, Oswald. *My Life*. New York: Arlington House, 1972.

Moran, Joe. 'The Two-minute Silence Keeps a Delicate Balance between Public Coercion and Private Reflection', *The Guardian*, last modified 11 November 2006. Accessed 27 October 2018. www.theguardian.com/commentisfree/2006/nov/11/comment.mainsection.

Mosse, George L. 'Shell-shock as a Social Disease', *Journal of Contemporary History*, vol. 35, no. 1 (2000). pp. 101–8.

Mulvany, Peter. 'Shot at Dawn; Justice Does Not Have an Expiry Date', *History Ireland*, last modified 10 April 2013. Accessed 18 July 2018. www.historyireland.com/20th-century-contemporary-history/shot-at-dawn-justice-does-not-have-an-expiry-date/.

Myers, Kevin. 'The Bitter Sting in the Tail of World War', *The Telegraph*, last modified 11 November 2001. Accessed 17 July 2018. www.telegraph.co.uk/comment/4266725/The-bitter-sting-in-the-tail-of-world-war.html.

Negron, Carlos E. 'Nomination of the Great Ocean Road for recognition under the Heritage Recognition Program', *Australia Engineers*. Accessed 18 July 2018. www.engineersaustralia.org.au/portal/system/files/engineering-heritage-australia/nomination-title/Great%20Ocean%20Road%20-%20Nomination.pdf.

Nicolson, Juliet. *The Great Silence 1918–1920: Living in the Shadow of the Great War*. London: John Murray, 2009.

Nicolson, Juliet. 'The War was Over – but Spanish Flu Would Kill Millions More', *The Telegraph*, last modified 11 November 2009. Accessed 17 July 2018. www.telegraph.co.uk/news/health/6542203/The-war-was-over-but-Spanish-Flu-would-kill-millions-more.html.

The Nineteenth Century and After, Vol. 95. London: Leonard Scott Publishing Company, 1924.

Nott, James J. *Classes, Cultures, and Politics: Essays on British History for Ross McKibbin*, Clare V. J. Griffiths, James J. Nott, William Whyte (eds). Oxford: Oxford University Press, 2003.

Noyes, Alfred. 'A Victory Dance', *Blue Ridge Journal*. Accessed 17 December 2018. www.blueridgejournal.com/poems/an-victory.htm.

'Occupation of Rhineland', *British Pathé Historical Collection*. Accessed 20 July 2018. www.britishpathe.com/video/occupation-of-rhineland.

'The Occupation of the Rhineland', *The Spectator*, published 27 August 1927. Accessed 20 July 2018. archive.spectator.co.uk/article/27th-august-1927/4/the-occupation-of-the-rhineland.

Oliver, Neil. *Not Forgotten*. London, Hodder & Stoughton, 2006.

Olusoga, David. *The World's Wars*. London: Head of Zeus, 2014.

'Oral History Audio Recording of Frank Gillard (b.1891) and His Experiences in the Army in World War One', *Living Archive*. Accessed 18 July 2018. www.livingarchive.org.uk/content/catalogue_item/days-of-pride-collection-2/oral-history-recordings-of-memories-of-world-war-one-by-people-from-wolverton-and-new-bradwell/oral-history-audio-recording-of-frank-gillard-b-1891-and-his-experiences-in-the-army-in-world-war-one-2.

'Oral History Recording of Sid Coles (b.1893) Memories of the Wolverton Park and Recreation Ground', *Living Archive*. Accessed 23 January 2019. www.livingarchive.org.uk/content/catalogue_item/days-of-pride-collection-2/oral-history-recordings-of-memories-of-world-war-one-by-people-from-wolverton-and-new-bradwell/oral-history-recording-of-sid-coles-b-1893-memories-of-the-wolverton-park-and-recreation-ground-2.

Orwell, George. *The Road to Wigan Pier*. London: Penguin Modern Classics, 2001.

Osborne, Frances. 'Sex in the Downton Abbey Era', *The Huffington Post*, last modified 14 August 2012. Accessed 18 July 2018. www.huffingtonpost.com/frances-osborne/sex_b_1597879.html.

Ott, Nancy Marie. 'JRR Tolkien and World War I', *GreenBooks*. Accessed 19 July 2018. greenbooks.theonering.net/guest/files/040102_02.html.

Palmer, I. 'Sexuality and Soldiery Combat & Condoms, Continence & Cornflakes', *J R Army Med Corps 2003*, no. 149, pp. 38–46. jramc.bmj.com/content/jramc/149/1/38.full.pdf.

Parker, Peter. *The Last Veteran: Harry Patch and the Legacy of War*. London: HarperCollins, 2010.

Parsons, I. M. *Men Who Marched Away: Poems of the First World War*. London: Hogarth Poetry, 1987.

Paxman, Jeremy. *Great Britain's Great War*. London: Penguin, 2013.

Pati, Budheswar. *India and the First World War*. New Delhi: Atlantic Publishers, 1996.

Payne, Dr David. 'Furthering Interest in the Great War 1914–18 Shell Shock: Genesis and Outcomes in the Great War', presentation at the Western Front Association, Thursday 22 May 2008.

'Peace Day', Peace Pledge Union. Accessed 26 December 2018. archive.ppu.org.uk/remembrance/rem03.html.

The People's Century, 'Episode 4: Lost Peace (1919)', (1995: London, BBC).

'Pilgrimage', *Aftermath*. Accessed 19 July 2018. www.aftermathww1.com/pilgrim.asp.

Piper, Edgar Bramwell. *Somewhere Near the War*. Portland: Morning Oregonian, 1919.

'Poetry, Peace & War', *Peace Pledge Union*. Accessed 19 July 2018. www.ppu.org.uk/learn/poetry/poetry_ww1_4.html.

Pope, Rex. *War and Society in Britain, 1899–1948*. London: Longman, 1991.

Read, Anthony. *The World on Fire*. London: Random House, 2009.

Reese, Peter. *Homecoming Heroes: An Account of the Reassimilation of British Military Personnel into Civilian Life*. London: Leo Cooper, 1992.

Reid, Fiona. *Broken Men: Shell Shock, Treatment and Recovery in Britain, 1914–1930*. London: Continuum, 2010.

Reid, Fiona. 'In Focus: Remembrance Day Traditions', *BBC History Magazine*, last modified 25 June 2018. Accessed 27 October 2018. www.historyextra.com/period/first-world-war/in-focus-remembrance-day-traditions/.

Report of the War Office Committee of Enquiry into 'Shell-Shock' (1922). Cmd 1734 by Great Britain War Office, Committee of Enquiry into 'Shell-shock'.

Reeve, Michael. 'Smoking and Cigarette Consumption', *International Encyclopedia of the First World War*, last modified 23 May 2018. Accessed 6 December 2018. encyclopedia.1914-1918-online.net/article/smoking_and_cigarette_consumption.

Richards, Andrew. 'Mobilizing the Powerless: Collective Protest Action of the Unemployed in the Interwar Period', Estudio/Working paper 2002/175, Juan March Institut, Madrid, 2002, last modified 2002. Accessed 26 August 2018. citeseerx.ist.psu.edu/viewdoc/download?doi=10.1.1.586.228&rep=rep1&type=pdf.

Richards, Frank. *Old Soldiers Never Die*. Uckfied: The Naval & Military Press, 2006.

Roberts, J.M. *Europe 1880–1945*. Harlow, Essex: Longman, 1995.

Rogers, Simon. 'First World War: Volunteers from the Colonies – the Forgotten Soldiers', *The Guardian*, last modified 10 November 2008. Accessed 17 July 2018. www.theguardian.com/world/2008/nov/10/first-world-war-colonial-soldiers-racism.

Rooke, Charles. 'A Few of My Experiences Whilst "On Active Service"', *First World War Diary of Charles Rooke*, last modified 1 October 2003. Accessed 20 December 2018. www.nigelduffin.co.uk/family/rooke.htm.

Rossy, Katherine. 'Shellshock, Suicide and Septimus: Illness as a Metaphor in Virginia Woolf's *Mrs Dalloway*'. Accessed 10 August 2018. text.desa.org.mt/literarycriticism/katherine-rossy-shellshock-suicide-and-septimus.

Roth, Andrew. 'Lord Morris of Manchester Obituary', *The Guardian*, last modified 14 August 2012. Accessed 26 July 2018. www.theguardian.com/politics/2012/aug/14/lord-morris-of-manchester.

Rothstein, Andrew. *The Soldiers' Strikes of 1919*. New York: Springer, 1980.

Roze, Anne, and Foley, John. *Fields of Memory: A Testimony to the Great War*. London: Cassell, 1999.

Rubin, Bret. 'The Rise and Fall of British Fascism: Sir Oswald Mosley and the British Union of Fascists', *Intersections*, vol. 11, no. 2 (2010).

Ruff, Alan R. *Arcadian Visions: Pastoral Influences on Poetry, Painting and the Design of Landscape*. Barnsley: Windgather Press, 2015.

Ruggenberg, Rob. 'Burials of the Great War: Near Ypres Newly Found Corpses and Mortal Remains are Reburied in Flemish Earth', *The Heritage of the Great War*. Accessed 19 July 2018. www.denblanken.com/ieper/burial.html.

Sassoon, Siegfried. *The Complete Memoirs of George Sherston*. London: Faber and Faber, 1972.

Sayers, Dorothy L. *Unnatural Death: Lord Peter Wimsey, Book 3*. New York: Hachette, 2009.

Schmidt, Karl J. *An Atlas and Survey of South Asian History*. Abingdon: Routledge, 2015.

'Scots Refused to Shake the Hand of Nazis Legion Members were Appalled at English "Naivety" over Dachau Visit', *HeraldScotland*, last modified 18 August 2001. Accessed 19 July 2018. www.heraldscotland.com/news/12172177.Scots_refused_to_shake_the_hand_of_Nazis_Legion_members_were_appalled_at_English__apos_naivety_apos__over_Dachau_visit/.

Seaman, Lewis Charles Bernard. *Post-Victorian Britain: 1902–1951*, Abingdon: Routledge, 1993.

Searle, G.R. *A New England? Peace and War 1886–1918*. Oxford: Oxford University Press, 2005.

Secret History: WWI's Forgotten Heroes. London: Channel 4, 2 November 2004.

Sewell, Rob. '1919: Britain on the Brink of Revolution', *In Defence of Marxism*, last modified 16 May 2013. Accessed 19 July 2018. www.marxist.com/1919-britain-on-the-brink-of-revolution.htm.

Sharp, Everett. 'The Etaples Flu Pandemic?', *World War I Centenary*. Accessed 17 July 2018. ww1centenary.oucs.ox.ac.uk/body-and-mind/the-etaples-flu-pandemic/.

Shephard, Ben. *A War of Nerves: Soldiers and Psychiatrists, 1914-1994*. London: Pimlico, 2002.

Sherwood, Harriet. 'Indians in the Trenches: Voices of Forgotten Army are Finally to be Heard', *The Guardian*, last modified 27 October 2018. Accessed 28 October 2018. www.theguardian.com/world/2018/oct/27/armistice-centenary-indian-troops-testimony-sacrifice-british-library.

Silbey, David. *The British Working Class and Enthusiasm for War, 1914–1916*. Abingdon: Routledge, 2015.

Simkin, John. 'Shellshock', *Spartacus Educational*. Accessed 18 July 2018. spartacus-educational.com/FWWshellshock.htm.

Simmonds, Alan G.V. *Britain and World War One*. Abingdon: Routledge, 2013.

Singh, Anita. 'First World War PoWs: Why Has History Forgotten Them?', *The Telegraph*, last modified 28 May 2014. Accessed 17 July 2018. www.telegraph. co.uk/culture/hay-festival/10861012/First-World-War-PoWs-why-has-history-forgotten-them.html.

'The Sinking of the SS Mendi', *History Today*, February 2007. Accessed 9 December 2018. www.historytoday.com/archive/sinking-ss-mendi

'Sir Frederick Maurice on the Allies' Decision to Accept an Armistice', *First World War. com*. Accessed 18 July 2018. www.firstworldwar.com/source/armistice_maurice.htm.

'Sir Oswald Stoll', *ArthurLloyd.co.uk*. Accessed 18 July 2018. www.arthurlloyd.co.uk/ OswaldStoll.htm.

Smith, David. 'A Book Lifts the Lid on the Carnal Comforts Sought by First World War Troops', *The Guardian*, last modified 23 August 2008. Accessed 18 July 2018. www. guardian.co.uk/world/2008/aug/24/firstworldwar.military.

Snow, Dan. 'How Did So Many Soldiers Survive the Trenches?', *BBC*. Accessed 18 July 2018. www.bbc.co.uk/guides/z3kgjxs.

'The Speech: David Lloyd George, 23 November, 1918', *Scotsman*, last modified 23 November 2007. Accessed 26 July 2018. www.scotsman.com/news/the-speech-david-lloyd-george-23-november-1918-1-700345.

Spingola, Deanna. *The Ruling Elite: Death, Destruction, and Domination*. Bloomington: Trafford Publishing, 2014.

Sprenger, Jeroen. 'The Triple Alliance', *The Triple Alliance: A Threat of Revolution That Never Was*. Accessed 20 July 2018. www.jeroensprenger.nl/Triple Alliance/chapter-ii---the-objectives-of-the-triple-alliance.html.

Stamp, Gavin. *The Memorial to the Missing of the Somme*. London: Profile Books, 2010.

'Statistical Bulletin: Divorces in England and Wales: 2012', *Office for National Statistics*. Accessed 18 July 2018. www.ons.gov.uk/ons/rel/vsob1/divorces-in-england-and-wales/2012/stb-divorces-2012.html.

Stedman, Michael. *Salford Pals: A History of the Salford Brigade*. Barnsley: Pen and Sword, 2007.

Stephens, John. 'The British West Indies Regiment Mutiny, 1918', *Libcom.org*. Accessed 20 July 2018. libcom.org/history/british-west-indies-regiment-mutiny-1918.

Stevenson, John. *British Society 1914–45*. London: Penguin, 1990.

'Stories of Britain's Forgotten Role in Russia's Civil War on Display', *University of Exeter*, last modified 18 October 2017. Accessed 22 November 2018. www.exeter. ac.uk/news/featurednews/title_616668_en.html.

Szreter, Simon. 'The Prevalence of Ayphilis in England and Wales on the Eve of the Great War: Revisiting the Estimates of the Royal Commission on Venereal Diseases 1913–1916', *Social History of Medicine*, vol. 27, no. 3 (2014). Accessed 18 July 2018. www.ncbi.nlm.nih.gov/pmc/articles/PMC4109696/.

'The Story of Africa', *BBC News*. Accessed 20 July 2018. www.bbc.co.uk/worldservice/ specials/1624_story_of_africa/page12.shtml.

Strachan, Hew. *The First World War Hew Strachan*. New York: Oxford University Press, 2003.

Taylor, A.J.P. *English History, 1914–1945*. New York: Oxford University Press, 1965. .

Thane, Pat. *The Foundations of the Welfare State*. Harlow, Essex: Longman, 1996.

The Times History of the War (Vol. 16). London: Printing House Square, 1918.

'This Month in History: Peace Day, July 1919', *The Gazette*. Accessed July 17, 2018. www.thegazette.co.uk/awards-and-accreditation/content/100215.

Thomas, David. *England in the Twentieth Century 1914–79*. London: Penguin, 1991.

Thomas, Pauline. 'The Mood of Edwardian Society', *Fashion-eEra.com*. Accessed 19 July 2018. www.fashion-era.com/the_mood_of_edwardian_society.htm.

Thorpe, Andrew. *The Longman Companion to Britain in the Era of the Two World Wars 1914–1945*. Harlow: Longman, 1994. .

Thorpe, Andrew. 'The Membership of the Communist Party of Great Britain, 1920–1945.' *The Historical Journal*, vol. 43, no. 3 (2000).

Torrington, Arthur. 'West Indian Soldiers in the First World War', *Imperial War Museum*, last modified 11 March 2013. Accessed 20 July 2018. blogs.iwm.org.uk/research/2013/03/west-indian-soldiers-in-the-first-world-war/.

Toye, Richard (Ed.). *Winston Churchill: Politics, Strategy and Statecraft*. London: Bloomsbury, 2017.

'Traffic to Stop in Inverness for Armistice Day', *BBC News*, last modified 7 November 2011. Accessed 19 July 2018. www.bbc.co.uk/news/uk-scotland-highlands-islands-15618855.

Tritton, Alec. 'Empire Settlement Schemes after WWI', *Exodus: Movement of the People*, last modified 2 July 2013. Accessed 19 July 2018. www.exodus2013.co.uk/empire-settlement-schemes-after-wwi/.

Trueman, C. N. 'Brothels and the Western Front', *History Learning Site*, last modified 31 March 2015. Accessed 18 July 2018. www.historylearningsite.co.uk/brothels_western_front.htm.

Trueman, C. N. 'Commonwealth War Graves Commission', *History Learning Site*, last modified 17 April 2015. Accessed 19 July 2018. www.historylearningsite.co.uk/world-war-one/world-war-one-and-casualties/commonwealth-war-graves-commission/.

Truda, Robin. 'Nightmares the Navel of Freud's Dreaming', *AJP Psychology*. Accessed 18 July 2018. www.ajppsychotherapy.com/pdf/26_2/RobinTruda_Nightmaresthe.pdf.

Turner, Alwyn. '"The Most Degrading and Bestial Business in the World"', *Lion & Unicorn*, last modified 25 November 2017. Accessed 19 July 2018. thelionandunicorn.wordpress.com/2015/11/08/the-most-degrading-and-bestial-business-in-the-world/.

Turnbull, Gordon. *Trauma: From Lockerbie to 7/7: How Trauma Affects Our Minds and How We Fight Back*. London: Bantam, 2011.

Tweedie, Neil. '"Sacred" Battlefield Still Gives up Its Dead', *The Telegraph*, last modified 11 November 2000. Accessed 19 July 2018. www.telegraph.co.uk/news/uknews/1373997/Sacred-battlefield-still-gives-up-its-dead.html.

'The Unemployed Ex-serviceman's Appeal', *Warwick Digital Collections*. Accessed 12 January 2019. wdc.contentdm.oclc.org/digital/collection/tav/id/4188/.

'UK Marriage and Divorce Figures,' *Kaggle*, last modified 20 March 2018. Accessed 11 December 2018. www.kaggle.com/osbornep/uk-marriage-and-divorce-figures.

Vernon, James. *Hunger: A Modern History*. Cambridge, MA: Harvard University Press, 2009.

'A Very Bitter Victory: Returning WWI Soldiers' Hatred for the Leaders Who Sent Them to Die', *Mail Online*. Accessed 20 July 2018. www.dailymail.co.uk/news/article-1084616/A-bitter-victory-Returning-WWI-soldiers-hatred-leaders-sent-die.html.

Walker, Stephen. *Forgotten Soldiers: The Story of the Irishmen Executed by the British Army*. Dublin: Gill and MacMillan, 2007.

'We are Making a New World', *Tate Britain*. Accessed 18 December 2018. www.tate.org.uk/whats-on/tate-britain/exhibition/paul-nash/room-guide/we-are-making-new-world.

Webb, Simon. *1919: Britain's Year of Revolution*. Barnsley: Pen and Sword, 2016.

Weintraub, Stanley. *A Stillness Heard round the World: The End of the Great War, November 1918*. New York: E.P. Dutton, 1985.

Welshman, John. 'Eugenics and Public Health in Britain, 1900–40: Scenes from Provincial Life', *Urban History*, vol. 24, no. 1 (1997).

Welsh Memories of World War 1. Cardiff: BBC Wales, 2014.

'What Tommy Did Next: Veterans' Activities and Organisations of the First World War, in the UK and Beyond', *Men, Women and Care*. Accessed 11 November 2018. menwomenandcare.leeds.ac.uk/what-tommy-did-next-veterans-activities-and-organisations-of-the-first-world-war-in-the-uk-and-beyond/.

White, Gerry. 'An Open Letter to Cork's Unknown Soldier', *Evening Echo*. Accessed 27 December 2018. www.eveningecho.ie/opinion/An-open-letter-to-Corks-unknown-soldier-c43d563d-42da-44d1-819a-d0bb91fece7f-ds.

Williams, John. *The Other Battleground: The Home Front Britain, France and Germany 1914–18*. Chicago: Henry Regnery, 1972.

Williamson, Henry. *The Wet Flanders Plain*. London: Faber and Faber, 2009.

Wilson, Brian. 'NEW YEAR'S DAY 1919 / A Private Tragedy at Lewis', *The Independent*, last modified 18 September 2011. Accessed 17 July 2018. www.independent.co.uk/voices/new-years-day-1919-a-private-tragedy-at-lewis-1397469.html.

'Wilson, Ernest J (Oral History)', *Imperial War Museums*. Accessed 17 July 2018. www.iwm.org.uk/collections/item/object/80004393.

Wilson, Trevor. *The Myriad Faces of War: Britain and the Great War, 1914–1918*. Cambridge: Polity, 1988.

Winter, Dennis. *Death's Men: Soldiers of the Great War*. London: Penguin, 1979.

Winter, Jay. *Sites of Memory, Sites of Mourning: The Great War in European Cultural History*. Cambridge: Cambridge University Press, 2014.

Winter, J. M. 'Britain's 'Lost Generation' of the First World War,' *Population Studies*, vol. 31, no. 3 (Nov., 1977), p. 449–66.

Winter, J.M. *The Great War and the British People*. Basingstoke, Hampshire: MacMillan Education, 1987.

Winter, J. M. and Baggett, Blaine. *1914–18: The Great War and the Shaping of the 20th Century*. London: BBC, 1996. .

Winter, J. M. and Robert, Jean-Louis. *Capital Cities at War: Paris, London, Berlin, 1914–1919*. Cambridge, U.K.: Cambridge University Press, 1999.

Wittenberg, Daniel. 'First World War Centenary: North London Historian Uncovered Stories of Survivors' Guilt in Rare Interviews', *Hampstead Highgate Express*, last modified 4 August 2014. Accessed 20 July 2018. www.hamhigh.co.uk/news/heritage/first-world-war-centenary-oral-historian-max-arthur-survivors-veterans-guilt-book-1-3712360.

'Why the Indian Soldiers of WW1 Were Forgotten', *BBC Magazine*, last modified 2 July 2015. Accessed 9 December 2018. www.bbc.co.uk/news/magazine-33317368.

Wohl, Robert *The Generation of 1914*. Cambridge, MA: Harvard University Press, 2009.

'Women's Clothing', *Landscape Change Program*, last modified June 2012. Accessed 23 July 2018. www.uvm.edu/landscape/dating/clothing_and_hair/1910s_clothing_women.php.

'Woodbine Willie: A Different Kind of War Hero', *Birmingham Post*, last modified 30 May 2013. Accessed 19 July 2018. www.birminghampost.co.uk/lifestyle/woodbine-willie-different-kind-war-3948562.

Wrigley, Chris. *Winston Churchill: A Biographical Companion*. Santa Barbara: ABS-CLIO, 2002.

'WWI Veterans Mark Armistice Day', *BBC News*, last modified 11 November 2008. Accessed 27 October 2018. news.bbc.co.uk/1/hi/uk/7720601.stm.

'WWII: Nell Martin', *BBC Northern Ireland.* Accessed 17 July 2018. www.bbc.co.uk/northernireland/yourplaceandmine/antrim/nell_martin.shtml.

Yanikdag, Yucel. 'Prisoners of War (Ottoman Empire/Middle East)', *International Encyclopedia of the First World War.* Accessed 17 July 2018. encyclopedia.1914-1918-online.net/article/prisoners_of_war_ottoman_empiremiddle_east.

Zakharis, Thomas. 'Book Review: All for the King's Shilling, The British Soldier Under Wellington, 1808–1814', *The History Website of the Fondation Napoleon.* Accessed 22 November 2018. www.napoleon.org/en/history-of-the-two-empires/articles/book-review-all-for-the-kings-shilling-the-british-soldier-under-wellington-1808-1814/.

INDEX

You may also enjoy ...

978 0 7509 9082 0

In this updated edition of his acclaimed study of the black presence in Britain during the First World War, Stephen Bourne illuminates fascinating stories of black servicemen of African heritage. Informative and accessible, with first-hand accounts and original photographs, *Black Poppies* is the essential guide to the military and civilian wartime experiences of black men and women, from the trenches to the music halls.

You may also enjoy …

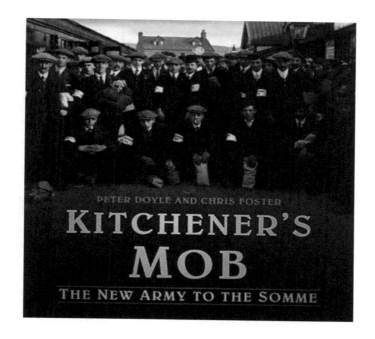

978 0 7509 6495 1

Kitchener's Mob tells the amazing story of 'Kitchener's Army' and its volunteer soldiers, the men of the 'First Hundred Thousand' and the many Pals' battalions that were later raised across Britain, in its industrial heartlands and leafy shires alike. Through artefacts and original documents, this moving tribute bears witness to the indelible imprint this memorable 'mob' made on our history.

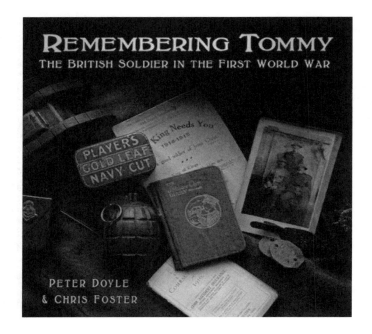